In 1947, at the United Nations Population Commission, the Soviet delegate Mr. Rabichko spoke unequivocally. "We consider any proposition formulated by this commission in favour of limiting marriages or births in wedlock as barbarous. Over-population is only a fruit of capitalism; an adequate social regime (socialism being understood), can meet any increase of population. It is the economy which should be adapted to the population, and not vice versa."

This view was often repeated, in almost identical terms . . . at other sessions of the same commission, at the Economic and Social Council and at the World Congress on Population in Rome in 1954.

"There cannot be any surplus population under a socialist regime, in spite of rapid demographic growth," says the Great Soviet Encyclopaedia.

This was certainly not the first time that the socialists attacked the Malthusian concepts. For a long time, these concepts were directly inspired by the fear that property-owners felt of having to share their goods with the poor who had become too numerous. Marx and the Marxists . . . assumed that overpopulation was caused by private property.

—from Chapter 23, "Communist Doctrine and Attitudes"

ALFRED SAUVY

FERTILITY
SURVIVAL

AND

Population Problems from Malthus to Mao Tse-tung

COLLIER BOOKS
NEW YORK, N.Y.

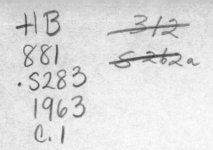
This Collier Books edition is published by arrangement with Criterion Books, Inc.

Collier Books is a division of The Crowell-Collier Publishing Company

First Collier Books Edition 1963

Translated from *De Malthus à Mao Tsé-Toung*, Editions Denoël, Paris 1958, by Christine Brooke-Rose
Translation © Chatto & Windus Ltd. and Criterion Books Inc., 1961

Contents

Part 3: The Demographic Solution; Prevention of Births

Part 4: Summary and Conclusion

Illustrations

Preface

THE LESS A PROBLEM is understood, the more passionate the opinions about it and the more solid the prejudices.

In the gallery of famous misunderstood men, Malthus occupies a notable position, for the confusions about him are numerous: confusions between the patrician and the dogmatist, between the moralist and the economist, confusions, even, between the various stages of his own development, and finally, between the prophet and all those who have spoken in his name.

The urge for simplification has produced a division of men into malthusians and anti-malthusians (or populationists), these terms being frequently loaded with a judgment value as solid as it is groundless. The mind is then at peace, having made or accepted this classification, but unfortunately the problem is not solved so easily.

Opposed and criticized for what is most valuable in him, praised for what is least edifying, Malthus is certainly a paradoxical figure. After a thousand-year-old technical stagnation, inevitably accompanied by chronic over-population, there began a period of progress which made it possible to feed more and more people; yet it was precisely then that Malthus' voice rose to advocate the limitation of numbers, and this in the very country which was fast becoming the foremost power in the world, with all doors opening before it.

A curious coincidence? Not at all. For this was also the moment when growing social awareness was slowly transforming the mass of the people into a responsibility; at this time too, after several thousand years of inefficiency and nil balances in terms of human life, medicine was at last entering into a period of forward impetus and success. As Mr. Philippe Ariès has perceptively shown, the techniques of struggling against death were bound also to favour the techniques of struggling against life. Or, in more precise terms, the very

9

idea that Fate was no longer the implacable enemy suggested the idea of fighting nature in other fields as well.

The problem of population arose somewhat suddenly after the war, with regard to the so-called "under-developed" countries. This new expression betrays its American origin. People have spoken, at various times, of barbarians, infidels, savages, natives, coloured men, etc., and, less pejoratively, of countries with different cultures. There was also "the yellow peril." In many ways the expression "under-developed" is even more cruel than its predecessors, with its scientific pretension and its implication of superiority. We shall use it nevertheless, since it is the current one.

In the book devoted to this problem by the Institut National d'Etudes Démographiques, the title "Le Tiers Monde" was used, by analogy with the "Tiers État," that mass which was at one and the same time almost everything and almost nothing. Does the analogy stop there? No, for an irreverent spirit has pushed it further, on the assumption that capitalism (or the capitalist world) is playing the role of the aristocracy and communism that of the clergy. But let us stop these dangerous comparisons; in any case the two worlds which have evolved, each in its own way, are nowhere near getting together to exploit the third, or even to resist its encroachments, or to come to its aid.

An abundant literature, mostly Anglo-American, has been growing in recent years on the subject of the "under-developed" countries. One anxiously scrutinizes each work in the hope of at last finding the key to the solution of this vast problem. Perhaps the reader of this book will feel the same nervous expectation and the same disappointment. I have sought neither to reassure nor to alarm, but only to describe the situation, particularly in its concrete aspects, which are not always easy to discover. Reliable documentation is essential to the correct construing of facts towards an indisputable conclusion. So many have dealt with the problem by giving more weight to prejudices and emotional reactions than they have to knowledge and understanding, that a description such as this, dry and factual though it sometimes may be, can surely serve a useful purpose.

Having spoken of Malthus, we should also mention Mao Tse-Tung. We can hardly avoid it, in view of the reversal in the Chinese attitude and policy on the subject of propaganda about contraceptives. The specialists, it must be said, expected this reversal, but did not know when it would occur or how speedily it would be put into action. Anyone who undertakes the presumptuous task of bringing social and scientific forces together must accept the risk even of violent changes once he has entered voluntarily into this whirlwind which frequently has little to do with university grades or even with the facts discovered. But the bitterness he may well feel when the blows come from the most unexpected quarters, revealing the worst possible moral collapses, is well outweighed by the purely internal victories he can enjoy when he sees political power, the strongest power of all, bow before an imperative it had rightly or wrongly ignored.

Demography includes fearful mysteries as well as fearfully certain areas of knowledge. I have attempted only to illuminate that which can be illuminated, including those awesome question-marks without which true science would no longer exist, since there would be no more frontiers.

PART 1
DATA AND
VAIN SOLUTIONS

Chapter 1

Two extreme theories

"The road to survival"

IN 1948 the American naturalist William Vogt made a sensation with his book *The Road to Survival*, in which he showed the contrast between the multiplying of mankind and the stagnation, indeed the decrease, of available subsistence-means, due to erosion and the destruction of natural resources. Humanity does not move towards progress, he cried; in the last four centuries it has in fact lived only by "consuming" an entire continent. This consumption, this dissipation, are drawing to an end, he concluded, so much so that the United States ought to refuse all aid to any country in which births are not being limited, and even medical progress ought to be slowed down in those countries.

This pessimistic pamphlet evoked some violent replies from, in particular, J. de Castro, Colin Clark, etc., from Catholics in general and, even more so, from the Communist world, which accused Americans and malthusians of being "cannibals" who wished to exterminate "inferior" races to benefit the lords of the earth, the only people with the right to live. It was, in fact, the old conflict between Marx and Malthus, but transferred from the level of social classes to that of world populations; this conflict is easy enough to understand, and yet is so very misunderstood, because impulses dominate reason so much and so often, on this subject.

Emotional reactions

Even the echoes of Vogt's book produced their own extremist reactions. After an article in a "Digest" which summarized the theory briefly but evocatively, the directing office of the French Securité Sociale received many eloquent protests, on the theme "Why do you encourage the birth rate with allowances for children if we are all going to die of hunger?"

Other reactions followed. To show their general trend, I shall imagine a scene (but am I really only imagining?):

An American industrialist comes home looking ravaged. His wife asks him if he is feeling all right. "Yes, I feel fine— And what about your business?—Business is fine, but things are much more serious. This morning I read an article by an eminent scientist; well, it seems that in a very short while we shall all die of hunger." And he quotes devastating figures. And as they sit down in silence to their meal, unsubtle perhaps but substantial, the couple listen to the wireless announcing Congress's vote of credit for the purpose of limiting agricultural production and reabsorbing excess foodstuffs.

By thus spreading anxiety among the Whites and fury among the Reds, Vogt at least succeeded in drawing the world's attention to a serious problem. But the posing of so grave a question in such unscientific terms, leading to reactions as violent and certainly unthought-out, is hardly the way to solve a delicate problem. The communists were not the only ones to protest at its ferocity, so lightly hidden beneath the coating of humanitarianism. The Catholics refused to accept the pessimistic thesis, and so did many scientists, each side in different terms but too incautiously.

The violence of the emotions that have been roused over "under-developed countries"—and this irrespective of the straight power-struggle between the United States and the Soviet Union—shows the intense interest the subject has and the importance of what is at stake.

Famine or abundance?

The optimistic theories rely on the importance of unexploited natural resources and on the scientific advances to be expected. Some, like the "abundantists," estimate that the world has reached such a degree of scientific knowledge and technical ability that only a redistribution of subsistence-means would be necessary, such redistribution to be achieved by abandoning the present system of exchanges and of private interests. This abundance, which has been the dream of so many, in so many different forms, from the goddess Ops through streams of milk to the weddings of Cana, would become a tangible reality, bringing with it other benefits and a veritable regeneration of mankind.

Thus on this one subject, with all the facts before us, some speak of famine and disaster, others proclaim an age of abundance and felicity in the near future. Between these two extremes lies, naturally, a whole gamut of more subtle positions.

When science is silent, confessing its impotence or its timidity, feelings march ahead, for they need not have such scruples. Certainly science has something to say on all this (that is the subject of this book), but it gives no last word, it can make no precise conclusion, as it could on certain problems of chemistry or natural history. On the other hand, the public is very ill-informed about the documentary evidence and ascertained knowledge that science *has* been able to collect, and on which all judgment ought to be based. The true data and the real aims hardly seem to come to light in the mass of partial, controversial but spectacular items of news.

Examples

The information given to the public is more suggestive than instructive. For instance:

"Every two seconds," say the more or less well-intentioned purveyors of information, "mankind increases by three inhabitants, that is, 90 per minute, 5,400 per hour, 129,600 per day, and 47,300,000 per year, more than the whole of France."

What does this string of figures prove? Nothing. In spite of appearances it has no statistical value whatsoever, because it does not attempt to relate two phenomena. But since education, which is two centuries behind the times, provides no lessons in statistics, the public, whether cultured or not, lives on prejudices. To give some sort of significance to a statement of this sort, one would have to say, for instance, that mankind increases by 1.7 per cent every year, say three times faster than France itself, and much faster than it ever did before. The mere repetition of the same figures by the hour, the day, etc., strikes suggestively without instructing.

Here is another example: "A strip of agricultural soil 32

inches wide has to feed more than two thousand million people." These two figures bear no relation to one another, since the length of the strip of land is not given. But the contrast between the huge number and the small one is effective in its intended suggestiveness.

Inversely, the anti-malthusians pose the problem of the Lake of Constance: if the whole of humanity were plunged into the Lake of Constance and the outlets of the lake were blocked, by how much would the displacement raise the level of the lake?

The answer (about 6 inches) astonishes by the modesty of the figure, and since the Lake of Constance takes up only a very tiny bit of the world map, the resultant feeling is that there is still plenty of room for mankind.

All exaggerated simplification plays for suggestion.

Two camps

In all this controversy, there are then two camps, both of which seem remarkably heterogeneous:

In the camp we shall be calling "pessimistic" or "malthusian" (without giving any pejorative sense to these two designations), we find generally speaking, Protestants, the Americans (of the United States), the social-democrats, the materialistic conservatives, persons belonging to juridical groups, individuals with logical minds, individuals with a dark temperament, etc.

The optimistic camp is no less heterogeneous, for it includes orthodox communists, obedient catholics, idealistic conservatives, many scientists, individuals with a generous temperament, etc.

In both camps there are the humanitarians, the altruists. In the second, the camp which trusts life (risking its own fate, as we shall see), can be found the men who are in love with human fellowship, including some Catholics of a deeply Christian spirit. In the first camp are to be found those who, like Malthus himself, wish to save their fellow-men from suffering. But this sentiment is inevitably accompanied by a less admirable fear of having to share with others poorer than oneself.

This fear can, in certain circumstances, take on a most unpleasant aspect; the malthusian attitude can recall that of the man on a raft or desert island, who says to his companions: "There is one man too many among us (or even, among *you*)." The weakest inevitably feels he is the one. It is this attitude, sometimes due to mere clumsiness, which has prompted the Soviet accusation of "cannibalism."

Such is the conflict. There are of course more subtly delineated positions; they will become, one hopes, more and more so as the concrete data spread.

But enough of motives, whether generous or not. We must look at the conflict. In the last few years it has diminished a little, after the initial fever. The danger of atomic and radiological warfare has, wrongly of course, eclipsed the dangers which are less close, but more precise. One of the many unfortunate effects of this war-threat is, then, to make people forget about mankind's means of subsistence. When death is near, one does not think of tomorrow's life.

And yet the threat of atomic war was already there when the question was first raised, some ten years ago. Since then, however, time passed and nothing happened: the men who were supposed to die of hunger did not die, at least not all of them. Their conditions hardly improved and their numbers increased, but this mere prolongation was enough to reduce the sensitivity of others.

I shall try to present the concrete data as clearly as possible. For this purpose, I must ask the reader to try and empty his mind of preconceived notions. If he has followed me so far, he can follow further still.

Chapter 2

An unprecedented anxiety

WHY IS this a contemporary problem, and were not our fathers, grandfathers and ancestors worried about it too? Has it become our worry because of our improved means of acquiring this kind of knowledge, because our statistical magnifying-glass has been perfected? Not at all, although the coincidence of the phenomenon and the means of observing it is not fortuitous.

Is it because we have become more sensitive and more humane? Not even that.

The fundamental fact is that important changes have quietly been taking place upon our planet for twenty years.

Over-population is certainly nothing new on this planet; one may even say more: for a long time it was the norm of humanity; a relative over-population of course, due to insufficient technical knowledge, sometimes also to social causes, but over-population nevertheless (see p. 22). But this situation did not, in general, trouble either the governments of countries or those who at the time constituted public opinion in any one country. Such preoccupations, when they existed, were purely local (Greece, China, Japan, American tribes, etc.), and sporadic. There was nothing resembling a world consciousness of population as a problem. It is not even found in Plato, who imagines his republic in curious isolation.

Collective consciousness

A society never knows itself well, for it is extremely difficult to judge from within. On a demographic level, however, measurement is relatively easy, but it does require an instrument, a method of observation, as well as a certain impassiveness, in other words, an essentially scientific attitude that is all too rare in the study of social problems, which everyone wants to solve in his own way, according to his prejudices and interests.

For lack of systematic observation which must, at first, seem exceedingly abstract, we are very ill-informed about our own social formation. The things we see everyday, the things we learn from rumour, from the press, the radio, official speeches, etc., are only the accidentals, the slightly salient facts. Knowledge of them not only fails to instruct us sufficiently, it also prevents us from seeing the real meaning of things and the true line of history. We are continually inducted into error by the truest news. Paul Valéry once said to André Gide: "Events bore me; events are only the froth of things; what interests me is the sea." The author of *Le cimetière marin* meant that the surface waves ought not to hold the attention, away from the deeper currents.

But the mind willingly grasps at detail, and prefers variousness which is more easily seizable; general phenomena, collected in statistical form, seem only abstractions. The death of a man may be a concrete phenomenon without social interest, but mortality is a phenomenon of abstract appearance which does not attract the mind. In this way the large deep currents remain unknown, even, sometimes, after this ignorance has brought about sensational disasters; these are then easily linked, by those who have suffered them, to some frail fact, and blamed on the government, the opposing party, the enemy of the moment.

It's movement that counts

The new factor in our world, let us repeat, is neither overpopulation—an imprecise term—nor misery—a partly subjective notion—nor hunger, or rather, under-nourishment, which is part of the data that can be measured scientifically.

The struggle for existence and the poverty of the greatest number have been part of the fate of mankind for a very long time. Of course, we might consider that the moment has come to stop this age-old tragedy, now that we have achieved so much in the way of dominating nature, and to say therefore that the new factor is our ability to conquer a scourge of nature. But there is another new factor, very new and very important: mankind has quite suddenly entered into a period of rapid growth in numbers.

Since we like the concrete, the solid, which we measure against the visible rather than against the future, we all tend to judge the events of a day a little too much against the day itself, and find it difficult to "place ourselves within a movement." Such placing is, in fact, an act of humility, a recognition of oneself as a small piece, a cog, in a larger whole.

Experts and specialists are by no means free of this fault: for a long time, on the subject of population, they held on to a static notion and, in particular, to an optimum notion that was more attractive than efficacious.

"If there are such states as underpopulation and overpopulation—too few and too many people," said Fairchild, "then between the two must necessarily be the state of optimum population, just the right number of people."[1]

This concept has been more or less abandoned today, at least as regards practical application. It remains a good exercise. Just as the teaching of mechanics begins first with statics, so it is useful to study the equilibrium of a population, before attacking the intricate machinery of its development.

What examples of the practical application of the optimum theory can we find in history?

After the Black Death of 1348 the number of men was suddenly reduced without any notable variation in technical achievement, or in any other factors. This swift reduction re-established France's economic equilibrium, Y. Renouard tells us,[2] and adds: "The sudden scarcity of manual labour brought about a rise in wages and, consequently, in prices; men of property and owners of inferior land, abandoned by their tenants . . . were ruined." Visibly, the population was superior to the economic optimum before the plague and no doubt even after it. Similarly in England, the improvement in the standard of living for survivors, especially manual workers, had the same result (Helen Robbins).

[1] Henry Pratt Fairchild: *People—the Quantity and Quality of Population*, New York, 1938.

[2] *Population*, July–September 1948.

Let us now speak in the future or the conditional: if an atomic bombardment or rather, a bacteriological war were to destroy part of the population of one territory, India, for example, or Canada, without at the same time causing any modification of natural or artificial installations, would the standard of living of the survivors be higher or lower than it was before? The answer varies, according to each case. One would say then that the population was above or below its optimal economic level.

The dramatic nature of these examples emphasizes the unpleasant aspect of the optimum notion, from the point of view of static economy. The practical applications of this notion are always linked with some disaster. At the core of the notion itself lies a hard condemnation of men who could be considered as "surplus." And dark hints hover around its usual developments: more often than not, authors have put forward the theory of optimum economy, thinking almost exclusively of this optimum being surpassed, that is to say, of over-population. And the people who are deemed to be supernumerary frequently belong to races or social categories thought of as inferior, so that a merely quantitative malthusianism is more or less explicitly shadowed by a severe judgment against "undesirables."

We know that many populations of the world are undernourished. What do we deduce from that? First and foremost, that their food must be increased, for all men existing in the world have the right to live.

Any attempt at an immediate or proximate decrease in their numbers comes up against great practical obstacles. It is difficult enough, as we shall see later, merely to slow down the growth.

Besides, any decrease of population and even any slowing-down of its growth, bring about other important phenomena, the most important of which is the ageing of the population, and this has its own numerous consequences. We shall return to this point.

In any case the sterility of static conceptions is obvious: it is movement that counts. And once again we come face to face with the new factor, which poses a new problem and dictates new solutions: this new factor, we repeat, is neither over-population, nor even hunger; the new factor is that after a long period of near-stagnation, the number of people in most parts of the world has suddenly begun to increase rapidly.

Growth of world population

After centuries and millenia of very slow increase the population of the world has suddenly, as it were, got going at a swift pace which must, however, be judged relatively and seen with a statistical eye. "Your figures are imprecise and valueless. How can you know the population of Rome or of cave-times?" This objection is groundless, for we shall see how little absolute precision is necessary in the light of facts which speak so clearly.

The first figures usually quoted go back to 1650, the very period, as it happens, of awakening consciousness. "The time of the world running out" was already a presentiment then. Here, anyway, are the most likely figures:

	Population in millions	Annual percentage of increase since preceding period
1650	545	—
1750	728	0.3
1800	907	0.45
1850	1,175	0.55
1900	1,620	0.65
1920	1,834	0.625
1930	2,008	0.88
1940	2,216	1
1950	2,476	1.12
1955	2,691	1.67
1960 (probably)	2,910	—

The Willcox evaluations for the period 1650 to 1900 are a little lower, especially for 1650. The evaluations quoted here combine those of Carr Saunders (1650 to 1900) and those of the United Nations Secretariat (since 1920).[3] These figures are not, of course, as satisfactory as they might be. Some

[3] See *Determinants and Consequences of Population Trends*, United Nations, New York, 1953.

of the observed growth could conceivably represent merely a reflection of perfected census techniques. Nevertheless the authors must have taken this classic phenomenon into account.[4] In any case, the twentieth century acceleration is obvious enough to deserve our closest attention. Our last figure, for 1960, is still to be confirmed, hence we have not indicated the corresponding annual increase in the right-hand column.

Fig. 1 illustrates the growth in the last three centuries, as

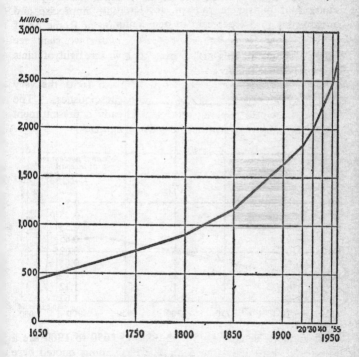

FIG. 1.—The population of the world since 1650.

[4] They have not, however, indicated how the relation was made between the Chinese census of 1953 and the Chinese Sections in earlier valuations of world population. The latter probably err towards under-estimation, at any rate the last ones.

well as the acceleration over the last few decades. But the detailed movement can be observed much more clearly in Fig. 2, which represents the annual increase (right-hand column of figure).

Not only has the population increased notably from one century to another, but the rate of acceleration itself has risen, after a slight slow-down due to the second world war: from 1951 to 1955, the population increased by 6.8 per cent, say an average of 1.67 per cent per annum.[5] The mere continuation of this same rate of acceleration would give an increase of 1 to 5.2 per cent in one century.

Fig. 2 shows all this and proves that we are truly facing an entirely new factor.

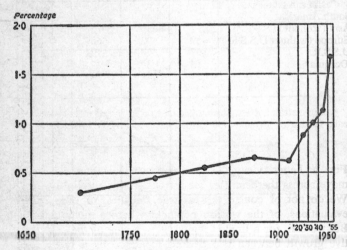

FIG. 2.—Average annual increase of population since 1650.

Forecasts

The United Nations have calculated the world's probable population up to the year 2000, following three different as-

[5] *Background Facts on World Population and Population Trends*, United Nations document E/CN. 9/139, February 1957.

sumptions of fertility. The main figures are shown in the following table.

The expected growth varies considerably according to the different areas. South and Central America are to increase rapidly, followed by Asia, whereas the growth of the European population will on the contrary be rather modest.

The question of Latin America will be taken up in greater detail in chapter 6.

	Population in 1955	Population in 2,000		
		high assumption	medium assumption	low assumption
		(millions of inhabitants)		
Africa	216	663	517	420
North America	182	326	312	274
Central America and Caribbean Islands	58	219	198	147
South America	125	432	394	298
Asia (without U.S.S.R.)	1,490	4,250	3,870	2,890
Europe (without U.S.S.R.)	409	592	568	491
U.S.S.R.	197	395	379	333
Oceania*	15	30	29	27
	2,692	6,907	6,267	4,880

* i.e. Australia, New Zealand, and Pacific Islands under American, British or French administration.

From Rome to the present day

For a better view of the recent acceleration we must move across the centuries "as a stone moves through water." We do not of course possess true statistics, or even rough evaluations, of the world's population before modern times. But we can, for a limited region, get an idea of the comparative growth between two periods separated by a fairly long stretch of time.

According to Beloch, the population of the Roman Empire must have reached 54 million when Tiberius came to power, in 14 B.C. There cannot be more than 300 million inhabitants over the same territories today. These are not precise figures, but we shall see that absolute precision is rather pointless in practice here. Let us even suppose an increase of 1 to 6 in nineteen centuries, which gives an annual increase below 0.1 per cent.

What would have happened if that population had increased, over the nineteen centuries, at the present rate of 1.7 per cent per annum, or even at a much lower rate of 1 per cent only?

One couple of the Tiberian age would by now have produced 130 million descendants. The population descended from that of the Roman territories would consist of about 3,000 millions, that is, 120,000 times more than the present population of the entire world. Even assuming that it might have exterminated the other populations, including China, it would have a density of 6,216,000 to the square mile, or approximately two persons to the square yard.

Such calculations are evidently right off the mark. Something has happened.

Growth is uneven

The developed countries do not, at any rate on a long view, contribute to the acceleration of the increase in world population. Their period of rapid growth was the nineteenth century and the beginning of the twentieth. Nevertheless the last decade, 1940–50, shows another spurt upward compared to the previous decade, with its great crisis.

It is in the "under-developed" countries that acceleration occurs, particularly in the last generation.

In fact, the average increase of 1.7 per annum for the population of the world is worked out from results that are very different for various regions. The 300 million Western Europeans multiply at a rate of only 0.7 per cent: the rate of 2 per cent, on the other hand, is surpassed in many countries: the whole of Central America, North Africa, the Middle East and almost the whole of Asia. Finally the rate of 3 per cent is reached in Mexico, Malaya, Turkey, Venezuela, etc. An increase of 2.5 per cent to 3 per cent per annum has almost become the norm in under-developed countries.

The rate 2.5 per cent per annum is equivalent to a doubling of population in under thirty years and to a multiplication by 12 in one century. Something has certainly changed.

Here, by way of documentation, is the approximate annual increase in various countries:

	%		%
Algeria (Moslems)	2.5 to 3	Iran	2.4
Brazil	2.5 to 3	Morocco	2.5 to 3
Ceylon	2.7	Malaysia	3
Chili	2.7	Mexico	3
China	2.5	Peru	2.4
Egypt	2.6	Philippines	2.8
Formosa	2.6	Tunisia	2.5 to 3
India	2	Turkey	3
Indonesia	2.5	Venezuela	3

I shall deal with the zones of strong growth and strong pressure in more detail in chapter 6.

"Natural" multiplying

To return to the world as a whole, or rather, to leave aside for the moment the question of individual countries, I shall now consider the conditions of growth for the human species.

A population which does not master nature and does not act either against life or against death, is designated as "demographically primitive" or "natural." Such a society is not quite comparable to animals: it cannot fight disease efficiently, any more than animals can, but it is assumed to have evolved a matrimonial and social order, which ensures a fertility not far removed from theoretical physiological fertility. For, contrary to appearances, a panmixia based on animal promiscuity would not produce such high results, nature being a great waster.

History is full of demographically primitive societies. Until now, demographic primitiveness has even been the norm.

Up to Jenner and the vaccination against smallpox, medicine had practically no effect, at least in terms of mortality, for it killed about as many people as it saved. The expectation of life in the early 18th century was no higher than that of Antiquity, and even no higher, possibly, than that of prehistoric times.

On the other hand, until quite recently, and with only very

local and temporary exceptions, the ways of slowing down natural reproduction were not preventive and voluntary; contraception, abortion or infanticide was nowhere a general rule. Such practices certainly developed in some societies in the course of history, but these subsequently became the prey of rivals who had remained more vital. For a long time, differential fertility selected people and groups of people precisely according to their fertility.

At what rate would a "demographically primitive" society multiply, assuming that its natural numerical expansion encountered no economic or political obstacle, that is to say, assuming that it had abundance of land and lived without interior or exterior wars?

In such a society, the birth rate is approximately 45 or 50 per 1,000, according to the age of marriage. (The differences in fertility between the various races are too slight to show up in practical statistics.) These rates are frequently met with today.

Mortality cannot be determined with the same exactitude. In a society without scientific medicine, the average life seldom lasts more than thirty years. The death rate is about 30 per 1,000.

Even less favourable figures have been quoted: average life of twenty years. But this figure, obtained in many places, at certain times, included more than just natural mortality. If the death rate had been as high, all these societies would have been doomed to vanish under the pressure of accidental causes.

This average life, however, should not mislead us: in a society where the average life is of thirty years, for example, few men die at thirty years old. Infant mortality plays an important part in such societies and easily reaches 20 to 25 per cent for the first year of life only; this murderous first year alone reduces the average life by nearly ten years.

We do not need absolute precision here either; it matters little, for this present purpose, whether this "natural" society develops naturally, that is, without accidents or resistance to surroundings, at an annual rate of 1.5 per cent or of 2 per cent; for we have seen that at such a rate mankind would multiply inordinately after a few centuries. The actual growth of populations has been much slower, about 0.1 per cent per annum, as we have seen, for societies included in the Roman Empire.

Let us take a brief look at prehistory, which is beginning to yield a few demographic secrets:

If it is true, as M. Louis-René Nougier has shown,[6] that during the third millenium B.C. the population of present-day France increased from 500,000 to 5 million, this represents only an insignificant growth of about 0.2 to 0.3 per cent per annum, several times inferior to natural growth.

In short, the actual growth of populations has in the past been considerably inferior to natural growth. Presumably then, accidental causes intervened. We shall look for them.

Fertility was high

Why did these populations, which should have increased by 1.5 to 2 per cent per annum, in fact increase at much lower rates? Migrations to new horizons could have played only a limited part in reducing the rate. These peoples must then have had either a fertility that was lower or a mortality that was higher than those of a "natural" society.

There is no confirmation at all of the theory of recently increased fertility, and it will not stand up to examination. Societies with low fertility may have existed for various reasons. The dissolution of morals and voluntary celibacy could, in general, play a more important role than health conditions, in this reduction of fertility.

Such societies were, in any case, exceptional. We know that, in the prestatistical periods about which we have information, the actual fertility was higher than that of present-day Western populations, and we have no reason to believe that the natural fertility of the species has increased. The only improvement which has occurred is sanitary and social (fewer miscarriages in a sufficiently nourished population where the women are not engaged on hard labours).

---

[6] *Essai sur le peuplement préhistorique de la France. Population,* April–June 1954.

The most satisfactory explanation of the slow increase in population through the centuries is the high death rate those peoples had to endure. In addition to natural mortality there was also an irregular excess mortality. And here we meet the three Fates, not those of Antiquity, but a more formidable trinity: Famine, Epidemics, Wars. They deserve some of our attention.

Chapter 3

The three fates of excess mortality

IN ORDER to see more clearly how a "natural" society evolves we will first take a look at the life of animals.[1]

A living species in its environment

Every living species is equipped with a faculty for reproducing itself, sometimes very rapidly. Even the least productive uniparous animals can, in favourable conditions, easily double their number in twenty years, and this doubling can then, with the play of geometrical progressions, lead to extremely high numbers even in periods of weaker vitality.

But this growth comes up against environment resistance.

Let us suppose that the living species is unique in the environment. Its growth cannot continue indefinitely. We may distinguish two ceilings, or upper limits:

(a) *Physical ceiling*. The total force of all the elements which constitute the environment cannot be overcome.

(b) *Biochemical ceiling*. Since the vital process requires non-instantaneous chemical transformations and the competition of non-assimilatable substances, the bioaggregate of the species can never represent more than a fraction of the substance entering the cycle or competing in it. This fraction is sometimes very small, so that this upper limit is, in general, much lower than the first.

Growth is not stopped suddenly by this second ceiling. The species comes up against a stronger and stronger resistance from the inert environment. The environment cedes a certain quantity of substance to the effort of the species; but the withdrawal is elastic; resistance reasserts itself, so that the sub-

[1] The reader will find more details on this subject in our *Théorie générale de la population*, vol. I, *Economie et population*, P.U.F., 1952 and 1956, pp. 9 to 24.

stances yielded to the species are not in proportion to its number. The reduction of substances per individual then reacts upon the species, provoking an increase in mortality, or a decrease in fertility, or an abandonment of the environment (emigration). Most frequently it is the shortage of food that provokes these reactions, but not inevitably.

Two phenomena occur:

An economic phenomenon. When the species increases, the means of subsistence per individual diminishes in quantity, because of the limitations of natural resources.

A biological phenomenon. This diminution of subsistence-means increases mortality and reduces fertility (leaving migrations aside).

The three fates

Animal excess mortality occurs in three ways: famine, epidemics, and violent death from the action of another species.

Famine is the most logical effect of the environment's resistance. It is a simple passive resistance. The environment refuses to yield anything more, therefore the quantity of substances taken from it by the species is enough to support only a certain number of individuals.

Epidemic illness is an accidental event which may appear quite unrelated to this equilibrium of species versus environment. But epidemics spread more easily when the species has multiplied, first because of the simple fact of number and density, and second because undernourished individuals offer less resistance to the illness.

Even when purely accidental, these epidemics counterbalance the multiplication of the species and help to maintain the species in a certain zone.

As for violent death from the action of another species, this is an *active* resistance of the environment. I shall return to it again later, when dealing with the equilibrium of two competing species.

The natural ceiling of animal species

An animal group placed in a specified environment cannot go too far above its ceiling without incurring a biological "punishment," except in favourable conditions. It oscillates around this ceiling, which it can surpass only precariously.

The oscillation around this level is not of the pendulum type characteristic of mechanical equilibria. Even though cyclical phenomena may introduce a certain regularity, the plus or minus variations are the result of chance phenomena.

A position of equilibrium can only be perfectly maintained if conditions remain constant, particularly the climate, and the aptitudes of the species in making the most of its environment.

If the climate becomes unfavourable—a gradual cooling, for instance, or drying up—the ceiling fixed by nature is also lowered gradually. This is a disaster for the species, victim of its environment.

Conversely, there can be favourable changes, and of course the species can adapt itself to the environment, learning where to find more food, reducing its vital needs, etc. The ceiling then becomes slowly higher.

These trends, however, are usually very slow, so that the equilibrium itself varies very slowly too. There is a maximal level for each group considered, a limit to the capacity of the habitat.

Two species in competition

I shall now deal with the situation in which two species are in competition, either because they both need the same food, or because the one feeds on the other. This may lead to the disappearance of one or the other, or a stable position of equilibrium may be achieved, allowing for the co-existence of the two species.

There is the classical example of the Juan Fernandez island: goats released on an island multiply and reach the maximal level allowed by the annual supply of grass.

If at this moment wolves are released on the island, these will eat the goats and multiply also. If the island is flat and featureless, without shelters even, the goats will disappear, and so, shortly afterwards, will the wolves, deprived of their food. The death of the last goat will mean the death of the last wolf. But if the island is rocky, with parts of it difficult for the wolves to reach, the wolves will miss their means of subsistence as the goats become rarer, and will diminish also. A position of equilibrium will be established between the two species. Similarly, any prey which multiplies through favourable conditions, finds less to eat and at the same time is more likely to be killed by the predatory species. Two factors work simultaneously towards equilibrium. This stable position of equilibrium is, like the previous one, subject to accidental variations, particularly meteorological variations (unequal vegetable growth in different years, epidemics that are more or less dependent on temperature, etc.).

It could happen that during one year the accidental variation is strong enough to cause the disappearance of the predatory species, or else of both species. The stable position of equilibrium of the two species cannot then be regained, except with outside help.

What can the wolves and goats do in their own interest? We must be careful here. In this fable I am naturally supposing that the animals are conscious of this interest and have the means to serve it.

If the goats possess both a retreat inaccessible to the wolves and some commonage or pasture land difficult for the wolves to reach, it would be in their interest to remain in the retreat for a time, although they may suffer and some may die of hunger. The wolves would then disappear as a species, leaving the goats free to multiply to the ceiling permitted by the island's means of subsistence, that is to say, far beyond the number that maintained them in equilibrium with the wolves.

And the interest of the wolves? Curiously enough, it does not lie in the development of a greater agility which would enable them to reach the retreat. Such a triumphant invasion would in fact lead to their early disappearance. This hypothesis deserves our attention, in spite of the unlikeliness of such a voluntary development. As a species, why would the wolves be going to their doom? Because they would be eating their capital instead of being content with a regular income, if they attacked the goat species, i.e., their machine for transforming vegetable into animal. The interest of the wolves would lie, on the contrary, in letting the goats graze in the whole island until they have reached their ceiling; the wolves, too, would reach a higher ceiling and would have to take care not to surpass it; if necessary, it would be in their interest to eat each other! and since we are making them so wily, they might also learn how to regulate their birth rate.

Better still: if the wolves became really intelligent and full of foresight, they would in practice start breeding and raising goats, in an attempt to multiply the species with which they would be living, in fact, in symbiosis.

The goats can also compromise their source of food and therefore their existence, by devouring all the tender and savoury young shoots.

It may therefore happen that an improvement in the preda-tory species provokes its own reduction, and even its disap-pearance, by enabling it to touch the very source of the regu-lar income provided by nature, in other words, to attack the "capital." The improvement, in fact, has given it only a dying spark of extra life, unless another improvement following from the first should enable it to make use of some other means of subsistence which had until then been inaccessible or unusable. In this way progress can condemn a species to progress.

Two species in equilibrium with each other can thus be limited by their own destructiveness, rather than by a lack of subsistence means. The food of one species, which is the basis of the whole, can remain throughout over-abundant.

If the concept of equilibrium and of the "limited capacity of the habitat" are the basic concepts of animal ecology, this is because the variations of tendency are slower than the multiplication of the species, so that the ceilings of each one can be maintained in a fairly static position for some time.

Violent deaths and natural deaths

Among animal species we must therefore distinguish between species that are prey to other species, and those which do not have to endure such severe trial. But is it in fact so severe? We cannot be sure, because failing violent deaths, the species are liable to famines and epidemics that lead, usually, to even more painful deaths.

I think I can safely leave aside this doubtful point, which is somewhat outside my subject, and mention only the fact that the numbers in domestic species can be limited by the will of man.

Back to the human species

I shall now transpose these considerations to the human species, or rather, I shall bear them in mind as I examine the way in which populations have evolved numerically in the past, during the "natural" epoch when men did not seek to limit their own descendance, when technical progress was slower than natural reproduction and when, finally, medicine was not as yet much help against mortality.

Information on mortality in ancient times is hardly available in statistical form, since parish registers rarely go back beyond the seventeenth century. Moreover, vast areas of historical material are still lying fallow. Nevertheless, the development of statistics in the last two centuries is so great that we can get a perfectly adequate idea of the conditions which prevailed for so long.

Natural cataclysms played an important role at various times. In some parts of the world, such as China, floods were often murderous. We cannot, however, draw conclusions of general applicability from such a factor. In historical times disasters of this kind have played only a very limited role.

On the other hand, we meet the three Fates again: Famines, Epidemics, Violent Deaths—the latter, however, due more often to the human species itself than to the action of another species.

Famines

Famines have long been in a sense the norm of mankind. But we must distinguish between acute famine and permanent under-nourishment (or even bad nourishment), although they frequently go together.

Acute famine results from three factors usually working together: insufficient agricultural technique in a growing population, irregular harvestings and insufficiency of transport.

The pattern can be summarized as follows: a society exists, on a given land, at a constant technical level. It increases naturally for a time, perhaps limiting its consumption a little, but not dangerously. Then a really deficient harvest occurs, and the privations are severe: everything must be saved on, even the seed. Thinly sown, the grain yields less the following year. Pushed by hunger, the people collect it earlier than they should, thereby reducing the resources even further; all that is needed is another inclement meteorological spell for the cycle of famine to start on its implacable course; nothing can stop it. A new cycle of growth and relative prosperity can only begin after the population has been thinned down by the famine. It is then easy to think that the losses were quickly made up.

Here again we have the struggle between two species, one being the prey (vegetation), the other predatory (man), and the second needs to know how to spare the first with foresight, how, in fact, to live on the income without touching the capital. The fatal failure of foresight is the absorption of seed as food, the corn eaten in the blade.

The term "cycle," used above, should not mislead us; there is no element of regularity in such alternacy, and all the less so because other accidents (wars, etc.) intervene in this more or less natural movement.

The unevenness of harvests from one year to another is much more emphasized in a country with under-developed technical methods. Progress enables a country to produce not only more, but more regularly. Moreover, it provides resources for compensation. A frost like that which occurred in France and Western Europe in February 1956 would have caused an extreme shortage in the past, and probably a famine. In fact, it merely halted the increase in agricultural product from one year to another and consumption was not diminished by a fraction.

Famines were often made more serious still by the lack of transport; there was no way of coming to the rescue of a particularly hard hit region. But ease of transport would only have postponed the shortages. A static or barely evolving technique made famine fatal, if not that time, then the next (unless a different scourge arose first).

Or else, technique remained more or less stationary; what we now call "productivity" increased only very slowly, whether the years were good or bad; the rhythm of increase was very far below the 1 or 2 per cent per annum necessary to counter-balance natural multiplying.

Epidemics

We are nowadays upset by a gentle epidemic of influenza, or by a surge of poliomyelitis which causes fifty deaths, and we may find it difficult to imagine the ravages caused by epidemics in the "natural" epoch.

Even without putting too much trust in the death figures quoted by the chroniclers of the time, we nevertheless find death rates that are far higher than anything we have seen in contemporary times, including the years of war. During the black plague of 1348 many regions and localities lost a third or half their population.

This evil, "that can enrich Acheron in one day," was often called the plague though no doubt it was often, strictly speaking, many different things. The devastation was so intense that one wonders how the human race avoided total extinction. The fact is that epidemics, like fires, always died out in the end, when the population had thinned out and the survivors had become more or less immune to the illness. But they also spread more rapidly inasmuch as the undernourished population offered less resistance to them.

A few examples

Because of epidemics and famines, the mortality rate could vary considerably from one year to another, even during a period of interior and exterior peace.

Here for example are the numbers of deaths, according to Sussmilch,[2] in two regions:

[2] *Die Göttliche Ordnung*, vol. I.

Prussia-Lithuania		Minden and Ravensberg	
1707	17,155	1721	3,191
1708	18,789	1722	2,556
1709	59,196	1723	3,758
1710	188,537	1724	4,196
1711	10,131	1725	3,386
1712	10,445	1726	5,774
1713	13,432	1727	3,992

Quite apart even from the extraordinary rise of 1710 in Prussia-Lithuania, it is remarkable that the death rate at Ravensberg in 1726 increased more than that of France in the year of Verdun and the Somme.

There are other examples of sudden and important increases in the death rate in France, in England, etc. M. Meuvret[3] has worked out the correlations between the death rate and the price of corn, the latter being itself closely related to the nature of the harvests.

These statistics naturally do not take war losses into account, which I will deal with now.

War and violence

Purely military losses, in the sense of men killed in combat, have only rarely reached figures of any demographic importance in history. In any case, writers only too frequently quote effects and losses that are far higher than the real ones. Lacking the means of finding out the real figures, they yield to popular feeling on such occasions, are themselves struck by tales of horror and uncontrollable rumours, and so reproduce these rumours or imagine a figure that tallies with the rumours.

On the other hand, until very recent times, wars have always been murderous for the civil population that watched the armies pass through. The shortage of supplies would force people to live on the land, and its method of doing this was far from being rationally organized. Great struggles ensued which led, even on lands previously friendly, to

[3] *Les crises de subsistance et de démographie de la France d'ancien régime, Population,* No. 4, October–December 1947.

mutual destruction, devastation and sometimes massacres. Wars in the strict sense of the word always brought other violence, sedition, repressions, expulsions, armed banditry, etc.

Various authors have suggested that over-population has been the chief cause of wars. This attractive theory turns out, on examination, to be a little too simple. If kings and rulers had intended to make war on their neighbours in order to fight overpopulation in their own territory, they would have taken the neighbouring territory by chasing out or exterminating its inhabitants. Yet in the whole of history we see them on the contrary seizing territory by force *with* its inhabitants. Any extermination of these was due, not to demographic density but to incompatibility (religion, and crusades, especially).

In a more primitive phase, however, pure conquests may well have taken place because of the demographic pressure of ill-exploited territories. The Angles and Saxons exterminated the Britons and took their place, because they needed land on which to live. But five centuries later William the Conqueror knew better. The Normans took the land and property, but carefully preserved the inhabitants, in order to make them work.

If the Anglo-Americans and the Anglo-Australians exterminated the aboriginal inhabitants of America and Australia, it was not on account of any demographic pressure; had the people in question been docile and capable of agriculture, they too would have been carefully preserved.

We have had to wait until 1945 and the agreements of Potsdam, to see a total, determined and premeditated expulsion of a whole population. And curiously enough, this taking of territory without its inhabitants was achieved by Marxist countries whose theories expressly condemn even the possibility of over-population! Even so, the motive was more political than economic.

We must therefore abandon this over-simple theory of rulers making war on each other in order to relieve the demographic pressure on their territory. Precisely because war is imperialistic, it is hardly likely to concern itself with the standard of living of individuals. This does not mean that there is no relation between wars and movements of population. After a period of destruction, the ruler is no longer in a state to make war. As soon as the population and its wealth return to normal he finds, on the contrary, new resources which enable him to attain his political objectives.

Besides, like the wind and the storm, war is the result of a difference in demographic pressures rather than of high pressure. The wars of 1914 and 1940 were largely facilitated by the French demographic decline in the face of the German increase.

Finally, extreme demographic pressure and the acute distress that goes with it, are less likely to generate a war than medium pressure, which leaves sufficient reserves to produce the necessary arms and food supplies. Here is an example from contemporary history:

The Second World War and its preludes included Italy's attack on Ethiopia, Germany's attack on Poland, and Japan's attack on China. In all three cases it was the country with the lesser demographic pressure and the lower birth rate which attacked the other.

There is a critical point in any population, which corresponds to its power optimum. A population that ensures maximum power is bigger than a population that ensures the highest standard of living for individuals. This is why the democratic countries, which are seeking a higher standard of living, are more "malthusian" than the imperialist regimes in search of power. And conversely, when a country is slightly over-populated, but not so much so as to be unable to arm, its temptation to find salvation in imperialism is greater than that of another country. And if such an imperialist country is surrounded with populated but under-armed countries the temptation is even stronger.

In any case, whatever the cause of war and violence, the effect is the same: a high death rate, a lowered birth rate, a reduced population.

Besides the Three Fates, Famine, Epidemics, and War, there is also a social phenomenon, which is little known, thanks to a more or less justified reserve or delicacy that screens it even from our retrospective gaze: this is the elimination of undesirables.

The elimination of undesirables

Every society is tempted to eliminate, in one way or another, any creatures thought to be supernumerary or inconvenient. This may lead to a higher death rate and sometimes to a decrease in fertility.

Primitive societies which eliminate the old are not in question here, since this does not lead to any durable decrease of the population. It is only when the eliminated persons are of procreating age that the demographic equilibrium may be affected by such practices.

The most classical methods are abortion and infanticide, practised on a certain scale, in various countries, either secretly or in accordance with law and authority. Abortion has remained and is now tolerated and even encouraged in some countries. But infanticide has come to be regarded more and more as a crime. Since society prefers to evade responsibility, it avoids positive action and tries to find a way of quietening its conscience. Here is an example:

Open infanticide is condemned in all societies with a violence that increases in proportion to the temptation; nevertheless a compromise has been found, at various times, by means of "exposition." If the child died it was the will of the gods. People appeased their conscience by playing the game of chance with a high degree of complicity. They then further smoothed their qualms by easily accepting the stories and legends about children who had survived and attained the very highest honours.

Is this time so very distant? In the eighteenth century (with sequels in the nineteenth and even in the twentieth), society had found a way of eliminating a large number of beings without actually killing them; abandoned children were taken in by hospitals, and kept there in such appalling conditions that a large majority of them died. In this way nobody had blood on their hands.

Another, even less conscious method of elimination was practised for a long time with regard to a-social beings.

Those who were unable to fit into the economic system, the moral system, etc., ran the risk of being eliminated.

Let us look, for instance, at France under the old regime. Because of fiscal, military, or other demands, because of infirmities too, men would "contract out," and become beggars, vagabonds, robbers, highwaymen, etc.[4] In Paris alone, the unclassed were still estimated at about 100,000 around 1900, so tragically called "la belle époque." What were their demographic characteristics? We are ill-informed on this point. In the case of mere poverty there would be the fertility arising from abject misery, together with a dreadful infant mortality. More often, however, illness, discomfort and the separation of the sexes must have been causes of sterility. In this way one part of the population would be eliminated, consisting of those who, according to the governing classes, did not want work.

Were they really undesirables? Certainly the governing classes tried to make use of these social failures. From the first Capets to Louis XVI or to Félix Faure, even to de Gaulle, the edicts forbidding and repressing mendicants are innumerable. But most of the well-disposed recognized the futility of pure repression and spoke of having new lands cleared or reclaimed by all these outsiders. It is the futility of these efforts which produces the expression "undesirables" and which allows one to say that society eliminated them by indirect means, without any apparent encouragement on the part of the authorities, which took no responsibility before God or man.

As for malefactors, madmen, etc., they were eliminated, not voluntarily or systematically, but more directly. Society was in no state to incarcerate all those who endangered it by infringing its laws or by committing acts of madness.

Without going as far as the Nazi gas-chambers, the repressive systems, ill-treatments, etc., certainly did their work. We are all the less well informed on the subject in that these practices were naturally not widely publicised.

---

[4] This not very widely known question is richly documented in *Histoire du vagabondage*, by A. Vexliard.

The natural ceiling of the human species

Finally, we must realize that "natural" human populations, without appreciable technical progress, cannot, any more than can animal species, go beyond a certain ceiling imposed upon them by nature.

This limitation is common, as we have seen, to all animal and vegetable species. But the feature which distinguishes natural human species from animal and vegetable species is that they are their own victims, through wars, whereas animal species are usually the victims of other species.

This natural ceiling is not an insuperable barrier. The population oscillates around this limit, increasing slowly, thanks to its capacity for multiplying, then drops suddenly, like the stone of Sisyphus, after some disaster or other.

Some populations can disappear altogether. There is, in fact, a minimum below which no population can subsist, even for biological reasons. But other groups, other races progress within this jungle.

The natural ceiling that weighs down upon the human race can of course be raised by an adaptation of man to his environment, by a better mastery of nature. Vogt estimates that there has been no real progress for three centuries, only a greater aptitude for consuming natural capital, in which case the progress achieved would only lead mankind to its doom. There is no evidence for thinking in this way. In many countries the natural ceiling has been raised thanks to technical progress. But because technical progress had, for a long time, been so slow that the increase in means of subsistence was less rapid than that of the natural population (2 per cent per annum at least), the ceiling has weighed heavily on mankind.

These age-old conditions have changed now that the struggle against nature has enabled us both to fight premature death and to raise the production of subsistence-means. A divorce has taken place between man and nature. A medical revolution and an economic revolution have destroyed and will destroy the laws and equilibria of thousands of years.

Chapter 4

A longer life

THE CURVES of birth rate and death rate, which have been intertwined for so long, are now widely separated in many countries.

In more than half the world, fertility has remained very close to natural fertility: 45 births for every 1,000 inhabitants per year is still the rate in most under-developed countries, after the errors due to people's forgetfulness in registering have been rectified. I shall return to this in the next chapter.

The death rate, on the other hand, has been considerably lowered, often settling below 20 for every 1,000.

The results of this lowering can be seen even better in the tables of survival than in the death rates; it is not mere coincidence that the first tables of survival were established (end of seventeenth and eighteenth centuries) at about the same time as the beginning of longevity itself. Measurement and control went together.

Such is the brutal fact; but the death rate of a population is the result of two very different factors:

(a) *Composition by age groups.* It is quite obvious that a home for old people will have a much higher death rate than a school for boys, even supposing the health conditions in the latter were deplorable. Similarly, health conditions being equal, a society containing few old people will be less affected by death than a society containing many. The failure to observe these facts can lead to some very curious errors.

(b) *Health conditions as such.* These are expressed in the tables of survival and the calculations of the average life or expectation of life.

In under-developed countries, the composition by age

groups has hardly changed for centuries. The recent lowering of the death rate shows only a longer duration of life.

Expectation of life

A classic method of observing and measuring this consists of calculating the average life or, more precisely, the expectation of life at birth. It is a somewhat abstract notion, but it has the advantage of combining all ages.

Two centuries ago a newborn babe had an expectation of life of about 30 years. This figure is already over 70 in many countries. Even more remarkable, many under-developed countries with a very modest standard of living have already reached an expectation of life of over 50 years (Brazil 52 years, Jamaica 56, Panama and Ceylon 60, Trinidad and Tobago 61, etc.).

Moreover, these levels of 60 and even of 50 years' expectation of life were reached only very recently in Europe: the 50-year level was not attained in England till about 1908, and in France till about 1913; the 60 year level in about 1935 in England, and about 1939 in France, that is to say, more than a century and a half after the death rate had begun to go down.

Thus the progress which has taken the Western countries a century or a century and a half to achieve, has taken one generation in some of the under-developed countries.

It is, in any case, only in the last few years that life has become longer. Consider Ceylon, for instance, a country in which the statistics are quite good. From 1901 to 1921, the expectation of life at birth had hardly changed: 37⅓ to 38⅙. From 1921 to 1946, in 25 years, it gained nearly 10 years (48). In 1953 it was over 56 and must now be higher than that of France before the war!

Progress in India, though not quite so rapid, has also been remarkable: a lengthening of 6 years in 20 years, from 1925 to 1945; similar progress can be observed everywhere, 9 years in 15 years (1930 to 1945) in British Guiana, etc.

Survival rates

This lengthening of the average life must be correctly interpreted. To say that the average life has risen from 30 to 60 years does not mean that death used to strike men at 30 and now allows them a respite of the same duration. The rise is in fact chiefly caused by the decrease of infant mortality.

The important thing from a demographic point of view is the proportion of survivors in various age groups, particularly among the under-fifties.

Here, in any case, is a very succinct summary of three survival tables; they concern:

A country before the demographic revolution (France)
An under-developed country today (India)
A developed country today (Norway)

	France Eighteenth century (Duvillard)	India 1941–1950	Norway 1946–1950
		(numbers of survivors)	
Birth	1,000	1,000	1,000
1 year	767	818	970
20 years	502	574	950
40 "	369	422	916
60 "	214	216	818
80 "	35	27	388
85 "	12	2	214

At 85 the number of survivors seems to be a hundred times higher in modern Norway than in modern India. In fact, the death figures are frequently imprecise with regard to the very aged, and the death rate between 80 and 85 is unlikely to be quite so intense in India. The high age groups are at one and the same time those in which science can offer only limited help and those which have no durable influence from a demographic point of view.

Comparing the eighteenth-century French table (which must have been approximately valid for Norway at the same period), we can see that in two centuries the number of survivors has almost doubled at 20 years of age and almost quadrupled at 60 years of age.

More important still is the fact that the proportion of people reaching adult age has risen from 50 to 95 per cent. The family of 5 children which, taking celibacy and physiological sterility into account, would have produced only two or three adult procreators, can produce 5 today. Instead of an equilibrium from generation to generation, there is a rapid multiplication.

The importance of this progress can be seen in the light of the following observation: until only very recently, longevity remained more or less the same. Leaving aside periods of war, we can find no essential differences between prehistoric men, the men of ancient times and those of pre-development modern times.

A stone, that has weighed upon the human race for aeons has now been lifted.

But many other things are being lifted at the same time.

Excess mortality disappears

Wars and violence, famines, epidemics, these as we have seen make up the formidable trio of scourges that decimated populations. Now progress has been achieved in all three spheres: the keeping of peace, economic progress and medical progress are the three counter-balancing factors to the above scourges.

(a) Public order is established in most states; internal struggles between clans, tribes, etc., have disappeared or have become considerably less destructive. As for international wars, it is indeed very difficult to formulate any principle of lasting value. Compilers of survival tables always leave them out of their calculations. But in most countries they have caused only slight losses over the last century. We shall later see a rather surprising world balance-sheet of the Second War.

(b) Acute famines are much rarer, on account of improved communications and, in extreme cases, the existence of foreign aid. If a real famine threatened 25 million Indians, the U.S.S.R., China and the U.S.A. would vie with each other in the sending of corn. I repeat, however, that we should not confuse acute famine with chronic under-nourishment. The first scourge has almost disappeared, but the second is still with us and may even have spread, as we shall see.

In developed countries the economic factor has played an important role. During the nineteenth and twentieth centuries, the production and the consumption of subsistence-means rose considerably in all social classes, so much so that the purely economic factor no longer exercises any appreciable influence on the death rate. In under-developed countries of the present day the question is much less clear. It will be further investigated later in this book.

(c) Finally, the killer-epidemics (the plague, cholera, smallpox, etc.) are in the process of disappearing. I shall be giving precise figures in due course.

But there is more: not only is the excess mortality which was constantly planing down the level of population disappearing, so that the human species is now re-acquiring its natural multiplying power, but the mortality one may call normal, natural, millenary—whichever one prefers—is also lowering noticeably.

"Normal" death moves back

The advances in modern medicine, especially in hygiene and preventive medicine, have everywhere lowered that dismal figure of 30 per 1,000 which seemed like a heavy stone laid on the head of mankind, and much lower rates have been reached, varying from 15 to 25 per 1,000, even among very poor people.

Societies, therefore, who have retained a natural birth rate, now dispose not only of a natural multiplying power of 1 to 1.5 per cent per annum which has never before been reached or retained for any length of time, but also of a supplementary multiplying power, so that in many countries the rate of increase has reached 2.5 or 3 per cent per annum.

I shall now examine the mechanism of the lowering death rate.

Moving back mortality is a destruction

Illnesses may be divided roughly into "exogenous" illnesses, due to exterior agents (tuberculosis, infections, etc.), and "endogenous" illnesses of an organic type (cancer, congenital debility, heart trouble, etc.). Medical action has been as successful in fighting the first group as it has failed so far in the second. Infant exogenous mortality has almost disappeared in certain countries—lower by 90 per cent or even more, in comparison with the "natural" period—whereas properly endogenous mortality has hardly been affected.

Man has admirably succeeded in destroying bacteria and viruses and in preventing their activity. On the other hand, his efforts with the actual functioning of the organism have so far produced only very modest results. The most important advances have been in surgery, which is also destructive.

Let us take a look at two extreme death rate tables, the one relating to a "natural" population with an expectation of life of 30 years, the other to a developed population, with an expectation of life of over 71 years. Between 10 and 15, an age group in which mortality is almost entirely exogenous, the death rate lowers by 90 per cent; between 80 and 85, an age group in which mortality is mostly endogenous, it lowers by only 35 per cent.

It would be as excessive to claim that all exogenous deaths have already been eliminated (there will always be accidents, in the widest sense of the word), as to affirm that no endogenous death has yet been prevented. But the tendency is in that direction. J. Bourgeois-Pichat has already thought of pushing this tendency to its logical conclusion in order to measure what he calls the "biological death rate" once all exogenous deaths have been eliminated. We may compare the survivors of such a survival table with those of a "natural" population and those of present-day France.

	Natural death rate (eighteenth-century France according to Duvillard)	Death rate of present-day France	Biological death rate (Tables of maximum survivorship)
		(number of survivors)	
Birth	1,000	1,000	1,000
1 year	767	960	989
20 years	502	940	987
40 "	369	901	977
60 "	214	754	904
80 "	35	298	500
90 "	4	40	169

The expectation of life would reach 78, no more. This calculation does not presume to constrict mankind with an irremovable ceiling. Cancer and arteriosclerosis may very possibly be conquered one day. But the struggle against exogenous illnesses proceeds more quickly, and some countries, in the vanguard, have already reached a stage not far removed from the provisionary "biological" survival table.

The limits of life

When Bourgeois-Pichat calculated that 78 years would be the average life of a population that had been rid of exogenous illnesses, he was not fixing a limit to the life of specific individuals, since that figure represents an average among men, some of whom would die of a heart attack at 50, or even of congenital malformation at 2 days old, and others of whom would live on after 78.

Until what age?

Like most demographic questions, the extreme longevity of the human species is deeply involved in prejudice and fable, and this from immemorial times. The myth of very long lives goes back to the night of aeons.

Every now and again rumour (that is to say the press) announces that an extremely old man has been found in a backward country, aged 130, 140, sometimes even more.

This is obviously not an impossibility. If such a fact were confirmed, it would break no known scientific law. But until now, such items of news have come only from countries without a registry office or at any rate without a registry office at the time of this exceptional creature's birth. In such societies, men did not know their own age and could only too easily mistake the memory of events told to them, for the memory of the actual events.

This belief in extreme longevity is often related to the myth of sovereign nature, which existed long before Rousseau. The men reputed to have lived 130 or 150 years are always rural people, often from the mountains, who would have been protected by the purity of the air and by their naturistic existence. This myth, which recurs century after century and is more or less related to the myth of degeneracy, has reappeared in a manner as official as it was unexpected, in the announcements of Soviet personalities and their official press, claiming that some men still living in the Caucasus had known the period of Napoleon's invasion!

Popular prejudice on health and longevity comes up against the obstacle of those great dream-destroying statistics that man cannot manipulate according to his desires; for instance, the statistics of death; even so, in spite of the eloquence of the survival tables, the myth of robust old men remains ("they don't make men of that stamp any more"). A compromise is made between the heart and the head, between belief and knowledge; everyone has the right to speak; that is why 54 per cent of French people polled on the question in 1947, though knowing that the death rate is going down, declared that man lives to a lesser age now than a hundred years ago (in actual fact, the average life has more or less doubled, that is to say, it has increased far more in one century than in all those preceding). In 1956, the public was better informed, but only 61 per cent of the questioned people said that life is longer in France than it used to be.

Of course, in those areas that are as yet untouched by science, with all its alarming measuring instruments, fancy, imagination and rumour have all the rights. And the imagination, in love with the marvellous, exaggerates ages when they are very advanced. Modern census methods have already shown that many of the centenarians entered as such in the civil registers turn out to be, on examination, a modest 95. What does science say on this point?

Without insisting on an absolute limit for the human species the works of P. Vincent[5] have shown that man has very little chance of living beyond the age of 109. We would have to observe several million centenarians, he says, in order to ascertain that several have died at the age of 110. Unfortunately there have been only about a thousand centenarians over 15 consecutive generations in France.

Racial differences, moreover, are not known; this does not

[5] *La mortalité des vieillards. Population,* April–June 1951.

mean that they do not exist; only that the differences due to
different modes of living (food, medical care, etc.) are such
that for the moment they obscure all intrinsic differences
that may exist between one race and another.

Besides, the important factor for the multiplication of the
human species is not the age limit assigned to it, but the age
limit of procreation. Apart from truly exceptional cases, the
evidence for which is sometimes unsatisfactory, this age
limit does not go beyond 50 years for women, and shows
no tendency to rise. The decisive factor, I repeat, is the function of survivorship among adult people.

Return to the death rates

These rates depend, as we have seen, both on health conditions and on the composition by age groups. The best health
conditions are still to be found in the developed countries.
But since their composition by age groups is much less favor-
able (15 per cent among sexagenarians, as against 6 or 7 per
cent in under-developed countries), their death rates are
sometimes higher. Here are a few contemporary figures:

France	12.4	Porto-Rico	7.3
Belgium	12.6	Ceylon	9.8
England	11.7	Japan	8
Federal Germany	11	Yugoslavia	11.2

The twentieth century, very different from the nineteenth

We must now come to the essential point: in what way can
the present-day increase of Asiatic, Latino-American, and
African populations be more dangerous than was that of the
European population in the nineteenth century? Since it is
accompanied by a rise in the standard of living, why should
it constitute a threat to that same standard of living?

There are two reasons, even leaving aside the question of
a civilization's greater or lesser aptitude for development,
which will be considered in Chapter 13:

(a) The present-day increase of under-developed countries
is more rapid than was that of the Western population during
the nineteenth century.

(*b*) A divergence has occurred between economic development and medical progress, between the *standard of living* and the *duration of life*.

The twentieth century's more rapid demographic growth

Between 1800 and 1950, in one century and a half, the population of present-day Western Europe has increased from 125 to 310 million inhabitants, which represents an average increase of 0.6 per cent per annum. During the nineteenth century this same population barely doubled itself.

At the present rhythm, however, an under-developed population can double itself in 25 to 30 years, more than three times faster. When I deal with the economic problem I shall show the full significance of this difference.

Why is the increase so rapid? For two minor reasons and one major reason:

(*a*) The birth rate of under-developed countries in the twentieth century is higher than that of Europe in the nineteenth: the latter never reached 40 per thousand (35 in general, 25 in France), it is over 40 per thousand and sometimes 45 in present-day under-developed countries.

(*b*) Overseas emigration slowed down the European rate of increase in the nineteenth century.

(*c*) The death rate is lower today. In the first half of the nineteenth century, figures like 25 per thousand were still frequent: 33 in Austria, 27 in Germany, 26 in Holland, 25 in France, 23 in England and Sweden. Today, at the dawn of world development, such a rate is already exceptional: 20 would be a more likely figure, if one could calculate a world average.

This third cause is the most important, although its quantitative effects may at times have been outweighed by the effects of the other two. But it enables us to put our finger on the essential factor: the death rate is and will be lowering without the help of economic progress.

Standard of living and duration of life

It is very interesting to compare, both in time and space, the standard of living with the duration of life.

The comparisons are naturally very rough, for we are dealing with very large concepts.

Since the standard of living cannot be measured in specific units (though suggestions have been made in that direction), I shall take as unit the average standard of living of Western European countries on the eve of the 1939 war, that is to say, approximately, the quantity of products consumed per inhabitant. We have a fairly good idea of this level, which is just a little below our present standard.

Taking then this level as a basis equal to 100, according to statistical usage, we have the following table:

	Standard of living	Duration of life	
		in years	in indices
France 1788	25	30 years	50
Western Europe in 1870	40	40 years	66
Western Europe in 1938	100	60 years	100
Present day Asia	10	40 to 45 years	66 to 75
Present-day Africa	12	40 years	66
Present-day Latin America	35	50 to 55 years	84 to 92

These are, I repeat, only very rough measurements. We are not in search of decimal-points. But the divergences are so great as to make narrower marking useless.

With a standard of living twice as low as that of France just before the Revolution, Asia and Africa have a considerably longer duration of life. This duration of life was not reached in Europe until about 1870, with a standard of living almost four times as high.

The poverty-stricken under-developed countries have, at one and the same time, a lower standard of living than that of Western Europe under the old regime, a higher birth rate and a lower death rate.

Latin America has the same expectation of life that Western Europe had around 1913 and the same standard of living that Western Europe had around 1850.

A starving Asiatic today can have a higher expectation of life than an aristocrat or a bourgeois of the old regime, well off and well looked after.

Medicine and economics

When Europe was developing, medical progress could hardly[6] ever advance beyond economic progress; both were dependent on the same source, the same inventions. All scientific discoveries (the thermometer, the microscope, chemistry, etc.), were serving both the technique of production and the technique of medical care.

And since medicine was then mostly commercial, the diffusion of methods was to a large extent dictated by economic progress.

Neither of these two interdependencies exists in the twentieth century in under-developed countries, or at any rate, not to the same extent. Medical techniques are mostly imported. An entire population can be vaccinated even though it may still be in the pastoral stage.

Furthermore, medicine has become more and more of a public service. Of course, the rich man not only can be better nourished, he can also consult the best doctor, buy the most costly medicines, etc. But the most effective remedies, in terms of mortality, have been widely diffused. For example malaria has been almost entirely wiped out from certain areas, thanks to the spraying of D.D.T.

A few examples

In the whole world, the effect of social-medical progress seems much more important than that of the economic level; here are a few examples from extremely varied countries and regimes.

First Spain: for twenty years, or let us say since the beginning of the Civil War, the people's standard of living has

---

[6] The word "hardly," which we here prefer to the word "not," softens the contrast between the nineteenth century and the world-scale twentieth century. It is possible, for instance, that medical progress in the first half of the nineteenth century (particularly the suppression of smallpox) slightly preceded economic progress —an important phenomenon. The poverty of the nineteenth century would be due, not so much to the birth of industry (which for all its horrors acted as a valve to the world of agriculture), but rather to the temporary surplus population resulting from medical advances. This point will be taken up again in chapter 13.

not increased appreciably. Nevertheless the death rate is lower by over 40 per cent, having come down from 15.5 per 1,000 to 9 per 1,000. The expectation of life must have risen by about 10 years.

In Ceylon, which we have already mentioned at the beginning of this chapter, the expectation of life has risen so fast that it is equal to that of France twenty years ago, whereas the standard of living must be three or four times lower.

Let us turn now to the U.S.S.R. In 1938, the death rate was still 18 per 1,000. Since then the material standard of living, in terms of food and lodging particularly, has improved only very slightly. Animal foods, especially meat and butter, are in short supply. The average amount of living accommodation in the cities is about 8¼ square yards per person, which is only half the allowance of French Council blocks. In spite of these rigorous conditions, which are hardly better than those of 1938, the death rate has lowered by more than half, having settled around 8 per 1,000. The average life has risen by more than 10 years.

This is the result of an important social-medical effort.

Infant mortality in France was once much higher in the big towns than in other localities. Now the position is reversed. Here for instance is the development in France in the last 20 years:

	1938	1957
Seine	67	21
The whole of France	65	30

In spite of very precarious housing conditions, the influence of the social-medical apparatus has been decisive and more important than sun and fresh air.

A few more examples: During the occupation, living conditions were difficult, but the maintenance of some social order and, in particular, of the more urgent medical aids (the isolation of infectious diseases, vaccination, etc.), kept the death rate at a relatively low level, 17.4 per 1,000 for the whole population, which is lower than the rate for the peaceful years 1911 to 1913. And we must add that, if we left out the population that had aged from 1913 to 1943, the death rate during the Second War would come out lower than that of peacetime thirty years earlier.

The standard of living (wages especially), is about a third higher in Belgium than in Holland. And yet it is in Holland that the expectation of life is higher (72 as against 66 in Belgium). In Amsterdam[7] itself, the death rate is higher among artisans and small employers than among workers. The former have higher incomes, but the latter benefit from more advanced medical and social services. An analogous inversion is found in France between small employers (food-supplies, commerce, etc.) and the lower grade clerical workers.[8]

It costs less to save life than to support it

The costs of collective food hygiene are relatively low. The World Health Organization has estimated the cost of the destruction of malaria at about 30 cents[9] per inhabitant. But the cost of keeping alive all the men thus saved is, as we shall see, much higher.

In 1947, for example, a cholera epidemic broke out in Egypt; in previous periods such an epidemic would have decimated the population. Help was rapidly organized, some from outside and some from the national health organization. The epidemic was stopped in time and only a few thousand died, a negligible number from a demographic point of view; but then the thousands or millions of men who would have vanished in previous periods had to be kept alive. And this is a much more difficult problem.

On the international level, feelings of pity and human solidarity are more easily roused by disease (or, at most, by

[7] See P. de Wolff and J. Meerdink: *La mortalité à Amsterdam selon les quartiers. Population*, 1952, No. 3, *La mortalité à Amsterdam selon les groupes sociaux. Population*, 1954, No. 2.

[8] See MM. Febvay and M. Croze: *Nouvelles données sur la mortalité infantile. Population*, 1954, No. 3.

[9] Sums expressed in francs in the French edition have been converted into dollars at the rate of 420 francs to the dollar, i.e. the rate ruling at the beginning of 1959.

acute famine), than by poverty. Outside help pours in to cure men or at least to prevent them from dying, but not to enable them to live.

The result of this advance of medical progress over economic progress is that it has become possible to make people live both longer and worse. Even with a lower standard of living than before, a man may have a longer life. These absolutely essential facts have not been widely disseminated, probably because they are unpleasant. Some are frightened of having to draw a cruel conclusion from them: that medical progress should be slowed down, according to Vogt's suggestion, which we shall be coming across again later. To observe is one thing, to act is another. A scientist must never, in any circumstances, be afraid of the truth.

The slow progress of the social sciences, and consequently the slow development of institutions, are the result of this refusal to face the truth, which is found even in the most eminent and often the most sincerely well-intentioned men, thanks to the solid defence-system of the unconscious.

Wars that populate

What has happened to war, which was once one of the three great murderers? In 1914–18 it beat all its previous records by killing several million men and causing breaches that remain from generation to generation and are only slowly being filled in.

And yet this war contributed to a great acceleration of progress and therefore to the struggle against death. Medical progress must of course have been appreciable during the hostilities, but it could not have had very important effects since the advances made were chiefly in surgery. And surgery saves many men, but at a fairly heavy cost. It is not surgery which is responsible for the great lowering of the death rate in backward countries.

But the general technical progress that arose out of the 1914–18 war (motor transport, aviation, radio, etc.) advanced evolution by a few years and thereby contributed to the acceleration of the increase in world population, which had already begun.

This paradoxical result can be seen much more clearly in the second war. The loss of human life is estimated at 31 million killed, to which must be added a civilian excess mortality of about 19 million persons; if we add another 10 million to account for reductions in births (in some countries on the contrary, births increased), we get a total loss or a minus-value of 60 million human beings.[10]

On the other side of this tragically negative balance-sheet, however, there is a positive account: the war accelerated the progress of hygiene and the diffusion of known methods, especially against malaria; so much so that the death rate is lower every year.

The use of penicillin, discovered in 1939, made considerable progress during the war, thanks to the American army which possessed powerful methods as well as subjects for experiment. This army was solicitous, not only about life but about comfort, and would spray all the Pacific islands one by one with D.D.T. in order to destroy the mosquitos before taking possession. After so many trials and tests, the technique was ready and perfected for use at the end of hostilities.

By how much has this fact lowered the death rate in the world? This is very difficult to measure, but we may safely say that the annual gain is 2 lives per 1,000 inhabitants, and this is a conservative estimate. Now 2 persons per 1,000 give 5 million a year, and 60 million in 12 years. From the thirteenth year therefore, that is, in 1957–1958, the general balance sheet of human lives for the second world war must have become positive. A truly extraordinary result.

Comparison with the estimates of world population (chapter 2) confirms this result and goes even further. From 1940 to 1950, world population increased faster than from 1930 to 1940; the acceleration of the increase already noticeable before the war, was hardly felt (Fig. 3). By an astonishing paradox, the war produced more people.

[10] See Frumkin: *Population changes in Europe since 1939*, New York 1951, as well as *Population*, October–December 1949: *Evolution démographique de l'Europe 1938–1947*, and July–September 1956, *La population de l'Union Soviétique*.

Chapter 5

The birth rate

LENGTHENING OF LIFE and a larger proportion of surviving adults are common to all countries. They start at different times and progress variously, but the movement is so general, as we have seen, that some under-developed countries, with a younger age group composition, already have a lower death rate than that of France and England, lower, even, than that of the United States.

The birth rate, however, is a very different matter.

Divergent behaviour

In the developed countries, the birth rate has nowhere remained at the old levels which more or less represented natural fertility. In France, contraceptive practices and the lengthening of life began at about the same time, that is, in the eighteenth century. In other countries, the lowering of the birth rate came later; it was the time-lag between the two lowering rates, the birth rate and the death rate, which caused the great demographic impetus in the nineteenth century.

In developed European countries the birth rate usually stands somewhere between 15 and 20 per 1,000.

This lowering is voluntary and the result of contraceptives and abortive practices. We know very little of the differences in natural fertility between peoples and races. But there is no evidence to suggest that such differences are even appreciable. They disappear, in any case, under the divergences due to anti-natal practices.

In undeveloped countries the birth rate has generally remained at the previous level, that is, around 40 to 45 per 1,000, which more or less represents natural fertility. We may even say, although the older statistics are imperfect, that the birth rate has risen slightly on account of improved health and hygiene.

The lowering of the death rate among young people has a favourable influence on the birth rate. Similarly the maternal death rate has gone down by large strides in twenty years, lowering from ⅔ to ⁹⁄₁₀, according to the World Health Organization:

	per 1,000 births
Ceylon	from 20.5 to 4.1
Mauritius	from 11.6 to 1.6
Chili	from 9.2 to 2.8
Colombia	from 8.4 to 3.7
United States (non whites)	from 8.9 to 1.3

Although these countries are still a long way from the rates of the developed countries (average of 0.5 per 1,000), the improvement is considerable.

This improvement helps to raise the birth rate: the average number of children gained per woman thus saved may be estimated at 2 or 3. From this fact alone the birth rate will have increased from 0.7 to 0.9 per 1,000 inhabitants.

On the other hand tribal wars, massacres, etc., must have cost the lives of many young men, the loss of whom would have reduced the number of procreating couples.

We may estimate on the whole that the birth rate may have risen, for these reasons, by about 4 per 1,000. In countries where it stood at just over 40 per 1,000, it must by now have reached 45.

In undeveloped countries, therefore, the situation is very different indeed from that which obtained before, as can be seen in Fig. 3.

This, we must emphasize, is a schema and not a table of statistical observations. Natural or violent mortality, in spite of strong oscillations, was not much lower, on an average, than the birth rate with its barely perceptible oscillations.

On the right-hand side we show that same type-population today. The birth rate is a little higher, while the death rate, which is considerably lower than before, continues to go down regularly, and with much gentler oscillations:

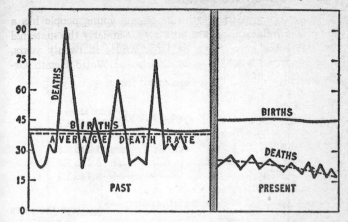

Fig. 3.—Birth rate and death rate in an under-developed population, in the past and today.

From 12 possible children to 2 or 3

A woman's natural fertility is, on an average, 12 children (L. Henry). In other words, if a woman marries at the moment of puberty and remains in a married state until she is nearly 50, the couple ought to have an average of 12 children. If that figure were reached for all couples multiplication would be extremely rapid.

But there are numerous obstacles to the attainment of this figure, arising from varying phenomena which are less or more important according to the countries and the periods: total or partial celibacy, widowhood, contraceptive practices, death of children before puberty, etc.

Here (Fig. 4), still according to Louis Henry, is the way in which these 12 possible children get reduced to about 2, both in an undeveloped European population (eighteenth century) and in a present day European population:

The undeveloped population

France has been chosen for the eighteenth-century population; since contraception as yet plays no appreciable part, the figure is more or less valid for other Western countries of the time (England, Germany, Italy, etc.).

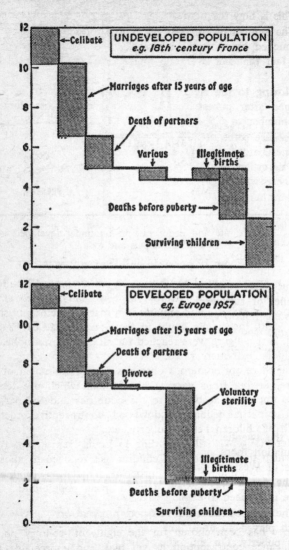

FIG. 4. Number of children surviving per couple, in an undeveloped European population of the eighteenth century and in a present-day European population.

This is how the figure reads (*left*);

The number of children per couple formed at puberty and untouched by mortality averages about 12 (*top left*); but the fact that not everyone marries reduces the average to 10.2.

Moving to the right: the fact that many marriages are formed after puberty causes an appreciable loss, lowering the number to 6.5.

Because some couples are separated by the death of one partner before the end of the procreation period, the number is further reduced to 5.0.

There was no divorce at this time, but various factors (separation, etc.) lowers the average figure to 4.5.

In the calculation of averages, we must add illegitimate children to the legitimate, which brings back the number to 5. This is the average number of children born per woman (or per man), legitimate or illegitimate, during her lifetime.

But these children do not all reach puberty, so that the number of survivors able to begin a new cycle is greatly reduced, falling to 2.4.

Note: The scale being arithmetical, the rectangles are not proportionate to the real waste. For example, marriage after 15 reduces the number of children by 36 per cent whereas death before puberty reduces the number by over 50 per cent.

The developed population

For the twentieth century, the diagram represents a type-population more or less equivalent to the average populations of Western Europe.

The figure reads from left to right, in the same way; there is no need to explain it in detail here.

The paths of reduction in the two figures differ profoundly; death played an important role in the past, particularly before puberty. On the other hand, voluntary sterility plays so huge a part today that the number of children surviving into puberty is a little lower than two centuries ago.

Present-day under-developed countries

It is not possible to draw up a sufficiently precise analogous table for a present-day under-developed country. The marriage figures, in particular, are missing.

We do know, however, that the final number of children per woman, surviving into puberty, is often more than 4, that is, twice as large as that of a developed country. The marriageable age is lower than in the European countries, developed and undeveloped. The death rate is lower than that of the undeveloped eighteenth-century country, but this

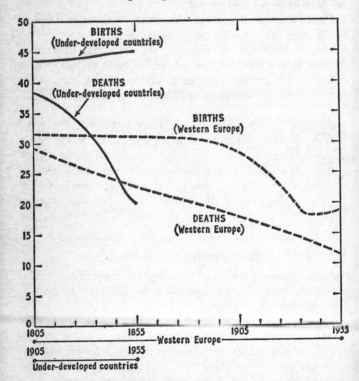

FIG. 5.—Comparison of birth rate and death rate, in a European population and in an under-developed population, placed one century back.

lower death rate is not counter-balanced by voluntary sterility, as it is in the developed European country.

Differences in evolution

In order to show more clearly the difference in evolution between the European and the under-developed populations, I have set out, on one and the same table (Fig. 5), both the birth rate and the death rate of each of these types of population, but putting the present under-developed population back a hundred years, so that its development can be approximately related to that of European countries.

Here again the figures are approximate, especially for the present-day under-developed population. For Europe, we are giving a weighted average of the figures discovered for France, England, Scotland, Germany, Holland, Belgium, Austria and Scandinavia.

Uncertain though these figures may be, they are sufficient to show the enormous difference between the two evolutions.

The death rate of under-developed countries has fallen below that of Western countries a century ago; in 1850 these had not yet begun their lowering of the birth rate, except for France. But the birth rate was lower, because of the later age at marriage.

All I have done here is simply to describe present facts. I shall take up the question of voluntary sterility in more detail later, in chapters 16 to 19.

I shall now complete the description with a quick look at the different areas of the world.

Chapter 6

Round the world

As WE HAVE SEEN, demographic growth varies considerably according to the country. Generally speaking, those countries which are able to support a larger population have the smallest growth. This apparent paradox is easily explainable. Those who possess, in other words, those who have something to lose, show the most foresight (I shall return to this question in chapter 16).

Europe

Europe can be roughly divided into three zones:

(1) In developed Western Europe, including Austria, Northern Italy and Scandinavia, we find a moderate growth, of about 0.6 per cent, except for Holland (1.5 per cent). This country is remarkable in several ways:

(*a*) It is the only country in which the fertility rate has completely separated from the death rate. It has the highest longevity in the world or very nearly, and at the same time has preserved a relatively high birth rate (22 per 1,000), so that its population is younger than other Western populations at the same stage of development.

(*b*) It has the highest density in the world; there are more populated zones (Java, Malta, some Far Eastern deltas, etc.), but no nation has such an accumulation.

(*c*) It is the only country in which one may speak of a real over-population, as opposed to an apparent over-population due to under-development. We have here a limit beyond which mankind can hardly go, in present-day conditions that is.

High densities are also to be found in other countries (England and Germany, more than 200), and even where the natural resources are not very great (Switzerland, Denmark). But these territories are organized; over-population has been fought by economic development. The example of Germany is particularly remarkable, inasmuch as ten million supplementary people have taken refuge there since the second war and found some means of living.

(2) Southern Europe is already affected by a certain degree of under-development which can be seen in both the more rapid growth and the greater poverty: Portugal, Andalusia, Southern Italy, Malta, Greece, Macedonia, Bosnia, etc. The increase is easily higher than 1 per cent per annum in these predominantly agricultural areas.

If we compare Southern Europe with Western Europe, which in general is more highly populated, we can see that *over-population may be merely one of the effects of under-development.*

(3) Finally, in socialist Eastern Europe, the rates of increase are rather high (1.7 per cent in the U.S.S.R.), but this is no longer considered as a wholly favourable sign in this country.

Under-development takes different forms here, while the apparent over-population is felt chiefly in the shortage of housing and the bad quality of the food. As in other countries, development has affected the lengthening of life more than the standard of living. Progress in social-medical organisation has caused an appreciable lowering in the death-rate.

The birth rate should normally be coming down, particularly in Rumania, Yugoslavia and Poland.

Forecasts for Western Europe

Calculations for the future have been made for various countries by Jean Bourgeois-Pichat.[1] The results have helped us to evaluate the way in which the general picture of Western Europe may change. We are using the term Western Europe in its political sense, excluding Yugoslavia and Turkey. Here are the results:

[1] *Les problèmes de population européenne. II. Perspectives sur les populations. Population,* January–March 1953.

	1950	1980	*Variations*
	Thousands of inhabitants		*over 30 years*
			%
0 to 20 years	93,500	90,500	—3
20 to 60 years	159,000	173,500	+9
60 years and more	40,500	56,000	+38
Total	293,800	320,000	+9

The oscillating movement around the medium ages will then continue. The adult population must always represent the same proportion (54.3 per cent), but the aged population will gain what the young population will lose (3.5 per cent of the total). The ageing of the population is therefore by no means over.

Jean Bourgeois-Pichat has pushed his calculations further, by studying the future of both active and non-active populations. I shall return to this problem in chapter 20, which is devoted to the population of developed countries.

America: two cultures, two attitudes

In America, the difference between Latins and Anglo-Saxons is very marked, from the point of view of both the increase and the attitude to it. In economic terms, the United States and Canada can easily support their natural increase of 1.5 and 2 per cent per annum respectively, but adopt at the same time a doctrinal attitude which is frankly malthusian. French Canada naturally occupies a special position. In the province of Quebec, which is under the authority of the Church, contraception is not officially allowed. These practices spread nevertheless, but the birth rate of the province remains a little higher than that of the United States as a whole, where the sterility of the North is counter-balanced by the fertility of the South, just as it is in Italy, in Spain and even in Yugoslavia.

It would however be wrong to believe that the white population of the United States is threatened by the fertility of the coloured population. Fertility is more a question of climate and lack of instruction than of race; the "poor whites" are also prolific, whereas the Negro soon sterilises himself in the big industrial towns of the North. The slight difference is partly counter-balanced by the higher death-rate among the blacks.

Besides natural increase, we must also consider immigration, which is higher in Canada than in the United States. In Canada, the British elements have watched the more rapid multiplication of the French with some apprehension; in order to counter-balance it, they call in foreign immigrants, most of whom adopt the English language.

Latin America is itself divisible into two zones:

(a) In Central and Equatorial America, the population is increasing rapidly, sometimes at a rhythm of 3 per cent per annum (Mexico especially), without yet attempting to reduce the burdens thus caused. But as spaces are wide and the un-exploited resources considerable, this growth does not raise anything like as many problems as it does in North Africa or in Asia.

(b) In the temperate and more developed zone (Argentina, Uruguay), the economic and cultural level is higher, the birth rate lower and growth less rapid.

Forecasts for Latin America

Calculations of "prospects" for Latin America have been worked out by the United Nations; here are the main results, first for South America:

These are purely demographic forecasts that leave aside the question of possible economic development and, with all the more reason, that of political reactions.

The calculations have been made on the assumption that the death rate will go down at the same rhythm as that so far observed in the developed countries. On this basis, the expectation of life which stood, at the beginning of the forecast (i.e. in 1950) at 44 years in Brazil and 66 years in Uruguay, would, by 1980, be somewhere between 57 years (Brazil) and 71 years (Uruguay).

As regards the birth rate—a more uncertain element—the calculations were made on three assumptions. The "high" assumption more or less represents stability, the medium assumption a slight lowering, and the low assumption a more rapid lowering.

CANADA 80%

UNITED STATES 60%

MEXICO 117%

BR. HONDURAS 84%
HONDURAS 100%
COSTA RICA 130%
PANAMA 112%

GUATEMALA 105%
SALVADOR 106%
NICARAGUA 127%

VENEZUELA 130%

BR. GUIANA 127%
SURINAM 96%
FR. GUIANA 70%

COLOMBIA 143%

ECUADOR 127%

PERU 145%

BRAZIL 103%

BOLIVIA 119%

CHILE 72%

PARAGUAY 130%

URUGUAY 32%

ARGENTINA 53%

Less than 100%

100 to 124%

More than 125%

Fig. 6.—Probable growth of population in America from 1950 to 1980.

Immigration has not been taken into account.

The difference in the rate of increase between the temperate zone (minus Paraguay) and the tropical zone (plus Paraguay) is considerable. At the end of the period the tropical zone would have a population four times as large as that of the temperate zone, and Brazil would have a greater population than France and England together.

Here are the main results in thousands of inhabitants:

	1950	1980			Increase over 30 years in medium hypothesis %
		Low birth rate	Medium birth rate	High birth rate	
Bolivia	3,020	6,158	6,627	7,147	119
Brazil	51,976	98,311	105,527	113,402	103
Colombia	11,260	25,438	27,388	29,514	143
Ecuador	3,156	6,662	7,174	7,733	127
Peru	8,294	18,896	20,370	21,992	145
Venezuela		10,678	11,476	12,338	130
Br. Guiana	420	884	952	1,026	127
Surinam	219	402	430	460	96
Fr. Guiana*	30	(45)	(48)	(51)	96
Tropical zone	83,756	167,874	179,992	193,663	114
Argentine	17,188	24,638	26,250	27,885	53
Chili	5,745	9,092	9,879	10,235	72
Paraguay	1,397	2,797	3,212	3,727	130
Uruguay	2,424	3,040	3,212	3,386	32
Temperate zone	26,754	39,567	42,553	45,233	59
South America	110,510	207,441	222,545	238,896	101

* For lack of evidence, we have assumed a slightly lower rate of increase in French Guiana than in the rest of the tropical zone.

And now for Central America and Mexico (the calculations do not include the Caribbean).

The method of calculation is approximately the same as for South America. The "high" birth rate is constant, the "medium" birth rate goes down by 5 per cent every five years and the low birth rate goes down twice as fast (10 per cent in

five years). Here are the main results in thousands of inhabitants:

	1950	1980			Increase over 30 years in medium hypothesis %
		Low birth rate	Medium birth rate	High birth rate	
Costa Rica	805	1,616	1,851	2,143	130
Salvador	1,856	3,354	3,821	4,398	106
Guatemala	2,802	4,989	5,759	6,715	105
Honduras	1,428	2,492	2,845	3,266	100
Nicaragua	1,057	2,091	2,402	2,788	127
Panama	798	1,491	1,697	1,953	112
Br. Honduras	67	109	123	141	84
Central America	8,813	16,142	18,498	21,404	110
Mexico	25,567	48,239	55,469	64,425	117
Together	34,380	64,381	73,967	85,829	115

Here again we find rates of increase as high as those of
tropical South America. The slight differences from one
country to another are not significant. But the increase in
Mexico is notable.

What are these forecasts worth?

We have already said that these are purely demographic
forecasts; they are based on the assumption that there will be
no very strong resistance from the environment. These forecasts, in fact, are worth what the hypothesis on the bitrh rate
is worth. This is precisely the great unknown factor, since it
depends on the will, even on the caprice of mankind.

Up till now, at any rate, *it is the high assumption which is
being followed.* It is even quite frequently below the actual
results.

These forecasts, we must repeat, leave the economic question aside; they do not tell us whether these men, who will be
twice as numerous in one generation, will be as poor as their
fathers or, on the contrary, powerful industrialists. But in any
hypothesis their number will weigh heavily on the future of
mankind.

Africa; the awakening people

Africa was long unknown from a demographic point of view, and posed no real problem before the 1939 war, at any rate no problem of over-population. Or, more exactly, the colonial powers were almost ignorant of these problems. Africa can be divided into three parts:

(a) Moslem North Africa has already entered into a period of great demographic development. From Marrakesh to Suez, the evidence is much the same: a birth rate now approximately at the level of natural fertility, that is to say, 45 per 1,000 (once the errors due to the under-registration of births have been rectified, naturally); a lowering death rate, around 20 per 1,000, sometimes less, as in Algeria. And since Algeria is the country in which the most advanced studies have been made, we will look at the results of the forecasts calculated by M. Jacques Breil.[2] He has projected the present-day trends, assuming that fertility would remain constant and that the death rate would continue to go down until 1975, especially for the young, with infant mortality decreasing from 11.5 per 1,000 in 1950–5 to 5.6 per 1,000 in 1970–5. These are the results:

	1955	1960	1970	1980
		(thousands of inhabitants)		
Under twenty years	4,606	5,282	7,215	9,730
20 to 60 years	3,692	4,208	5,388	7,182
60 years and over	482	590	850	1,068
Total	8,780	10,080	13,453	17,980

Thus, in spite of nearly 100,000 young men away in France, most of them without their wives, the population would double in less than 25 years, more or less preserving its present composition by age groups, with more than 50 per cent of young people. These calculations do not take war losses into account; no balance-sheet of these is yet available.

The other countries of Moslem North Africa are undergoing a similarly rapid growth, which sets very serious prob-

[2] *La population des départements algériens. Complément No. 2.* —Statistique générale de l'Algérie 1955.

lems in those lands where water is scarce and trees not much respected. Industrialization has hardly begun and faces considerable obstacles: shortage of motor energy, lack of capital and, especially, lack of qualified personnel.

The situation in Egypt is particularly difficult; only an expensive programme of dam-building can increase the present surface of arable lands, over which the density is already extremely high; unemployment and under-employment are very widespread.

In all these countries, the rapid demographic growth is closely related to the movement for emancipation. The latter is frequently attributed to obvious and immediate political factors, but these factors would have had only a very slight influence without the demographic surge.

(b) *South Africa.* As in North Africa, the white population is vastly out-numbered by the increasing Indian, half-caste and Bantu populations.[3] In thirty years, the European population is expected to increase by 50 per cent, whereas the coloured increase will be 75 per cent for the Bantus, 100 per cent for the half-caste, and 150 per cent for the Asiatics. In pure figures, the increase would be of 1,200,000 for the Europeans and of 7,800,000 for the non-Europeans. A situation which is all the more explosive because segregation aggravates the social pressure.

(c) *Black Africa and various regions.* In other areas, including Madagascar, over-population has not so far been considered to be a serious danger. It was depopulation even, that was denounced, resulting either from epidemics (sleeping sickness, malaria, etc.), or from a lower fertility than that of Asia, North Africa or Central America.

This difference between Asiatic exuberance and the relative sterility of the blacks has long remained a mystery which has not yet been fully explained.

The problem is not one of race; as we have seen, there is no scientific evidence for any difference in fertility or in natural longevity.

Rather must we turn to social-physiological factors: con-

[3] See *Le problème démographique et racial en Afrique du Sud. Population,* October–December 1957.

sanguinity in certain tribes, sexual prohibitions and taboos, polygamy, prolonged breast-feeding, etc. And these factors change in importance from one region to another, from one tribe to another.

Depopulation has today become exceptional, as much in Madagascar as in the rest of black Africa. A phase of long-lasting increase has begun in all areas where economic circumstances are not too unfavourable. But the risks of over-population are less marked than in Asia or the Far East, not only because the growth is, in general, less rapid, but because the natural resources are much less exploited. It has even been observed that at certain points the growth itself brings about an increase in productivity. Erosion, however, is the great "overpopulator," against which it will be necessary to fight hard.[4]

Asia: immense, populated and populating

The great migrations came out of Asia, and the greatest human masses are now in Asia, as well as the greatest expansions in numbers. This part of the world is therefore our largest field of experience, with regard to the three principal areas where effort is being made to reduce over-population by birth control: China, India, Japan. I shall return to this in chapter 22.

In Asia as a whole, the growth of population is fairly rapid; but there are great regional variations in the relationship between the population and the natural resources, at least as these are at present exploited. Whereas Iran, Irak, Burmah, Vietnam and even Turkey and Syria apparently still have, like Soviet Asia, vast resources at their disposal, India, China and Formosa, Japan, Israel, Korea, Pakistan even and Malaya, are finding it difficult to cope with their demographic growth.

We are very badly documented on Soviet Asia, but there is good reason to believe that its rate of increase is higher than that of the Soviet Union as a whole, 1.7 per cent per annum. It is very probably over 2 per cent per annum, including

[4] Over-population is always relative; it is a relationship between man and his resources.

immigration. On the other hand Siberia, like all hard and inhospitable regions, has long remained unexploited, so that it could provide some sort of habitat for a higher population if a certain organization of the territory were undertaken.

India[5]

We must pay special attention to this country, which is so often considered to be the poorest in the world and that which suffers most from food shortages. Famines and epidemics have been so widespread that from 1891 to 1921, in thirty years, the population increased only by 12 million inhabitants, that is, by 5 per cent. During the following thirty years, the increase was of 113 million. But the death rate remains one of the highest in the world; and in spite of recent improvements, the average expectation of life must still be below 40 years.

Calculations of prospects have been made by Mr. Coale and Mr. Hoover;[6] Mr. Gilbert Etienne has compared them with those that would result from the type population of India and Pakistan according to the norms given by Mr. Henry and Mr. Pressat.[7]

Here are the figures:

	Coale and Hoover		Henry and Pressat	
	Constant fertility	Average fertility	Constant fertility	Immediately and rapidly lowering fertility
		(in millions)		
1956	387	387	387	387
1966	476	476	470	464
1976	605	573	584	538
1986	782	634	743	615
Increase in 30 years	102%	64%	92%	59%

[5] This country's situation is described in more detail in chapter 21.

[6] *Prospects for population growth and their implications for economic development in India 1956–1986*, Princeton University, September 1956.

[7] *Le Tiers Monde. Sous-développement et développement.* Cahier no. 27 de l'Institut National d'Etudes Démographiques, Paris, 1956. P.U.F.

The rate of increase is lower than in South America; environment resistance is already being felt. But even thus limited, this increase is higher than that of previous periods and raises economic difficulties to which I shall return later (see chapters 17 and 21).

Oceania, sparse and various

In spite of a few weak and tardy efforts at immigration, the vast expanse of Australia remains sparsely populated, and an obvious temptation for the poverty-stricken Far East. During the war there was a threat of a Japanese invasion; the economic and political obstacles to international migrations would be partly removed if violent troubles were to enable Malayans, Chinese, Japanese or Indians to penetrate this continent which is both sparsely populated and sufficiently developed to allow for rapid settling.

The East Indies, whose political unity is purely the result of colonialism, are full of demographic contrasts: whereas Java is heavily over-loaded (more than 1,036 inhabitants to the square mile), Sumatra is half empty and Borneo almost a virgin country. But the difficulties of an organised mass-transplantation are enormous, and although it is encouraged by the political authorities, the human trickle from one island to another remains very thin.

Future development

The United Nations have worked out some forecasts, or rather, some prospects, for the different areas of the world. The results were summarized on p. 27.

Wealth and poverty

The poverty of a people can be described in many ways, with accounts of the life of peasants or workers, their food, their clothes, etc. Statistics summarize all this in one bare figure: the national income per inhabitant. It is usually calculated in American dollars. Here are a few partial results:

From nearly 2,000 dollars per inhabitant in the United States, the income per head scales down to 600–1,100 in

Western Europe (850 in France), in Australia and New Zealand, and falls to below 150 in the poverty-stricken under-developed countries.

Rhodesia and Nyasaland	100	dollars
Thailand	80	"
South Korea, Pakistan, Belgian Congo	75	"
Kenya, India, Uganda, Burmah, etc.	60	"

These figures must be considered only as extremely rough, with a margin of error of as much as 25 to 30 per cent; but they do underline the enormous variation of wealth from one country to another.

They are, moreover, averages per inhabitant, but since the national income is often very unequally distributed in under-developed countries (India, especially), the income of workers is in fact below these figures. I shall give more detailed information and show the consequences of this inequality in chapter 15.

Another method of comparison consists in measuring the quantity of food consumed per person per day. In Western countries, the figure is frequently higher than 3,000 calories, and higher than 80 grammes of proteins. Far Eastern and other countries do not always reach a daily ration of 2,000 calories, or more than 60 grammes of proteins. Moreover these are national averages. J. de Castro's work, *Géographie de la faim,* has shown how widespread is the under-nourishment and physiological debility of the world.

Chapter 7

Possible developments

WE ARE THUS FACING a phenomenon which is unprecedented in history. Already in the nineteenth century, medical progress was a truly new factor since the life of man, after an age-long stagnation, had suddenly entered a phase of increased longevity; but now medical progress is significantly ahead of economic progress, and this produces not only economic problems, but social and political problems which are so new that the old national and international structures are considerably shaken by them.

Continuation is impossible

Can the movement continue for long? Is there any need to worry about it?

The simplest knowledge enables us to answer these two questions easily:

To the first, *no*.

To the second, *yes*.

A population combining the natural fertility observed in so many countries with "biological" mortality, that is, a mortality limited to endogenous illnesses only, would double in fifteen years or even less. Or, leaving aside this somewhat hypothetical combination, we will assume that the rate of present increase remains the same in the world. Between now and the year 2000, the population would more than double, for the present 2,800 million would become 5,700 million. In 2100 it would be 31,000 million, and 170,000 million one century later.

Geometrical progressions are so obliging that with a few more turns of the handle, that is, pushing the calculations a few centuries later, one may produce the most extravagant results. We would very quickly reach the stage in which space would be lacking, not only for culture, but for actual standing-room. A little later we would reach the moment when the weight of mankind would exceed even the mass of the earth's substance.

One may therefore easily reply:

A new factor will emerge, which will modify present conditions and the present rhythm of growth.

We must worry about it, however, in order to prevent this new factor from being a destructive cataclysm.

Must we limit the horizon?

Something new will emerge, we know; we worry only about the nature of this new thing, and try at least to avoid disasters or aggravations. But should we approach the problem in its entirety, including the night of aeons, or with a more limited horizon?

These long-term calculations of geometrical progressions are condemned as vain by some. Let us do our best during our lifetime, they say, within the traditional horizon of one generation, and our children will take over their own responsibilities.

For most questions, this position is tenable, but for the problem of population it has certain weaknesses.

For one thing, the life of man does not last for one generation only, but for 60 to 70 years, sometimes more. When society promises a young man of 18 a fixed pension at 65, to last until his death (75 to 80 years on the average), it is in effect making a forecast over half a century. It would be fairly logical for this society to look ahead, not only at the undertakings it makes, but also at the resources it will have at its disposal to face these undertakings.

Many human actions (revolutions, the building of cathedrals, of hydraulic dams, etc.) are destined to last far longer than merely one generation.

By limiting our role too narrowly, we run the danger of merely procrastinating the difficulties and leaving our children with far more difficult tasks. If, because of our negligence, any part of the world should become twice as populated in twenty-five years, having yet remained as poverty-stricken, the problem will be that much more difficult to solve.

Ah, but the developed countries, you will say, will by then have even more technique at their disposal to solve difficulties which today seem insoluble.

Such a hope is too naïve, for it neglects the actual proportions and, especially, the very growth of needs, which are inevitably modelled on the consumption of the developed countries, particularly in terms of energy. The developed countries will certainly be richer and more powerful, but they would also, in this hypothesis, be facing men not only more numerous but also more lowly placed, in relative values, than they are today. The way people are spaced over the planet might then lead to explosive situations.

On the other hand, it is obviously fairly futile to build the world too long in advance, and those who in the past have tried to pierce through the thick clouds of the future have certainly been greatly discomfited.

It may, however, be useful at least to examine the question without specifying a precise date, a limited horizon. Time will after all intervene anyway, for every particular problem.

Not one world, but nations

Another preliminary observation: to argue about "world population," as many do, is surely to betray singular optimism (or pessimism, as you wish), on the solidarity of man. This solidarity will of course increase, for progress reduces distances. The recrudescence of nationalism may even be considered as a reaction of the weak against international links that are becoming closer and closer. But for the moment, we are dealing with ferociously independent nations which do not seem ready yet to bear the burdens of others.

The problem of population is therefore one of individual countries at the moment. We have seen in our "trip round the world" in chapter 6, how varied were the individual situations. The same geometrical progressions can therefore be repeated for Egypt, India, Brazil, Mexico, South Africa, Pakistan, etc., but the very results will show how vain such

long-term calculations can be, since they give themselves the
lie in the very act of reaching these fabulous figures.

But what lie?

The different possibilities

I am avoiding the word "solution" here, on purpose. The
present situation can develop in various ways, which are not
necessarily desirable. It is among these ways, these possibilities, these eventualities, that a solution must be found.

I am starting, for the moment, with a simple arithmetical
observation. A group of men increases in a given country.
What will happen during the next, or the next two, or three
generations?

(1) *Return to an increased death-rate,* either voluntarily,
according to the more or less clearly expressed desire of
some; or involuntarily, as a result of shortages or of cataclysms, such as war.

(2) *Emigration to other lands.* The population decreases
by exits from the territory. This would be a geographical
solution.

(3) *Progress in production* of subsistence-means, sufficient
to feed everyone and even to improve welfare. This is the
so-called economic solution. The rhythm of growth remains,
but without harmful results.

(4) *Reduction of the birth rate,* sufficient to slow down or
stop the growth of the population. This is the so-called
demographic solution.

The various developments can naturally combine, so that
the possible permutations are infinite.

The last two developments (3 and 4) have been perhaps
prematurely called "solutions," because they are, as we shall
see, the two most debated methods.

I do not want to neglect any of the possible means, and
will therefore examine in turn each of the four enumerated
above.

A word of warning! We must avoid a frequent misunderstanding: there is no other way but these four (except, of
course, the scale of intermediary methods combining two or

three of them or all four). Many writers try to escape from this prison of facts and figures by suggesting solutions which appear to be quite different, concerning the political regime, the spiritual state, imponderables, etc. This attempt at evasion is only an illusion. All suggestions or possible hypotheses about political regimes or evolution, social, familial, cultural bonds, etc., must in the end be reduced to figures which bring us back to one of the above possibilities. It is always a question of knowing which of the four parameters will be set in motion: death, emigration, economic level, birth.

One of these four stands a little apart from the others: the resort to death. However unpleasant the idea may be, we have no right to neglect this possibility. Needless to say, it is not from preference that we are dealing with it first.

Chapter 8

Death's revenge?

THIS POSSIBILITY, this development, should perhaps be mentioned last, for it would in fact be a sanctioning of nature, if men confessed themselves incapable of dominating her.

Nevertheless, I prefer to deal with it first, perhaps in order to be rid of it, but also in order to emphasize, at the end of the first part of this book, the two great solutions which are to be the subject of its second and third parts.

Death's revenge could occur in several ways, all unpleasant of course, but I do not wish to neglect a single hypothesis.

(a) *Voluntary or semi-voluntary mortality*, through the stopping of medical progress, as suggested by Vogt and his followers, and through a more or less discreet elimination of "undesirables."

From a certain viewpoint the solutions based on abortion, as in Japan, could be included in this group. These, however, will be examined under birth-control.

(b) *Involuntary mortality*, through lack of subsistence-means in certain countries, with a return to famines, illnesses due to debility, and epidemics.

(c) *War, atomic, bacteriological, radiological*, etc.

(d) *Radioactivity* escaping from man's control, or other accidents causing an exceptional death rate.

I shall examine these in turn.

Voluntary stop to medical progress

Although an actual stop to medical progress is rarely advocated explicitly, there is no doubt that the general effect of what is today called "progress" has raised much opposition.

This progress threatens to disrupt old civilizations. The beginning of industry in nineteenth-century Europe had already produced many social evils in town and suburb, such as slums, alcoholism, prostitution, etc. What horrors, it is argued, might we end up with if people now in a feudal or tribal stage have to reach the industrial stage in such a short time and in great disorder? Already the ravages of "detribalization" are evident in Africa and elsewhere (see chapter 16). Let loose in a conglomeration without form or faith, men who have until then been protected by a close system of traditions can suddenly give way to every weakness.

In the face of such dangers, voices are raised, more or less discreetly, against what used to be called civilization, which is now called progress. They take up the Virgilian *O fortunatus nimium* and at the same time emphasize the destructive nature of this development.

This point of view is put out or suggested, either by conservatives who are terrified that this world commotion will seriously upset the established order, or by sociologists, aestheticians, ethnologists, etc., who mourn the possible destruction of this or that group, harmonious or solid, which had proved itself and shown great aesthetic vitality. There exists a whole literature in this vein, which has its public and its echoes.

Vain regrets

The destructive character of some of the innovations resulting from medical progress is incontestable. All progress, in whatever field, destroys some established order. Those destructions that originated in medical progress may certainly be regretted, and even cursed, but they cannot be stopped.

Why? Because it is impossible to prevent medical progress from spreading, at least in its general and collective techniques. What government is going to remain indifferent to a group of men, however primitive, decimated by illness and dependent on its authority? What doctor is going to face disease, his enemy, and allow it to do its worst, even for the sake of "humanity"? Even those who advocate such brutal methods would be unable to bear the sight of children covered with sores, or stop the hand that was about to relieve the pain.

Of course, if it was only a question of pushing a button to ensure the disappearance not only of the mandarin but of all the million hungry people who threaten to become "dangerous," this button would not remain inactive for long. But fortunately the destiny of these people does not present itself in this light.

Will anyone get up to suggest that the work of the *World Health Organization* or of U.N.I.C.E.F. should be suppressed? Perhaps, if he could evade all responsibility on the subject and know, moreover, that his advice would not be followed.

Such facts are sufficient to decide the question, even apart from all humanitarian or moral considerations; only on the day when these national and international organizations decide to abandon the struggle against death, and to take death as an ally, only then will it be time to revise this judgment.

This said, there remains a certain lack of precision: the effort to save men may vary in importance. In every country there are choices, frequently of a financial kind. Such a choice may lead to the (discreet) sacrifice (more or less) of the medical services, in favour of other expenses, which might even be investments in a future ability to support human life. Theories can even be erected over the best solution, that which will finally ensure the highest standard of living for the greatest possible number of people. Such a calculation might lead as far as a deliberate sacrifice of individuals on the altar of collectivity, as an army in wartime sacrifices a patrol or a garrison to save the rest.

But it is very unlikely that such unpleasant designs should be put into effect. Under cover of social honesty, they would on the contrary quickly turn into social hypocrisy which would not stand up to the sight of the sufferings that would be, from then on, "willed." Besides, these primary medical expenditures are, as we have seen, considerably less than economic investments. The primary medical expenditure would have to be enormously lowered in order to benefit the economic expenditure only a little. The death rate may lower at varying rhythms, but it is impossible to conceive the country in which it would go up again by a voluntary decision.

An unconvincing example

The late Montagne, who had studied Morocco for many years, did not think that the demographic problem there was very serious; he first pointed out that the natural resources, the land especially, were unexploited, and here I can but agree with him, reminding the reader, however, that considerable investment would be needed for any realization of assets. Further, he estimated that the increase in population was slight, as a result of the following process: the demographic excess of the country pours into the towns; as for the towns, their population is decimated by illnesses and physiological sterility (venereal diseases). The situation is more or less that of eighteenth-century France, when writers accused the big towns of being "the graveyards of the race."

But these observations are not based on any documented figures. "They melt away in a thick absence," one would be tempted to comment. Similar judgments have been pronounced for other countries, but they are hardly worth pursuing: the observation of demographic phenomena by sight and impression leads to seriously erroneous judgments. It is better to use statistical documentation, with all its imperfections, and then to apply the necessary correctives. Wherever such work has been done, a fall in the death rate has been observed, even in the poorest areas such as India.

The open circle

With the age-old closed circle of life and death now open, the advance of medical progress will destroy all the ancient civilizations, and all the undeveloped religions, or will at least profoundly change them, in the name of the same thing.

Preserving ethnical groups, as one preserves animal species in national parks, is like piously preserving illnesses in front of a locked cupboard full of medicines; the idea may be tempting, but will not stand up to examination.

Certainly we should avoid sudden and destructive jumps, we should control transitions, and save as many cultural values as possible; this task requires all the more attention because it is a delicate one, but such precautions are progressivist ones, and very different from the fiercely conservative conception which too frequently inspires the opponents of advancing development.

Lack of subsistence-means?

However strong curative medicine may be it cannot keep men alive below a minimum subsistence level. This minimum should not be confused with the normal ration, often called minimal, which is, in fact, a maximum. It varies from 2,400 to 3,500 calories a day according to the region, the race and, also, the writer. Qualitative factors further complicate the picture (proteids, vitamins, etc.).

The level beneath which under-nourishment directly influences the death rate in any appreciable way (apart from indirect causes like tuberculosis), is lower than is generally thought. On this point as on many others the war was a cruel but instructive experience.[1] Observations were made, notably in Spain (1937–9), Malta (1940–3), Budapest (1945), Holland (1945), especially as regards infant mortality.

It is true that only short famines were in question. If the situation in Holland in 1945 had lasted for a few more months, no doubt the results would have been far more murderous.[2] Nevertheless some very fixed conceptions on the physiological minimum have had to be revised.

Can we really expect a nation simply to stifle beneath its own vitality, to consume its inhabitants in a sub-vital poverty, with death winning over birth? This view is too simple.

First, can under-nourishment, without appreciably reducing the genetic capacity as such (I shall consider Dr. J. de Castro's ideas on this point in chapter 18), notably reduce the number of births through the exhaustion of the mother

[1] When the Germans imposed rations in France in September 1940, a great doctor and politician, speaking to high officials, was extremely pessimistic: "350 grammes of bread a day, 300 grammes of meat a week, I leave you to imagine what will become of the race in six months."

[2] See Hélène Bergues: *Répercussions des calamités de guerre sur la première enfance. Population,* July–September 1948.

(miscarriage, still birth, etc.)? If so this would really be an end of human beings, that is to say, death in disguise.

Whether we call this failure a lack of birth or a premature death, there would come a moment when the population would cease to increase, and would simply maintain its number, living in abysmal poverty. The production of subsistence-means would be further reduced by lack of health.

But this "possibility," even as here described, does not seem probable in such rudimentary form. Such a development has never occurred because, as we saw in chapter 3, natural populations were the victims of inequalities in nature, such as cold or dry periods, which brought about alternating spells of relative prosperity and famine, the latter resulting from both bad harvests and lack of forethought, each adding to the effect of the other.

If such a degree of under-nourishment occurred, it would certainly arouse world public opinion.

A period of bad luck is of course always possible, but the process would be very different from the classic process. The speed of material and other communications would prescribe quite a different course. It would not be possible for the developed countries to let millions of men die of hunger. Even failing true feelings of humanity, the competition between two rival worlds would cause help to pour forth, exactly calculated perhaps, but sufficient to prevent a cataclysm. If there was a serious shortage of corn or rice in India, the U.S.S.R., China and the U.S.A. would compete to ensure the people's susbsistence.

A serious epidemic would also produce the same reaction. The Egyptian episode of 1947 would be repeated (p. 60).

Even on this pessimistic hypothesis, therefore, it is impossible to imagine a simple revenge of death in a specific zone. And once international organizations or the big powers have taken charge of a population it would be as difficult to abandon it as it is to abandon the Arab refugees in Palestine today, who are supported by the United Nations.

Such an action would represent a deepening of world solidarity, but it would inevitably be accompanied by political intervention in the threatened country. These intervening forces would then be faced with the other three possible developments enumerated in the preceding chapter and described in the next three.

Thus, an acute lack of subsistence-means would not "resolve" a local problem without causing the over-population to cease; it would simply re-create the problem on a wider scale.

Atomic war

Needless to say, such an eventuality nullifies all the forecasts and prospects given in this book. It is of course always difficult to extrapolate from or plunge into a totally unknown future. Nevertheless everybody agrees that far from resembling the previous war (see p. 62) a third world war would destroy both subsistence-means and people, in a proportion which is beyond our grasp.

Radiations

I am here considering this danger only on the hypothesis of peace being maintained. Experimental atomic explosions have alarmed men of science and public opinion many times. Even without further explosions, the danger subsists, since radioactivity is cumulative.

The real danger is very difficult to calculate, since here too we are dealing with an unknown situation. We do know, however, how difficult it is for any collective force to stop before it reaches an ungrasped, ill-defined obstacle, when it is pushed by other forces in the direction of that obstacle.

The possible sequence is as follows:

Among the scientists of the world some may give the alarm out of prudence, without in fact being certain that the dangerous phase is truly in sight. They will think, not without reason, that it is better to be on the safe side than to enter the mortal zone.

After a moment of emotion, but not of hesitation, humanity will perceive that the announced disasters are not occurring, although the use of radiation has been stopped by no one. It will become absorbed by other worries.

The episode may be repeated two or three times, finally

creating a false sense of security, so much so that when the evil really begins to unfold, scepticism will be supreme. Has not the alarm been given so many times, in vain? It will be all the more difficult to stop the emissions of radio-activity because each nation will reproach the other for its misdeeds and the world duality will certainly not favour the setting-up of one single power.

This hypothesis may appear pessimistic. But who can deny its possibility?

If, because of the radiations, the world death rate should begin to rise, after two or three centuries of steady fall, the question of population would be profoundly changed. If, for instance, infantile cancer, leucaemia, etc., were to multiply, the birth rate of the developed countries would be insufficient, whereas on the contrary that of the under-developed countries would merely cease to be excessive. This would considerably upset present conditions; we can only hope that humanity will be wise and good enough to avoid such a calamity, or strong enough to be able to fight its effects.

Conclusion

Apart from catastrophic developments, which are more or less beyond the range of any real forecasts, we can see that a return to a high or rising death rate is hardly possible, not only because it does not constitute a human "solution," but *because it is beyond probability*. On the contrary, all the present efforts to bring down the death rate even further will continue and will be increasingly successful. At the same time, they will reduce physiological sterility and, especially, miscarriages and dead births, thus contributing, in an initial phase, to the rise of the natural birth rate and the acceleration of the increase in population.

The other three solutions enumerated in the previous chapter remain to be considered:

Emigration.
Increase of subsistence-means (economic solution).
Reduction of births (demographic solution).

We will begin with emigration.

Chapter 9

Illusory emigration

EMIGRATION IS OFTEN suggested as a solution of the difficult subsistence problem in a country with a growing population. It is a solution which comes all the more naturally to mind because it seems the easiest and most instantaneous as a safety valve.

In the past it has frequently served to overcome the difficulties arising from excessive multiplication. And in the last four centuries it became such a classical method for European countries that many have been tempted to regard it as the prescribed universal remedy.

In the eighteenth century French writers on the subject rarely believed even in the possibility of over-population. The contrary danger was, according to them, much more serious. But those who admitted the possibility of inhabitants exceeding resources regarded emigration as the ideal safety valve. And people have continued to think in this way right up to the second war, in spite of the gradual closing up of the New World.

In fact, however, mass emigration is now only possible in the most exceptional cases, for many changes have occurred in half a century. In particular, the emigration from Europe to America which took place during the 16th to the 19th centuries, cannot continue into the 20th, for the following reasons:

(a) For a long time America was a jungle open to all newcomers. It was not in the interest of the newcomers to lock away immense unoccupied territories. Even if they had wanted to do so it would have been physically impossible. Today that world is entirely appropriated by nations which carefully regulate all entries into their territory.

(b) This disorderly immigration was carried out at small

enough cost in money, but at enormous cost in human lives.

Today all immigration is "organized" and thereby costly, in economic value. The method of counting has changed.

I will begin with the second point:

The cost was once in human lives

Even in the relatively well-organized nineteenth century, people would pile up on the decks or in the holds of ships without knowing just where they would be going after they had disembarked. In such a huge lottery, some succeeded, others vegetated, others succumbed. The loss in human lives was considerable.

Such human waste, which must have had considerable after-effects, was not in the least shocking at the time. Not only was it almost unseen, unknown, and certainly unmeasured, but it also corresponded to the human wastage within, which was the rule in all countries: each family giving birth to 5 or 6 children for two or three to survive, the elimination of undesirables, etc. Perhaps there was a certain selectivity about this massacre of the innocents, but it is hardly in keeping with present-day notions.

An organized migration is costly

The conditions of migration are very different today. The country of destination, the country left behind, international organizations, all want to proceed in a wise and orderly manner. The immigrant must obtain in advance, a work contract, lodging and guarantees, or even an agricultural settlement already well in order, with a year's advance revenue for the expected first harvest. He must himself fulfil certain conditions.

No organization concerned with immigration could today permit the disorderly and murderous methods which obtained for so long. As soon as a third party takes over the responsibility, as soon as conscience takes part, one must be absolutely logical and renounce all appeal to natural selectivity.

Furthermore the necessary investment per person is much higher than it used to be, both in private goods and tools and in public services (lodging, hospitals, etc.).

This double technical and organic development has considerably raised the financial cost of any immigration. In several countries it can easily reach 10,000 dollars. An immigration of only 10,000 persons costs several million francs. France, for instance, is finding it immensely difficult to populate Guiana with Caribbeans and Madagascar with Reunionians, in spite of the proximity of territories and climates and the great differences in demographic pressure.

Ready-made but onerous adults

A priori, immigration would nevertheless appear to be, for the country of destination, less costly than the rearing of nationals, since it receives "ready-made" men.

But even if we leave aside the various moral, familial and national problems (which are yet important enough!), we find that such a reckoning is entirely contradicted by practice. The investments necessary for an immigrant are in fact higher than those necessary for a native individual, because of the question of adaptation, because the immigrant cannot be satisfied with fortuitous solutions which a native might at a pinch find acceptable, and, especially, because these investments are more easily charged to collective funds, creating financial needs, whereas the investments needed for a native are frequently made without State intervention and even, in the case of peasants, without any keeping or rendering of accounts. As for the actual rearing of men, which is obviously more costly for the native, it is borne by the family, with the possible exception of education.

Besides, whatever the result of those calculations, one fact remains: native children must have priority over foreigners. If the demographic growth is already too rapid, it will naturally be immigration which must be slowed down; it is an immediate measure, generally approved of by public opinion, whereas a policy of birth limitation raises numerous difficulties, as we shall see, and would give only long-term results.

It is difficult to see how a country like India, whose

population is increasing by 6 million a year, could alleviate its demographic pressure through emigration. Even Indonesia is finding it difficult to organize an emigration from over-populated Java to empty Sumatra, although it has the political authority. Nor will it be any easier for Egypt to discharge some of its population into Syria.

Let us now look at the political aspect and the system of regulations.

Strict rules on entry

The countries which take immigrants strictly control all entries into their territory, either because they have enough difficulties to face with their own problem of growth (Mexico, Brazil, etc.), or for racial or political reasons. The only welcome immigrants are qualified workers or those possessing capital. These are precisely the two categories most wanting in the under-developed countries with a rapidly rising population. Poor workers with only their hands to offer are the least welcome, even in countries short of manual labour, and the development of trade unionism can only accentuate this tendency.

In fact, the sense of property is much more developed than it was two or three centuries ago, and is opposed to such transfers. The protection of work, which is no less justified, has now been added to the protection of property.

This appropriation is as visible, in other forms, in the socialist world. One can hardly imagine the Soviet Union opening up its immense territories to give China some land for cultivation. And yet from an economic and financial point of view, such a transfer would be no costlier than that of Russians or Ukrainians to Turkestan.

Emigration considered as an evil

Even in the over-populated countries there is a resistance to emigration, which is considered as a barbarous remedy or at most a precarious palliative. At the United Nations Economic and Social Council the Soviet representatives condemned this method as useless except, they said, to mark the failures of capitalism.

Poland and Yugoslavia have suspended all emigration and have even tried to encourage the return of their own nationals. Similarly the U.S.S.R. has reclaimed "her" Armenians. In Holland and even in Italy, emigration is regarded only as a makeshift arrangement in the hope of more constructive solutions. The essential aim is to find work for people in their own country.

Everyone at home

In fact the time of a finally arranged world has begun, and we must abandon the idea of resolving the demographic problem of Asia or the Far East by emigration. There are, it is true, vast unpopulated regions in Asia and in South America, where Indians and Malayans could find a life less arduous than their own. But such transfers would cause considerable economic and political difficulties. Emigration can only work for small territories; it may even be a successful remedy in certain islands associated with a much larger territory (Mauritia, Reunion, Malta, Formosa, Porto-Rico), but it cannot go any further.

Staying on earth

The imagination is always able to escape from the cruel dilemma which is the object of this study. Science fiction has partly become a reality since the launching of the first satellite, in October 1957, and by facile analogies, many hypotheses of exodus to other planets have been thrown out, vague enough to evade detailed criticism but exciting enough to break the vicious circle that surrounds our minds and forces us to make such painful decisions.

There is, however, a vast gap between the launching of projectiles or even of explorers and the possibility of a massive emigration—not to mention the huge economic problem. The satellites have been backed by budgets of wartime dimensions. But high though their cost has been it is infinitesimal compared to that of settling any portion of mankind in areas where the entire environment would have to be conditioned. At the lowest estimate, such a settlement would cost far more in those areas than in the polar regions, which are at the moment out of the question as regards population. Let us therefore stay on earth.

The real dilemma

Having put emigration aside, we now face the great dilemma: *economic solution or demographic solution.* Should we adjust the resources to the population or adjust the population (by lowering the birth rate) to the resources.

There is no escape-route

At first sight, on reflex perhaps, we may well prefer the economic solution; it seems more opportune, more humane, whatever happens, to adapt the economy to the population than vice versa. Besides, since mankind is already under-nourished, the need for a great economic spurt is incontestable. But it should be examined statistically. I shall therefore begin by analysing the "economic solution."

Chapter 10

General considerations

THE "ECONOMIC" SOLUTION consists in increasing the means
of subsistence at least as fast as the number of human beings.
It is a natural aim. The container must be made to expand at
least as fast as that which it contains.

At the rhythms now reached, however, the increase in
the number of human beings would, by geometrical progressions, produce such high figures in a few centuries that all
physical possibilities of containing them would be surpassed.
However splendid the progress of future science, it would
not allow for an indefinite increase in means of subsistence
at the rhythms foreseen. Is then the "economic" solution
really a "solution"?

It deserves to be examined for three reasons:

(a) An improvement in the standard of living is, as we
shall see, an essential condition for the limitation of births,
or at least a very favourable factor. The "economic solution"
can therefore facilitate the "demographic solution."

(b) In any case, even on the most optimistic hypotheses,
we must expect an important increase of population in under-
developed countries for at least a generation. It is therefore
essential that the means of subsistence should be increased.

(c) Even leaving aside the question of a lowered birth rate,
an improvement in the standard of living is of the utmost importance; it would be inhuman and dangerous to allow human
beings to multiply in wretchedness.

Since the standard of living is continually rising in the
developed countries (which are both richer and less prolific), a vast gap may occur which would generate political
complications.

What is needed therefore is a *considerable* and rapid improvement in the standard of living.

In the following pages we shall be studying the conditions in which the quantity of subsistence-means per person can be increased in the years to come.

In the whole world or by country?

This economic problem is often examined on a world scale. The growth of world population, for example, is compared with the increase in the production of subsistence-means.

In chapter 17 we shall be giving the results obtained by the F.A.O. for the whole world, and we shall be able to see just how inadequate this method is. It is all very well to rejoice if the world production of corn increases faster than the population of the world, but the problem is not solved thereby. It would only be solved if there was a world government to distribute the goods according to the needs. In present conditions the economic superiority of one country inevitably entails political subjections.

A world view is also used to discuss possibilities (and impossibilities). The economist Colin Clark, for instance, has written: "If all arable land were cultivated with as much skill and care as is the land in Holland, if individual consumption of agricultural products were also on the level of present-day consumption in Holland, the world could feed 10 to 15 thousand million human beings, instead of the 2.3 thousand million inhabitants it consists of at the moment."[1] Even allowing that the calculation might be blameless from an agronomic point of view, it is almost valueless in practice. To cultivate the soil everywhere as it is cultivated in Holland is not merely a question of machinery but of agronomic and other wisdom among the peasants. Certainly we must try to instruct those who are cultivating the soil in India or in the Brazilian sertao; but how long will it take to see any results? An elderly and unlettered peasant is not educable. Therefore we must get hold of the young ones, teach them to read, and then give them the required agronomic knowledge. All this must obviously be done, but it will take a generation or perhaps two, and in the meantime

[1] B.B.C. Talk, March 1953.

the population will have increased . . . together with the yield of the fields in Holland. We can see how unpractical this calculation is; like most economic doctrines it omits or underestimates the notion of time.

We must base our studies on a given country: how can a country of an under-developed type manage to increase its production more rapidly than its population by acting upon the former and not on the latter? That is the economic problem.

The imperialist way

I am anxious not to eliminate any possible method and must therefore mention, for the record, the solution of imperialist development. Two classical examples are still before our eyes: that of England, and that of Japan. These two countries, especially the first, succeeded in enabling a large population to live on a reduced territory, by means of political domination. This method no longer offers the same opportunities as it did in a colonial economy. Moreover, even if it could be practised by any given country, it would only aggravate the situation of all the others. It cannot therefore be retained.

In certain cases, however, an economic improvement could be brought about through sudden and even brutally achieved economic freedom, with a repudiation of debts and previous undertakings. The case of the Middle East and its oil-wells inevitably springs to mind. I shall return to this in chapter 15.

The mercantile, industrial or commercial solution

There are, of course, intermediary solutions between imperialist domination and the solitary exploitation of one's own interior resources. A country which transforms foreign raw materials and consumes imported foods may manage to nourish a large population by drawing, thanks to its skill, on the natural resources of other countries. Such an attitude in any given country is blameless, both morally and politically. Nobody would criticize Switzerland for selling watches throughout the world and therewith buying the corn and petrol it needs. Nevertheless the question has been asked, whether the developed countries as a whole are not in this way exploiting the under-developed countries as a whole. This question too, will be taken up again in chapter 15.

In any case, this solution of Switzerland or England cannot be practised by all countries at the same time. If a world government were set up, it could certainly resort to a division of work among nations, but it would be obliged to establish a general balance-sheet of natural resources, which are the basis of all wealth, even "tertiary" wealth.

In practice, we need not take too much notice of such a suggestion. The under-developed countries are finding it extremely hard to exploit their natural resources adequately. Their task consists in catching up on a technical handicap, not in overtaking the others.

The curious case of the Lebanon, however, should certainly be mentioned, for it lives on outside commerce and on the activity of its citizens who have settled abroad. But such an exceptional solution is only within the reach of a small country.

Within a horizon of one or two generations, which is in fact our horizon in the majority of cases, our main objective in this Part Two is the adequate exploitation of natural resources in each country, adequate, that is, to increase the production of riches faster than the population. We must not lose sight of this main objective.

The programme outlined

In this second part of the book, which is devoted to economic development, I shall examine the economy of a type of under-developed country, in the following order:

I shall first study the demographic growth, more or less in its pure state; and then its cost, as well as the advantages it may sometimes present.

I shall then turn to the improvement in the standard of living in its most general and simplest form.

These two factors taken together should enable us to measure the intensity of the effort needed to meet the increase or, better still, to improve the standard of living as the increase is being met.

The next two chapters are devoted, respectively, to internal resources, that is, the national capacity for development, and to the possible exterior aids.

Finally we shall examine the choices facing us and the priorities to be established (chapter 16). Such is the proper function of all government, the essence, even, of all politics.

Results will then be set forth and conclusions proposed (chapter 17).

Chapter 11

The cost of growth

WE ARE DEALING HERE with fairly new factors, and our way of seeing things is also new, that is, our technique, which has advanced so much in the last few years that it finds more and more to do ahead of it and is, moreover, still unfamiliar to many writers on the subject.

A plant, or an animal, has two kinds of feeding needs: there is the need to live, to maintain the organism and, for some, the need to grow in size. The young need not only a ration for maintenance, which is approximately proportionate to their weight, but also a ration for growth, which dieticians are nowadays able to measure with a high degree of precision. This notion may be transferred to the social body.

Present and future: investments

A society also has different needs, some of which correspond to the notion of maintenance, others to that of growth.

Economists make a classical distinction between those efforts that have quick results and produce consumer goods, and those which create new methods of production for the future. The latter are called "investments" (a fairly new term, since it does not figure in L. Say's economic dictionary of 1896, but an ancient notion explicit enough in Quesnay, who has proved such a rich source of ideas).

Quesnay and the physiocrats who followed him were not populationists like the men of his time. He estimated that in order to support more human beings or an excess-population, land would first have to be cleared, reclaimed or improved so as to produce the necessary subsistence. He called such acts of foresight "advances" made to the earth (a just image and a better term than the clumsy "investment" which has prevailed today).

The question is now a little more complex, but can nevertheless be directly modelled on Quesnay's schema.

Two kinds of investment

Among man's economic activities, we may distinguish those which:

(a) produce consumer goods (for example, the production of foods).

(b) keep up the maintenance of productive equipment, so as to avoid or compensate its wear and tear (this is more or less the equivalent of the sinking-fund, well-known to every tradesman, industrialist, peasant, and even to any housewife with a minimum of foresight).

(c) aim at improving this equipment, in order eventually to raise the standard of living (for instance, the construction of hydro-electric dams to produce better light, electricity for refrigerators, washing-machines, etc.) These are the *economic investments*.

(d) aim at giving the supplementary inhabitants (from population growth) the necessary installations for a standard of living equal to that of the others (housing, schools, factories, arable land, etc.). These are the *demographic investments*.

If a population that has long been stationary and used to a certain standard of living suddenly begins to increase it must, initially, enlarge its investments *merely to maintain its previous standard of living*. It is possible (but not certain, and it depends on circumstances) for the growth in population then to have positive economic effects, either because a denser population was desirable, or because the rising of the sap (I shall return to this point) brings with it an extra vitality and a development of the creative spirit. But for a time, these quantitative or *demographic investments*, like all investments, cause an initial impoverishment. This is what has happened in France today, for instance.

The cost of growth includes not only investments proper (the building of schools, for example), but the actual cost of bringing up the "surplus" children, i.e. those exceeding the number necessary to ensure the maintenance of the population at the same level, or the renewal of generations.

I am leaving aside the more complex phenomena such as ageing and the cost of pensions for men whose lives are prolonged, etc., because this phenomenon is not at present operative in the under-developed countries.

It is of course very difficult to distinguish in practice between an "economic" investment and a "demographic" investment. For example:

A new school is being built to replace an old one which has decayed: this is an "economic" investment.

Elsewhere, or in the same place, a new school is being built to meet the increase in the number of pupils; is this only a "demographic" investment? In fact, the school is being built on modern principles and improves the average standard of schools; even if it were being built as an exact imitation of the old ones, the very fact that it is new lowers the average age of school buildings and reduces decay; this investment is therefore partly "economic" or qualitative.

It is however useful to make the distinction, in order to disentangle the cost of growth from other costs.

We can see the importance of demographic investments in one particular field, for example, that of housing:

We will assume that a house lasts one century.[1] A stationary population need only cope with renewal and, therefore, build a number of houses equal to 1 per cent of the housing patrimony.

A population which increases by 1 per cent per annum must, *in addition*, build for the newcomers and increase the patrimony by 1 per cent. For the same result, therefore, its effort must be twice as high as that of the stationary population.

Who foots the bill?

These investments are not necessarily assured by the State, nor are they necessarily financial ones. We may distinguish three main categories:

(*a*) *State investments,* financed by the Public Treasury (or

---

[1] This estimate applies to fairly developed countries.

local funds). This usually covers roads and their maintenance, numerous public works, schools, universities, sanitary installations and, in some countries, a part of housing.

(*b*) *Capitalistic investments,* which are in financial form and appear in private accounts (sometimes as self-financing, if a company is in question).

(*c*) *Investments in kind*; for instance, if a peasant with two sons digs a well and clears a forest to produce new arable lands for them, he is making an investment which does not appear in private accounts. But taken altogether these self-investments may become assets for a global evaluation, in the accounts of the Nation.

As always in such circumstances, one has to simplify in order to get an idea of the phenomenon without losing oneself in a multitude of considerations which, however interesting, are like the trees for which one cannot see the wood.

Rates of national interest

The notion of "national income," conceived at the end of the seventeenth century and already clear in the mind of Vauban, has recently been greatly restored to favour after an eclipse of a century. It is in terms of "national income" that we have to think. The national income is the amount of wealth produced by a territory in any given time (usually a year); it does not matter whether this wealth is sold, consumed by its own producer or invested in the improvement of equipment and of patrimony. The "national income" per inhabitant represents the standard of living.[2]

It is generally admitted that a 1 per cent increase in population requires demographic investments representing 3 to 5 per cent of the national income. Conversely, it is said that the rate of national interest is between 33 and 20 per cent. The rate of a country possessing rich natural resources is higher than that of an already heavily populated country

---

[2] Strictly, the standard of living is represented only by the quantity of goods consumed per inhabitant, investments being only a promise of improvement in the standard of living. I am here using the term "standard of living" in a more general sense, as a defined level of wealth.

where new land is rare and the natural resources are already fairly well exploited. For example, the cost of growth, in investments, is higher in Egypt than it is in Argentine or even in Turkey.

But then, once the investments necessitated by the population growth have been made, will the standard of living be maintained, raised, or lowered? Here the effect of the growth itself is felt.

Growth has its own advantages

Demographic growth sometimes produces economic advantages. Such as the following:

(a) *Qualitative improvement.* If growth is due to a lowering of the death rate, it is often accompanied by an improvement in health. This is the case, for instance, in the suppression of malaria.

(b) *A redistribution of the nation's "general expenditure"* among a larger number of people. This argument is particularly valid in the developed countries, where the fixed responsibilities are large (military, administrative, etc.), but it is by no means negligible in the under-developed countries. An increase in density reduces the cost of transport.

(c) *Specialization, better division of labour* and more facilities for exchanges; here too a higher density may allow for many more exchanges.

(d) *An easier adaptability of the structure.* We are thinking especially of the structure of the population in its occupational activities. This is the most important argument, and the least studied.

All development, all economic progress, means de-formations, and these are chiefly made through the renewal of generations. In a stationary population, the annual contribution of the younger generations is of about 2 per cent. In a population which is increasing by 2 per cent every year the contribution is about double. But its effect is even more important than that, because young people are much more mobile, and readier to take up *avant-garde* occupations.

Growth therefore favours development by giving a certain flexibility to the social body.

This argument, which is not to be identified with the preceding one, is more important for the developed countries. Moreover, it ceases to be valid beyond a certain rhythm of growth, because expansion must not exceed a certain volume.

These various advantages of growth, which counterbalance the disadvantage of environment-resistance, can become more or less cumulative. Mr. Maldant has noted that in certain regions of French black Africa an increase in the population has itself led to an increase in productivity and this without any appreciable investments. Must we then admit that the cost of growth could be nil in these regions? Not necessarily, because in these fairly primitive societies investments are not a matter of book-keeping but of supplementary efforts. But since these efforts would not have been made if the population had remained stationary, its growth has in fact been productive.

Growth and quality

For a complete analysis, from the economic productivity viewpoint with which I am here concerned, the human qualitative factor should also be taken into account.

I am leaving aside the *moral* factors, to be examined later, in order to consider the physical or intellectual vigour expressed in the aptitude for work.

With my terms thus defined, the question is as follows:

Does growth go with quality or against it? Does it improve or reduce man's capacity to produce wealth?

There is no uniform answer. Growth may be the result of a medical improvement which has caused a reduction of both mortality and debility. Such is the case, for example, with growth arising from the fight against malaria or sleeping sickness.

The position is not so clear in the case of growth due to a victory over other illnesses, such as tuberculosis. If it were a preventive struggle, through better food, aeration, etc., quality would go with quantity. But the curative struggle may have the effect of prolonging human lives and increasing the number of patients, convalescents and delicate people.

This remark is not intended as a criticism of the curative

methods. Human life remains above economic calculations. But we must take all the facts into account. We have already seen (chapter 4) that medical progress unaccompanied by economic progress can simply enable a poorer and weaker man to live as long as before, if not longer.

But I am assuming, throughout this second part devoted to the "economic solution," that the standard of living is rising, together with the cultural standard. And from this it may be inferred that man's physical and intellectual state is also to improve, after a few years of development, and this allows for a little more optimism than is provided by strict calculations.

These should, of course, take all factors into account and summarise them in one single figure. But there are always untamable elements, approachable, that is, but impossible to cipher.

The most frequent rate of national interest[3]

Since this study is particularly concerned with countries that are already strongly populated, we shall keep to an average investment figure of 4 per cent of the national income, which is to meet a demographic growth of 1 per cent per annum, maintaining the same standard of living.

Thus, a population which is increasing by 2.5 per cent per annum must devote (on the average) 10 per cent of its national income to the mere maintenance of its standard of living. People must contribute one out of ten working days, that is, pay a tithe, in order not to be impoverished by the increase. The standard of living cannot be raised except by an investment over and above this 10 per cent.

The cost of forming a man

To these investments, which require new installations, must be added the cost of rearing children, over and above the number necessary for the simple renewal of generations.

Since currencies and prices vary considerably from country to country, gross comparisons in the currency of each coun-

[3] See p. 124, and footnote.

try would be pretty meaningless. I shall therefore take the working year per person as a unit, in each country; the working year is simply the national income divided by the active population. Thus in France, in 1957, the working year is 15 thousand million francs divided by 20 million active people, i.e. 750,000 francs approximately. Two questions arise at once, for any period or country:

(a) What part of the national income is devoted to the formation of men?

(b) What is the total cost of forming one man, in working years?

A western population

For a developed Western population the following estimates may be given:

The cost of rearing the young (before they start working) is about 15 to 20 per cent of the national income. These figures include family expenditure on children, whether or not they are covered by State grants. State expenditure on the health and education of the young (not including therefore, family expenditure) is about 4 to 5 per cent of the national income.

These figures do not include the cost of maternal care; not only is this difficult to evaluate, but it never appears in the national account. If an attempt were made to estimate it, in terms of commercial expenditure, the resulting figures would naturally be much higher, and perhaps somewhat unreliable.

From these figures, we may deduce the cost entailed in the formation of one man from his conception to 18 years of age:

Actual rearing: 4 to 5 working years.

Education and public health: 12 to 13 working months.

Thus the total cost of forming a man may be estimated between 5 and 6 working years, nearer to six than five.

Variations in time

For France these figures are roughly equivalent to a sum of 10 to 11 thousand dollars in 1958, or, in other terms, 2,750 hundredweight of corn.

In 1910-1911, Alfred Barriol estimated the social value of a man at about 1,171 hundredweight of corn.[4]

In 1748 Claude Dupin[5] estimated the value of a man at about 353½ hundredweight of corn. Of course these figures, which have been reached by different methods and upon different definitions, cannot easily be compared. Nevertheless they do express such great variations that we may assume a steep rise in the cost of man-formation, with the development of education, hygiene and general welfare. But though the cost has risen in terms of merchandise, it is not certain that it has also risen in terms of working years, for the working year expressed in terms of merchandise has itself risen a great deal.

The total cost of growth

The above figures do not represent the precise cost of growth, but they do enable us to evaluate it.

Up to a point young people merely represent the maintenance of the population at the same level, that is to say, the renewal of generations. Growth proper consists of the number of young people over and above that point which ensures this stable level.

This surplus differs, according to whether one is working out the total maintenance of the population or the integral replacement of one generation by another.

Under the second calculation, in a Western European population with a birth rate of about 17 and a death rate of 11, about a third of the children could be considered as the surplus number. On this hypothesis, the percentages of the national income devoted to growth are as follows:

	%
Family upbringing	6
Public education and health	1.5
Demographic investments	2.5
	10

[4] *Revue économique internationale*, years 1910 (p. 552) and 1911 (p. 356).

[5] *Oeconomiques* (re-edited in 1913).

On this hypothesis therefore, the total cost of population growth is 10 per cent of the national income. But this estimate errs in one important point: since the renewal of generations is only barely assured, without any notable surplus, the growth of the population is due almost exclusively to the lengthening of life.

The European population, however, oscillates around the medium ages (see chapter 6) and, in 30 years, the increase will be chiefly among adults and especially the old.

In these conditions, the cost of growth is dissociated from the cost of youth. We would have to call it rather "the cost of survival." And the cost of increase can in fact be seen in the demographic investments. The prolongation of life makes us provide a few more instruments of labour and, especially, more houses and sanitary installations. The cost of growth can be described as follows: there is no longer any surplus youth to bring up, but the number of old age pensions to pay becomes higher and higher. The demographic investments remain about the same although the building of educational establishments is less, other things being equal, in a population which is increasing by lengthening the life of its members, than in a population which is increasing through the birth rate.

Increase in under-developed countries

We have seen that population growth is often more than 2.5 per cent per annum, which means a levy of 10 per cent on the national income for demographic investments alone. The national income, therefore, is already amputated by one tenth, a sum which we found (on the highest hypothesis) was sufficient to meet all the costs of growth in a developed country.

Furthermore, the number of surplus children to bring up, that is, the number exceeding the level necessary for the replacement of generations, is high. An increase of 2.5 per cent per annum means a doubling of the population in 28 years, that is, at a net reproduction rate of 2; in other words, 100 women give birth during their lives to 200 women reaching the average procreation age. Half the children must be considered as "surplus."

It would be radically impossible to apply European norms. More than half the national income would have to be devoted to children, that is, about 60 per cent including demographic investments, and even more if we include the cost of children who die before reaching procreation age, a cost which is negligible in Europe but which can be as much as 10 to 15 per cent in under-developed countries.

How then do these countries meet such extraordinary costs? They somehow manage in two ways:

(a) by putting children to work very early.

(b) by bringing them up very frugally.

The first method is more important than the second because, since the national income is very low, the number of working years devoted to a child is worth less in terms of care and food. It is not even certain that the cost in working years is lower, given equal ages, in the under-developed country. But children frequently work from the age of 10 or even 8, as in eighteenth- and even nineteenth-century Europe.

The way they are brought up is sometimes so rudimentary that the following fact has been established: in various tropical and subtropical countries excess mortality and illnesses due to debility are particularly high among children between 1 and 5. This anomaly has been explained thus: up to the age of 1 the child gets his maternal milk and so lives without shortages. After 5 he is strong enough to "earn a living" by looking for birds' eggs, grasshoppers, fruit, etc., or, in towns, grubbing in the dustbins, begging, etc. But the period between 1 and 5 is a critical one, with shortages of proteins and vitamins.

Such poverty processes cannot help the general development. The growth is then beyond the capacity of the population, which faces it only with a qualitative failure. For lack of resources, it wastes human beings.

Let us assume that a child costs no more than two working years before reaching his own working age. The upbringing of the young (under 10) then works out at a cost of about

12 per cent of the national income. Since only half these children represent the actual growth, the cost of this growth is as follows:

	Under-developed countries %	Developed countries %
Upbringing of children above the equilibrium	6	—
Demographic investments	10	0.5
Health, public education	1	2.5
Total	17	3

Thus the cost of growth (not to be confused with the cost of the young) absorbs a much higher proportion of the national income in the under-developed countries than in the developed countries. Those who have the least resources also have the greatest liabilities.

The calculations are contradicted

Such data would lead one to believe that growth is "expensive" and that from an economic point of view it is in the interest of a population to remain constant. Would it not in this way avoid demographic investments and the cost of surplus upbringing, all in one? We will see whether experience supports such views.

Here is the most striking example: during the nineteenth century, Western European populations (outside France) increased by about 1 per cent per annum.[6] In France the increase was only of 0.25 per cent. Consequently, demographic investments cost only 1 per cent of the national income in France and 4 per cent in the other countries; France thus economized 3 per cent on her revenue. In addition she also economized on the upbringing of children, but I will even let that go and consider only the first economy.

[6] This figure is obtained from the difference between the death rates and the birth rates. In fact, the population increased a little less, on account of emigration. But the latter is costly, since society forms men without benefiting from their produce. My figure is therefore valid if this phenomenon is taken into account.

If this sum had been put into economic investments, the national income per inhabitant would have increased 0.75 per cent faster in France than in other countries. In one century this would have produced a supplementary increase to double the original sum.

But there was no special improvement in the French standard of living at the beginning of the twentieth century, compared to other countries. Perhaps this annual 3 per cent bonus was just consumed; but in that case a French superiority in standard of living would have made itself felt during the nineteenth century. Yet nothing of the kind occurred.

Where then did this great source of wealth vanish, which appears in the calculations and yet is nowhere to be found in the reality? What do you think about it, J.-B. Say, who advised the French in no uncertain terms to "save money rather than produce children"?

The example of France is far from giving the only lie to the hard and cold calculations. Many others can be quoted: Ireland, and Gascony, for example, ought theoretically to have benefited from the decrease in their population. But decrease has nowhere enriched, nor has stagnation, although the gross calculations predict that they ought.

Moral factors

The explanation may sometimes be sought in the advantages of growth itself, which were enumerated earlier. But we must also mention other factors, called "moral" factors for the simple reason that they are not easily assimilated into calculations of annual income. Scientists, or at any rate those who rely on statistics, have too frequently shown a tendency to neglect any factors of which they cannot easily measure the effect. They remind one of the water-diviner who said: "Sir, there is water here at a depth of exactly 25.5 feet, *apart from the clay.*—That means 25.5 feet plus the layer of clay?—Precisely, sir, there may be 600 feet of clay, I have no idea, because of course I cannot divine clay."[7] But one

---

[7] An authentic story, which occurred about 1921 in the South of France.

should at least describe, enumerate these factors which escape statistics, and try to show how far they may change, if not destroy, the conclusions drawn from large-scale calculations.

In any case, some of these factors are really economic factors and could in fact be brought into the calculations if methods were improved.

Among those factors that are so difficult to measure and to bring into line with mathematical reasoning, the most important is the strength of youth. An increasing population is in a way pushed by its youth, by the love of life. The father of the family is constantly compelled to be more resourceful than he would have been and to make more efforts than he would have made without children, and is in this sense being pushed by his children. The children *push*—it is well said—but whom? The adults. Moreover, an only son does not have the same virtues as the child brought up in the rough and tumble of brotherhood. Brothers and sisters are splendid educators.

A stationary population gets older, since the death rate is going down; it replaces, in effect, the youth with the old, it has less and less aptitude for progress. To a certain extent, demographic pressure favours emulation and competition.

But these various factors on the whole cause only a moderate increase, of 1 to 1.5 per cent per annum, for example. Beyond that, growth may have the opposite effect, breeding discouragement and resignation. This is not a question of nuance, for there is a genuine dividing line. Up to a certain point demographic pressure stimulates; but if it is too great it has the opposite effect, and the breaking point is reached.

Chapter 12

The cost of improving the standard of living

If, FOR ONE REASON OR ANOTHER, a country goes on trusting to its natural fertility, it has somehow to meet the great cost of population growth. It may devote one working day out of six to these costs but this will considerably amputate its already very modest income. How then will it be able to make further sacrifices to improve its standard of living and, especially, that of its future generations?

The two basic facts of development

I must now leave aside the various costs of growth. In order to raise the standard of living, a certain fraction of the national income must be saved. Improvement in the standard of living depends on only two factors: the intensity of the effort, and its efficacy.

(a) The intensity of the effort is measured by *the quantity of economic investments,* which is expressed by the proportion of the national income devoted to them: 5 per cent, 10 per cent, etc.

(b) *The efficacy of these investments* is measured by the resulting future increase in the national income. In relation to the investment which has yielded it, the increase in the national income is called "rate of national interest." If, for example, 1,000 dollars of investments increase the national income by 200 dollars in each succeeding year, their "rate of national interest" is said to be 20 per cent.[1] This new no-

---

[1] The Anglo-Saxon world generally reverses this rate and calls it the coefficient of capital intensity. This somewhat clumsy and inexact expression corresponds to the interest or "denier" of our ancestors. (We may recall Harpagon who lent money at the "denier quatre," that is to say at 25 per cent.) It is better to keep the terminology of income yield used in capitalist accountancy.

tion is really only a transposition of the old notion of capitalistic interest.

A money-saver knows that his future income will depend on his savings and on the rate of interest he receives. Similarly a country must know, or should know, that its income will depend on these two factors, the quantity of the investments and their efficacy.

The use of these two parameters—the quantity and efficacy of investments—will considerably simplify the presentation of a country's economic development.

The capitalist's interest and the nation's interest

The "rate of national interest" of any operation is generally much higher than its capitalist rate of interest, since it is expressed in terms of production while the other is expressed in terms of financial profit.

Take, for example, a hydro-electric dam costing 20 thousand million francs. It will produce 4 thousand million francs worth of electricity. But the cost of maintenance, personnel, distribution, etc., brings down the actual profit to 1 thousand million.

The rate of interest is thus 5 per cent for the (public or private) concern in charge of the work. But for the nation the profit is 20 per cent. It may even be higher than that if the electric energy produced has "multiplying" effects and allows for a new increase in the national income. I shall return to this point later.

Let us suppose that the concern has to borrow initial capital from private persons at 6 per cent. It will be unwilling to undertake the operation, since it will be paying out 1,200 million per annum for a profit of only 1,000 million. Should the operation then be abandoned? Not necessarily. For the State, the annual balance-sheet can be presented as follows:

Interests to pay	−1,200 million
Sale of electricity	+1,000 "
Increase in tax returns due to increase in national income resulting from operation	+1,000 "
Net profit	+ 800 "

The increase in the tax returns is the result of the direct increase in the national income of 4 thousand million, and a fiscal rate of 25 per cent. In fact the fiscal receipts will be higher because of the indirect increase in the national income arising out of the "multiplier."

Therefore the interest of the capitalist may be very different from the interest of the nation.

How high is the rate of national interest?

The rate of national interest of an investment is usually between 15 and 40 per cent, naturally supposing the chosen investments to be the best possible. If the country is already very populated and does not possess rich natural resources that could be exploited, the rate is low. If, on the contrary, new land is available, or new sources of energy are easy to tap, the rate may rise to above 30 per cent. In schematic calculations the rate of 25 per cent is usually adopted. But it is below 20 per cent in many under-developed countries.

Therefore assuming that the two basic facts of development are known, it is easy to forecast the increase in national income in percentages per annum:

Rate of national interest %	Economic investments expressed as percentage of national income			
	3%	5%	10%	12%
15	0.45	0.75	1.5	1.8
20	0.6	1	2	2.4
25	0.75	1.25	2.5	3
30	0.9	1.5	3	3.6
35	1.05	1.75	3.5	4
40	1.2	2	4	4.8

If *economic* investments only are in question, this table also gives the increase in the standard of living per annum. If both demographic and economic investments are in question, the figures no longer express the increase in the standard of living, but that in the national income, that is to say, in total production.

Most writers in fact assume, on a rough estimate, that the rate of national interest is the same for economic as for demographic investments. In other words, they assume that the same quantity of investments is needed, in any given country, to increase production by 1 per cent and to meet a population increase of 1 per cent.[1]

As with the demographic investments, we must distinguish three categories:

Investments financed by the public Treasury,

Private investments giving rise to financial operations,

Private self-investments, without rendering of accounts, particularly in the country. These are not always certainly included in the usual statistics. By leaving them out it is possible sometimes to work out extremely high and even infinite rates of national interest. Let us take, for example, the eighteenth and nineteenth century colonists of Canada. All they had to do to invest was to cut down trees and work the plough to create new land and build their own wooden

---

[1] This identification is only a convenience, but it is untrue in many instances. We may take for example, the case where only one type of merchandise is being produced, say, rice, and where the population is under-employed for lack of land. Without investments (clearing of new land especially), the surplus inhabitants produce nothing, since there is already under-employment. In these conditions, an investment which increases the available surface of land by . . . *n* per cent allows either an increase of . . .*n* per cent in the production of rice per inhabitant (economic investment), or a maintenance of production by meeting a *n* per cent increase in population.

These conditions are naturally never realized: for one thing, the national income represents, in the least inaccurate manner possible, a heterogeneous assortment of very diverse products and services. The goods needed to improve the standard of living by 1 per cent per annum, for example, are not the same as those needed to meet a 1 per cent per annum increase in population. The extra production necessary for the latter includes a much higher proportion of foods, housing, etc.

This diversity is rather to the benefit of economic investment. But we must also take the actual effect of population increase into account; in certain cases, as we have seen (p. 114), increase may favour productivity, and hence the standard of living.

These two rates are not in fact sufficiently precise in measurement for clear distinction. They are therefore frequently regarded as equal, in rough estimates, so as to simplify the schema.

houses. The national income was increasing yearly without any investment being accounted for.

In general economics, one should always try to include self-investments, as one includes auto-consumption. But in other perspectives (that of a bank for instance), only audited investments are taken into account.

Miracles and mirages of the multiplying factor

After a period of somewhat relative rationalism, mankind has again sought refuge in myth. Constriction always creates an evasion myth; financial difficulties are no exception to the rule.

These difficulties seemed particularly absurd during the big slump, when shop-windows were full and purses empty, so that various doctrines emerged suggesting means of escape that were characterized by a certain scientific caution.

If Schacht was the true executor, the great prophet was Keynes. Like all prophets, he was ambiguous enough to leave ample room for interpretations, he was sufficiently far from the truth to give creative imagination a chance, and sufficiently brutal to destroy a whole set of fetishes with which the most apparently realistic doctrines were encumbered.

One magical name in particular was retained by the non-specialists: the multiplier.

Let us return to the example of the hydro-electric dam. A new quantity of electricity is going to be produced in that country. If the electrical energy is simply consumed by individuals, the increase in wealth stops there. But if it is particularly needed in that country, like water in a dry land, it will lead to other increases. Workers so far unemployed will be put to work; others so far producing little will produce more. National production will therefore increase in two ways: through the electricity itself and through its use. The total increase will therefore be, not 4 thousand million, but perhaps 6, 7, 8, etc. This is one effect of the multiplier.

There are others, and this is where the mirage often begins. The distribution of supplementary means of payment will, it is said, provoke chain buying which will increase business and incomes like the loaves and fishes. This doctrine is not absolutely new, for it is already explicit in Law and implicit in Boisguillebert (about 1700). But it has been sufficiently rejuvenated to cause both miracles and havoc.

An artificial demand creates activity only if part of the population is both widely unemployed and *capable of work*. The first condition is unfortunately too often fulfilled, the second much less. The people may be adept at producing something that is not much in demand, or they may, through lack of instruction and technique, be able to produce only at a very high cost. In such a case the artificial extra demand causes the prices to rise or becomes, through the shortage of foreign exchange, as it were a false coin ejected by an automatic machine. This is the situation of many under-developed countries, not to mention others.

When people speak of a rate of national interest of 20, 25, or 30 per cent (whatever it is), it is often objected that "the multiplier has been forgotten," as if reality was too unpleasant and could only be "carried forward" with an agreeable and indeterminate myth.

I cannot take up more space discussing this question which raises numerous difficulties and would lead me to formulate a complete economic theory, that is to say, . . . pursue a phantom.

Suffice it to emphasize that the "rates of national interest" quoted above include or should include all increase in production, direct or indirect, resulting from any given investment. Experience will show whether higher rates can be reached in the future. If an economy starts off with unexploited productive forces, any investment which helps to exploit them, to bring them within the circuit, naturally has a high rate of national interest. An irrigation which enables a more or less unemployed group of people to work and to produce, obviously has a high return, if it is not too costly, but there are many other cases.

Cost of the whole

I shall now go back to our population which is growing fairly rapidly and has to face a high total of expenses. Below are the results of a new calculation, which shows how the national income of a population which is increasing by 2.5 per cent should be used, and this on two hypotheses, that of maintaining the standard of living, and that of raising the standard of living by 2 per cent per annum.

	Standard of living maintained	Standard of living raised by 2% p.a.
Consumption of the young:		
Renewal of the race	7.5	6.8
Surplus above renewal of race	7.5	6.8
Consumption of other non-active persons (old, sick and infirm)	11	10
Consumption of active persons	64	58.4
Demographic investments	10	10
Economic investments	—	8
	100	100

These figures are approximate of course. The first column is in fact equivalent to "multiplying in wretchedness." It is not a real "solution" and yet the active persons have to contribute more than a third of their other production to the rearing of the young, the maintenance of inactive persons, and to demographic investments.

On the second hypothesis—always assuming that no outside help is at hand—*even poverty has to be economized on.* Consumption must be reduced by nearly a tenth in order to provide for the 8 per cent economic investments.

The present must be cut into in order to improve the life of tomorrow. The active persons are left with only 58 per cent of their meagre production.

Moreover, the share which returns to the capital or capitalists must be taken into account. The necessary conditions for an exact calculation are lacking, but we should note that the investments are mostly taken from this very deduction, and should therefore not be counted twice. The capitalists themselves, however, consume part of the production. What proportion? It is very difficult to judge. From the existence of nabobs and fellahs of wretchedness, one would be tempted to quote exceedingly high figures. But the nabobs are very much less numerous than the fellahs: if they consume 6 per cent of the national income for themselves, the worker is left with only 52 per cent of his production.

Illustrated below is a very similar case:

Consumption by the young	Consumption by old, sick, infirm	Consumption by active persons	Consumption by inactive capitalists	Demographic investments	Economic investments
13	9	52	8	10	8

Possible distribution of national income in a country with a population growth of 2.5 per cent per annum and 2 per cent per annum increase in the standard of living.

Am I too pessimistic? These calculations have been made with an assumed rate of national interest of 25 per cent. But in many countries the rate cannot be higher than 20 per cent. On this hypothesis, the total investments would move from 20 to 22.5 per cent, the total consumption would be reduced from 82 to 77.5 per cent, which would leave the active persons with only about 55 per cent of their production, and the consumption of owners still to be deducted.

I have moreover assumed that children are working early, from the age of ten, on an average. In fact, modern technique demands a minimum of instruction, with which this system is incompatible. And since any lengthening of tuition temporarily reduces production and at the same time increases the needs, the balance is upset, as it were at both ends.

These figures give some idea of the difficulties a country may have to cope with before it can get out of the rut. It means that the healthy adult man must absolutely renounce the notion of working for himself and his family alone. And already we can see the difficulties that a capitalist system based on individualism may encounter when attempting to make the necessary provision. But let us not anticipate.

Chapter 13

Is it easier than it was for Europeans?

THE CALCULATIONS in the two preceding chapters were somewhat abstract. Is it possible, in practice, to evaluate the costs of growth as I have tried to do? It is fairly difficult, but even on rough and purely qualitative estimates, some writers have argued that the Asiatics, Africans, Americans, etc., should *a priori* succeed in the twentieth century more easily than the European countries did in the nineteenth.

This optimistic view rests on a very solid argument: the technical short-cut.

A model before one's eyes

Backwardness is often humiliating to one's self-esteem, but it has one advantage: it is possible to catch up, and the direction is clear. If American economy is sometimes a little uncertain, it is partly because, being ahead of all the others, it does not quite know where to go.

The under-developed countries have examples before their eyes, one might almost say models, which make very valuable guides. Whereas the European countries had to feel their way, others benefit from "technical short-cuts." They are as it were given 200 years' worth of accumulated efforts, and are not obliged to pass through Stephenson's "Rocket" or the Pacific locomotive and all the intermediary stages, in order to acquire a modern engine.

It has been calculated that if anyone wanted to build a modern car with the technique of 1913 (let alone that of 1850), it would cost about 71,500 dollars; if it were made by hand, with the technique of 1650, the price would be so high that even Louis XIV or Aurangzeb could not have afforded it. But now it comes to us ready-made, out of an enormous accumulation of brain work and experience.

But during the nineteenth century (see chapter 4), medical progress and the lengthening of life came more or less together with technical and economic progress, whereas today they usually precede it; penicillin and vaccination can reach completely feudal populations. Should it not be the same for economic techniques? Why do we not contribute to an economic rise as rapid as the decrease in the death rate?

We must not go so fast. At the risk of appearing to denounce medical progress as an evil, and of being therefore violently reproached by inattentive readers, I shall analyse the facts.

Was Europe so wonderful?

Population growth is much more rapid in the twentieth century than it was in the nineteenth. If Europeans had had to meet such a swift rise in the population, their economic progress would perhaps have been completely stifled.

In any case, is it so certain that population growth in the nineteenth century was in total harmony with economic development, and resulted only from improved welfare? Vaccination against small-pox and various other hygienic measures may have caused a small rise in the population, difficult to register, which generated poverty. Contemporary writers have attributed the latter to the greed of industrialists and the unfairness of the regime. That is how it seemed. Did these industrialists belong to a special race with particularly long and crooked claws? Did they not rather simply take advantage of circumstances which were exceptionally favourable?

These workers who lived in such deplorable conditions partly came from the country; why then had they left it? Because of great difficulties there and a shortage of land. They preferred exhausting work to no work at all.

It is only from about 1850, at least in France, that wages have frankly been going up faster than the cost of living.

The quarrel between Proudhon and Marx on the one side and Malthus on the other was less about the facts than about the attitudes and intentions of the owning class. "There is only one man too many on earth," said Proudhon, "and his name is Malthus." Neither side was wholly right or wholly wrong. In fact the demographic and economic history of that half-century still remains to be written.

Nor should we forget the intensity of European emigration and the great relief given by this outlet, not only to the conquistadors who were weary of their proud poverty, but to all "marginals" of all countries.

Back to under-developed countries

Let us assume however that medical progress and economic progress were more or less even in the nineteenth century. This is no longer the case today, for it is a question of imported techniques, not of discoveries made within a fully developing population.

Economic technique cannot be transmitted as speedily as medical technique, for several reasons. Economic technique is in the hands of only a small number of specialists. It is something which a society submits to but does not utilize. It takes far longer to spread Danish agricultural methods among ignorant and illiterate peasants than to teach a few nurses and doctors how to inoculate vaccinations, which are nearly always imported.

Widening these tenets a little, it is possible to argue that the techniques of consumption are much easier to assimilate than the techniques of production. An unlettered person is perfectly capable of using a refrigerator or a television set. The production of these things is a very different matter. Without the accumulated science of the West, the Middle East oil-fields would yield only an infinitesimal fraction of the wealth they actually produce for the interested states. Since, however, the rhythm of demographic growth is so much higher, the rhythm of economic development ought to be higher too, the transformation ought to be more rapid. Of course, the existence of very numerous young age-groups strongly favours the transformation; changes occur only through the young, whether it be the active population or those still being reared. Even so, these young people have to be sufficiently well trained, and such a task may well fail if the effort is too great.

There are other differences, of which I will mention three:

(a) the difficulties of civilization-grafting,
(b) a much higher density to start with,
(c) the contribution of other countries.

I shall take these in turn.

The grafting of a civilization

In the nineteenth century, progress was the logical result of a long cultural evolution. Descartes and Newton were already two hundred years old and Copernicus three hundred. The Church, for a while surprised and shaken by science, soon learnt to allow science its share, thus avoiding too deep a chasm between tradition and innovation.

In the under-developed countries, on the other hand, it is more often a question of *civilization being grafted*, a new culture irrupting into the old with its efficiency which, though incontestable on some levels, is nevertheless destructive of values and therefore difficult to impose.

Higher density at the start

The under-developed countries are not all more densely populated than were the European countries around 1750, and here again we must differentiate Asia and North Africa from Latin America and black Africa. But it is precisely in the great Asiatic masses that the high densities apply. Of course, the density or number of inhabitants per square mile is only a very rough measurement, since there are square miles and square miles. In Egypt, for instance, only 13,510 out of 386,000 square miles are habitable. And even though the sea is more productive than the desert, it is not included in calculations of density. In spite of this important reservation, however, a comparison of density can still be fairly significant, for the differences are extremely striking.

	Density *about* 1800		Density *about* 1800
Belgium	261.6 to sq. mile	Egypt*	1,657.6 to sq. mile
United		Korea	323.7 " "
Kingdom	168.4 " "	Ceylon	287.5 " "
Netherlands	168.4 " "	India	284.9 " "
Italy	158 " "	Japan	
France	132.1 " "	(c. 1870)	246.1 " "
Germany	116.6 " "	Pakistan	207.2 " "
Switzerland	93.2 " "	Philippines	165.8 " "
Spain	51.8 " "	China	155.4 " "

* Not including the desert.

The population of India, for instance, starts off with a density higher than that of Belgium in 1800, which was already partly industrialized and had a higher standard of living. We should also beware, as Mr. Pierre Gourou has shown, of our own illusions on the exuberance of tropical land, which is frequently of superficial appearance only.

The contribution of other countries

If the backward countries of today can benefit from the previous experience of others and sometimes from outside credit and gifts, we must not forget that (in a different sense of course) European countries leant heavily on the rest of the world to lay the foundations of their famous progress.

First of all, they found a field of emigration in the new world, which provided a great deal of employment. The "system" may of course seem onerous for the emigrating country, which bore the cost of rearing and training numerous men without benefiting from their adult contribution. But this argument is tantamount to saying that it would have been more "economic" not to give birth to persons who would be lost as soon as formed; such a view is contestable, to say the least. Apart from the moral factors examined in the preceding chapter and the favourable conditions created by a certain degree of growth, these emigrants were not totally lost; by creating new activities they opened new markets and became purveyors of raw materials which were very much needed.

In any case, I am not here concerned with finding out what

would have happened if the emigrants had not been born, but what would have happened if they had not found such an outlet. Unemployment was chronic throughout the nineteenth century, and when Marx talked of a "reserve army" of workers, he was relying on factors that were essentially real, however imprecise and unmeasured.

If all the Swedes, English, Germans, Italians, Spanish and Frenchmen, who found a life outside had had to stay in their own country, would the lowering of the birth rate have begun earlier? Such a hypothesis is plausible for the leisured classes that had long been affected by the "market," but very problematic for the working-classes; proliferation and pauperism might have led to serious disturbances.

But we still have to determine the value of the colonial contribution itself, a very delicate task! The Soviets have sometimes regarded it as the decisive factor in European development. But here we must allow for their obvious desire to reduce the merit of capitalism, or rather that of the West, as much as possible. In fact, the purely colonial contribution has been modest. From 1815 on, most of the American colonies emancipated themselves. The contribution of the black continent has been slight. That of India was certainly more important, but the difference between a political subjection and an economic dependence is not a determining factor. In short, countries without colonies, such as Switzerland, Sweden and even Germany, have benefited as much from the outside contribution as the others, with the exception of England. Similarly the countries which were not politically colonized did not develop more quickly than the others.

The real advantage to Europe has been the existence of a market, an outlet for men and products which has not only allowed for profitable exchanges, but has also brought about a certain fermentation, a faith in continuous progress. The sometimes mythical character of these eldorados did not destroy their creative power. Donogo is far from being a joke. Europe in fact benefited from great new openings which are quite simply unavailable to countries like Pakistan or Malaya.

It is quite clear at any rate, that unless strong outside contributions are made, of a very different kind this time, the progress of the under-developed countries has to face much harder conditions than those that European progress had to face at the end of the eighteenth century.

Chapter 14

Interior strengths and resources

AT ITS SIMPLEST, economic development consists in finding as many means as possible for the realizing of investments and in applying these means in the best possible place. I have already spoken of this schematic operation. This chapter will deal with the gathering up of interior forces and the various problems raised by economic development.

Investment presupposes some unpaid work

In the perspective of finance, it is often assumed that any investment presupposes a *previous* saving. This proposition is not very exact, because various forms of credit create means of payment *ex nihilo*. When economic problems are discussed in this form, error and sophistry are almost fatal. Contrary to appearances, it is "money" which is an abstraction, and the statistics of products and especially of persons, which express the concrete aspect of the matter.

To invest means that men are going to work, without producing an immediate result; this includes not only the men who build the dams, the factories, and the men who teach others, but also those who produce the cement for the building, the coal to make the cement, etc.

All these men must be paid, or, more exactly, they must be enabled to live. Therefore other men will have to produce consumer goods, especially food, and themselves consume only a part of these; the surplus must be given up, either unwillingly and definitely (i.e. as taxation in various forms, and the profit of capitalist interest), or voluntarily in exchange for promises (i.e. as loans).

In any case investment means gratuitous work, work without immediate fruit. The real question is who bears this cost and by what means.

Can the poor man save?

In all these countries, income is very low, often lower than 95 dollars a year per person; this income (or rather this produce) is seldom enough even for purely physiological needs. How then, or by what magic, can this under-nourished and debilitated man renounce part of his vital food and that of his children? Can a voluntary saving equivalent to 300 calories a day really be expected from a man who hardly has 2,000?

Asking a poor country to save raises in fact the same objections as does the moralist who advises a needy family to put some money in the savings bank.

And yet the 15 per cent saving on the national income which was quoted above represents a minimum; two-thirds of it, i.e. 10 per cent, will meet demographic needs and maintain the same standard of living, and the remaining third will enable the country to raise its standard of living by an average of 1.25 per cent per annum—a very modest result which means a whole half-century to double the standard of living and bring the annual income to a still abysmal level of 190 dollars per person!

Perhaps part of this saving can be made through extra work: pushed by the need to feed his children, a poor farmer may, in certain cases, clear some uncultivated land, dig a well, etc. Will he have the strength for it?

The savings of the poor are certainly not to be relied on.

The savings of the rich man

If the national income is unequally distributed among rich and poor saving is more easily achieved. For example, if instead of 100 persons with an annual income of 95 dollars we have one with 4,750 and 99 with the remainder divided equally between them, the rich person will without much difficulty be able to save 15 per cent of the whole.

But this solution is appallingly expensive. It means creating a strong inequality of incomes and lowers the income of the poor by far more than 15 per cent. It even seems a simpleton's solution. The rich man will never save 100 per cent of his income; the inequality therefore leaves him with sums which he consumes, and it starves the workers all the more.

It is also objected that inequality of incomes is necessary for other reasons. All the countries in the world resort to it, including the U.S.S.R.

No doubt some inequality of incomes is necessary for increase in production, *but not any kind of inequality*. It must be a reward for merit, not for birth, for the future and not for the past. In most under-developed countries, however, inequality of incomes is quite simply the result of inequality of fortunes and particularly of a very unequal sharing out of lands. The solution should be reproved as too burdensome, which consists in maintaining a high degree of inequality in the hope of saving more. The saving function is paid too dearly. The man of property behaves rather like a tax-collector who levies much from the mass of the people but returns only a little to the public treasury.

This return need not necessarily be made in the form of financial saving, that is, by subscribing to various types of State borrowing; it can be made as a private investment or a self-financing, but the result is the same.

Taxation

When this source proves inadequate, voluntary subscription must be abandoned and taxation is resorted to. But the difficulty is much the same: it is not easy to milk an egg. The property-owner manages to impose levies on the poor, only because the poor man does not control his production, at any rate when he earns a wage and can be sacked if he does not pay his farm-rent. Consequently public authorities tend to favour the inequality of incomes, which makes the task of tax-collectors easier. But the operation as a whole is as defective. We fall back on the tax-collectors, but with the aggravating circumstance of discontent and resistance in the owning class which, far from regarding itself as exercising a sort of public function, thinks it is being plundered and tries in every way to impede the fiscal task.

I cannot here attempt to deal with questions of choice

between possible taxes. I must recall, however, that direct taxation of acquired fortune is not only more equitable than indirect taxation of consumption, but that it encourages development by hitting the inactive element and freeing the active one. This elementary principle is often forgotten, particularly in France.

Credit, multiplier, inflation

I have already spoken of this question in the previous chapter. To what extent can a country do without savings and realize investments by issuing paper money, of whatever form and name? What would be the consequences of this extra artificial demand?

It could happen that this demand might put men to work who were waiting for but one thing to increase their activity: the unblocking. Appearances always favour such a situation. In fact, however, it is rare for the extra demand not to meet with some sort of bottle-neck, some island of resistance just strong enough to provoke a rise in prices, in other words, the feared inflation or a demand for foreign goods.

Indeed, it is fairly futile to look for the "real motive force." Both investment and the training of men can be useless, if no mechanism is set in motion to stimulate demand. But this mechanism, which is more of a catalyst, a lubricant, than a source of energy, must be regulated with the greatest care.

When faced with all kinds of claims, governments always tend to open the financial sluice-gates rather more than they should; this is as much the case in Poland as in France, in Yugoslavia as in Brazil, in Turkey as in Finland. The result is an overflowing demand on the outside world, that is to say, on foreign currency.

The situation can be summed up as follows: an artificial demand when met by a potential offer, an unused factor of production, irrigates the economic field and creates prosperity; in the contrary case, it provokes a financial crisis frequently followed by an economic slow-down. In an unlettered population, such a crisis arrives long before full employment.

The rich man's duty

According to a traditional and persistent popular opinion, the rich man's duty is to spend, in order to keep many people working, so as to return to society what he has taken from it. The parable of the bad rich man, the anathemas and satires against the miser counting his gold, are of all times and of all countries.

But although this sentiment survives tenaciously even in the most unexpected financial circles, reason dictates very different attitudes.

How can the rich man use his possessions and especially his income? Here are the ways, in order of national benefit:

(a) *Destruction or sterilization of his credit.* When the money is made of paper, that is to say, unpaid for, the best thing the rich man could do with his notes is to burn them. He would thus destroy, not wealth, but his rights over the wealth of others. The national bank could then issue notes for that same money, without committing the *lèse-monnaie* crime of inflation, and it could devote them to the public interest.

(b) He could also accumulate them, without consuming anything. When he dies, others will consume; the public would benefit from the death duties.

(c) *Investment.* Then comes a procedure which is just as favourable to the public: to invest, on condition that these investments should be nationally useful. The good rich man follows the advice of the marquis de Mirabeau: "A property owner who leaves the gable of one of his barns uncovered murders the whole population."[1]

But, it may be objected, is this totally unphilanthropic action really useful to society? Some day or other, the rich man will want to enjoy his income, to consume his riches. No doubt, but as long as the process lasts, the public benefits because there is always more employment.[2]

The legal and moral difference between this solution and

[1] *Les économiques,* 1769.

[2] This is where Marxist theory and instinctive opinion both err. In a general way, productivity and mechanization increase employment. Experience is irrefutable.

that which consists of State investments financed by taxation of the rich is very great, but the economic result is about the same. And since the most important thing may be to "hold out" for a generation, this solution is theoretically defensible. The interest of the capitalists as a class is anyway in the same direction.

(*d*) *Consumption of work.* In this solution, which conforms to popular desires, the rich man spends money all around him, enabling not only his own servants to stay alive but a whole world of artisans and workers. It is a luxury of subsistence, a solution which favours the population of the time but sacrifices the future. It can last—and has in fact lasted—as long as the population does not increase. But an increase in the population destroys the feudal regime, or any regime, however generous and solid, which is based on the maintenance of available resources.

(*e*) *Consumption of subsistence-means.* If the rich man's consumption is chiefly of natural products, this world of artisans and workers disappears. A short-circuit is established between nature and the rich man which leaves no room for others. This is the case of the man who owns horses, hounds, etc., and uses arable land for hunting, of the princess who bathes in milk, etc.

In such conditions the active population and, consequently, the total population, is less important that that of the previous case, and remains stagnant too.

The order followed here is certainly not that of popular opinion, which has always insisted that the good rich man is the one who spends and not the one who hoards. Even if it was true once it is no longer true today. That great prodigal, the State, is only kept back from creating new means of payment by the rise in prices. Any person who does not consume enriches the public Treasury. The latter can certainly make a mediocre use of its resources; but any economic development presupposes in the rulers a minimum sense of the public good, otherwise they would soon go the way of Farouk.

Leaving aside the very hypothetical case of destruction and even sterilization (for a bank account is not inactive), we can see that the best way to use wealth is to invest it in works which are in the national interest.

If the rich man has little inclination to consume and little desire for power, he will in effect devote most of his income to investments. But his choice, which is inspired by considerations of profit, will not always fall upon the investment which would have been the best for the nation.

The fiscal solution

In the solution which may be called fiscal, the State heavily taxes high incomes, especially incomes from property. The landowner's expenditure is thus replaced by public expenditure. If the latter is aimed at the general interest, it is more favourable to economic development than the former, which served, in effect, as luxury consumptions, or as private investments; so that, even if the landowner amputates his private investments in order to maintain his consumption, there still remains a certain public advantage, always providing that these public investments are properly selected. Moreover, these investments will not be burdened with annual interest charges.

The financial transfer has a counterpart in the change of activity. Instead of working for some lord, like the servants, artisans, etc., people are employed in some work of public interest. The active population is therefore transformed as a result.

The benefit of such a transfer lies in the aptitude of the public authorities to use the sums received with foresight and probity. A condition like this of course inspires grave doubts; between mere nonchalance and pure corruption lies a vast zone of bureaucratic carelessness and technical ignorance. But a squandering regime cannot last long in a country with a growing population. Failing virtue, the pressure of an increasing number of mouths to feed will sooner or later inspire some sort of prudence.

This is the wise solution which any enlightened governing class conscious of its interests ought to adopt. To feed the horse in order to stay in the saddle. Such consciousness is only too evidently lacking in more than one country. But in such cases the road is open to more radical solutions.

The revolutionary solution

A revolution is a change of governing personnel. There are several ways of conceiving such a replacement; in our day, the attraction of the communist system, or at least of Soviet protection, plays an essential part. It is always important to know whether the new governing body will rely on the communist party or put it out of harmful action. But I must leave aside the political aspect and deal only with the economic schema of such an overthrow.

In losing power, the governing class loses its property and its income, which are transferred to the public treasuries and used for development. This is how the popular republics of Europe and China have been transformed. From a purely technical point of view the difference between this and the preceding solution is only one of degree; the procedure in either case aims at replacing superfluous consumption by necessary investments. In principle, it is faultless; in practice, it may carry with it bureaucratic and other wastes and losses heavy enough to counterbalance the advantages.

This solution however, seems more attractive to the under-developed countries than it does to the developed ones. People who have never known liberty cannot be sorry to lose it; lacking the strict necessities of life, they find themselves facing fairly easy technical choices and can be content with an unsubtle planned economy.

What Marxist would declare today, following Marx, that England will be the first country to turn socialist, simply on account of industrial concentration and maturity?

Communism offers the under-developed countries a rough and efficient solution.

The redistribution of land

The redistribution of land is often favoured by those who support both conservatism and social progress. The theory of land for those who cultivate it, when applied, certainly creates a stable and stabilizing class.

Attractive though it is, this solution has its dangers if used incautiously, and may even go as far as causing famine in the towns. By imposing a levy on the income, that is, on the subsistence of the cultivators, the landowner or the feudal lord did, in effect, enable other people to live. The suppression of this transaction leaves these people without income and without subsistence.

Such an elimination can go further, for food consumption is extremely elastic among overtaxed peasants. The consumption of meat leads to a consumption of intermediary calories and, subsequently, of land, which is six times higher than the consumption of milk. Moreover, animal-breeding requires fewer men on an equal surface, so that once freed from the levy, the land tenant is able to sack some wage-earners.

A radical sharing out of land not accompanied by other measures to protect the public safety would therefore be a dangerous solution, in spite of appearances. By getting rid of the rationer together with the rationing, it runs the risk of starving part of the population, in spite of the freeing of the rations consumed by the rationer.

The first Soviet famines, at the beginning of the Revolution, have been attributed to the voluntary retention of products by the peasants. It was not a question of sabotage, nor of mistrust of currency. The under-nourished peasants were simply ready to consume more calories than under the old regime.

Learning from this experience, China was clever enough to back the redistribution of land with a high tax in kind, which has ensured the feeding of the towns. The problem was all the more acute because the monetary unit, the Yen Min Priao, was defined in terms of a certain amount of products in which grain and rice were particularly prominent. To pay ten million communist officials and soldiers meant the same, therefore, as to promise them a certain quantity of food. The 1950 budget included 41 per cent taxes in kind on peasants.[3] A straightforward sharing out of the land, without important levies by the central authority, would have meant the death of

[3] See H. Brenier: *La réforme agraire en Chine. Revue de politique étrangère* (April–May 1951).

numerous town-dwellers, or rather, social and political up-heavals of exceptional violence.

It is true that the re-distribution of land is rarely as radical as this. In the hands of a conservative government, it is always very limited and progresses slowly. It is only in the case of revolution that the risk is serious.

Conclusion

Whether it is voluntarily used, claimed or confiscated, can the income of the rich be sufficient to ensure the development of a backward country? Does it cover a great enough part of the national income to prevent any extra deprivation from being imposed on an already very deprived nation? No certain and general answer can be given. The Soviet Union succeeded only by imposing very severe privations. China seems to have avoided them. But in such a country, with its corrupt governing class and its perpetual wars, some improvement was fairly easy to bring about. Moreover, Soviet aid to China has been important.

It seems therefore that in many under-developed countries the population is increasing too fast for them to get out of the rut by their own means. No country consists entirely of heroes. It is therefore necessary to look at the possibilities of outside help. This is the subject of the next chapter.

Chapter 15

Outside forces

THERE ARE two very distinct aspects of this question:

(a) Are the present under-developed countries the victims of an economic exploitation on the part of the more developed countries?

(b) In what ways can the latter give positive aid to the former?

The role of force in production

Inside a country, social-economic relationships are called "production relationships." Without the serf, the slave or the wage-earner, the rich man would not be rich; however immense his factories or extensive his land, his existence would be very modest indeed. From this fact alone it is very tempting, and certainly very easy, to expose the injustice of the system; the demonstrations of Marx were more or less superfluous.

In any case, whatever the doctrines, changes are taking place everywhere, either to modify the production relationships (communism), or to make them more humane. Nobody now defends the pure force of ownership, without strikes or social legislation.

But how does this problem appear on an international scale?

Great inequality in the world

Between rich and poor nations, the inequality is very marked. Here is the population and national income, evaluated in dollars, of the world's large regions:

	Population in millions	National income in thousand million dollars	National income per person in dollars
I. 16 developed capitalist countries	385	536	1,390
II. U.S.S.R and European countries of medium development	450	198	440
III. Latin America	195	41	210
IV. Africa, Oceania (without Australia or New Zealand), Asia (without U.S.S.R.)	1,800	195	108
	2,830	970	342

Even with averages taken over such large areas, one can see a privileged group with an income twelve times higher than that of the immense and wretched block of under-developed countries in the Bandung world.

Here are these same figures in percentages:

	Population	National Income
I. Developed countries	13.6	55.3
II. U.S.S.R. and European countries of medium development	15.9	20.4
III. Latin America	6.9	4.2
IV. Africa, Oceania (without Australia or New Zealand), Asia (without U.S.S.R.)	63.6	20.1
Total	100	100

Thus 14 per cent of men have 55 per cent of the income, whereas 64 per cent have only 20 per cent. This fact is relatively recent; inequality among nations was less pronounced at the beginning of the nineteenth century; and, in particular, the inequality between wage-earners has increased considerably.

It is evident that conflicts between social classes have become far less important than conflicts between nations.

Is it a matter of production relationships?

But is this inequality as shocking from the legal-social point of view as it is from a humane one?

Let us hear the developed countries first: Our wealth, they say, is the result of our work. We are rich because we are better than other countries at exploiting our natural resources, cultivating our land, etc. We are ready to help the other countries, providing this is regarded simply as help and no more. They have no rights over us. Relationships between nations are very different from those between social classes, which are closely and jointly binding.

We exchange our products, the under-developed countries reply. Without our raw materials and our oil your factories would not function and your wealth would be dramatically reduced. You value our working hours at a ridiculous price when you buy our products, whereas we pay very dearly for yours.

The argument of the developed countries would be perfectly tenable only on two conditions:

(a) If no natural resource of an under-developed country were in the hands of a developed country.

(b) If there were no outside trade.

In such isolation, they could oppose all claims, just as Martians could oppose all our claims if their standard of living were extremely high. The whole business would be a pure matter of charity and human solidarity, not to mention the possible risk of violence (invasions, etc.).

In fact, however, outside trade exists, though it does not play as important a role as the relationships between social classes. The capitalist owes almost all his wealth to his wage-earning workers. This is not the case with the developed countries.

Similarly, if the capitalist were to double the wages of his workers he would have no more income; whereas the developed countries could double the price they pay for their raw materials without being ruined by it, and such a change would be very far from doubling the income of the under-developed countries.

As for natural resources, the problem of ownership is particularly relevant with regard to oil. Of course, the world of Bandung is incapable of consuming all the oil in the Middle East. But it can nevertheless demand a higher and higher proportion of the income or even nationalize the wells and refineries. It was extremely unwise of the capitalist world to base its prosperity on a product that does not belong to it. The consumer of motor energy in the form of road petrol ought to be paying a very high security premium as part of the accountable price. But the power of the oil-men was too great for any precautionary gesture of this kind to be even suggested.

Raw materials?

More generally, the developed countries might well be accused of monopolizing all the raw materials and thereby limiting the industrial opportunities of other countries.[1]

The consumption of motor energy per inhabitant is forty times higher in the United States than in the under-developed countries; this ratio is approximately the same for steel.

In order to bring the under-developed regions to the European level, world production of raw materials would have to be more or less doubled. The realization of such an aim would certainly not be impossible, but while it was being realized the consumption of European countries would have risen again considerably.

In a general way, the United States consume more than half the world's raw materials, and produce only about 40 per cent; and the gap is tending to increase.

Development in the world is held in check by the developed countries. A country which sells twenty tons of mined copper and which, with the money received for it, can only buy one ton of products made with this copper, can hardly hope for more than very slow progress, unless it possesses important agricultural surpluses or huge mineral resources that are already being exploited. Such conditions presuppose a certain degree of development; it is a vicious circle.

The developed countries can reply, but is it our fault if synthetic rubber costs the same to produce as natural rubber:

[1] See especially F. Tabah: *La population du monde et les besoins en matières premières. Population,* October–December 1953.

And why should we pay more for it than the net cost inside our own countries?

However strong this argument, which is limited to certain products only, it is difficult to resist the feeling that unless world production of raw materials increases enormously, and is accompanied by the kind of progress that would economize those materials (reduction in the weight necessary to any given production), the mercantile policy of the developed countries is in direct competition with the growth of world population. It would be a coherent policy only if, quite suddenly, the population of the under-developed countries were reduced, for example, by half.

The opposition between the two movements—increase of production in the developed countries and growth of population in the under-developed countries—is all the more dramatic in that international tension and armament lead to an immense destruction of raw materials.

Poverty and wealth can, while simply juxtaposed, raise no more than a problem of charity. But any social link between them changes the perspective and forces a different orientation. This relation is becoming more and more precise. The link is visible, for instance, between the immense consumption of newsprint for sterile ends (most of it being for publicity, and economically useless from a global point of view), and the education of the illiterate. And others are no less close for being less apparent.

Legal discussions are, in the end, rather pointless, in the absence of an international tribunal that would judge these things on well-established principles. The question will be solved by force, which does not necessarily mean by war.

Outside aid

Relationships being what they are, just or unjust, the problem before us is really that of the aid given by developed countries to the others.

In theory, nothing could be easier. A certain capital, put into well chosen investments, brings about 25 per cent in terms of production, or national income—as we have seen.

If the interest, in capitalist terms, is 5 per cent, only one-fifth of the surplus production need be deducted and exported to pay the interests. With a slightly higher deduction, the loan could be redeemed in twenty or twenty-five years.

In fact, a deduction of 20 per cent on surplus production is much heavier than it appears. The operation seems to consist simply of lowering the national interest rate from 25 to 20 per cent. Could one not, by choosing the necessary investments very carefully, retrieve the 5 per cent which make up the repayment of the foreign capital?

The operation is not the same, at any rate in a capitalist regime. All production determines increases in wages and other income which are difficult to take back once distributed. Moreover, this production must be exported in order that the lending nation may be repaid in kind.

A difficulty is not an impossibility. Assuming the complete good faith of the borrower, even to the extent of heroism, one may conceive a series of classic loans from Croesus to poor but honest Job, and loyal repayments from Job to rich but unphilanthropic Croesus.

Conceive, yes, but can it be realized?

The lion in the mouse-trap

The present international atmosphere does not lend itself to such operations. The control of currencies, the fear of nationalization, of a change-over to communism, or quite simply of the borrower's failure to repay, all these factors do in fact restrain the possible lenders.

About 1955 a proposition was laid at the United Nations, suggesting that all nationalization of foreign property invested *after this agreement* should be forbidden. In other words, any countries borrowing from then on would undertake to respect such an agreement.

In the spirit of liberal capitalism, such a proposition is based on a strong natural bond: the undertaking and the given word underlie the whole transaction. In this capitalist spirit, public power exists only to ensure that property and contracts will be respected. Since an international political power was being created, it was perfectly natural to demand that it, too, should ensure the observance of international agreements.

The proposition, however, was condemned as interfering with the sovereignty of nations, which is incontestable, and it was therefore rejected.

This event, which passed almost unnoticed, marks an important date, for it sanctioned the breaking of a legal right, the end of a system.

The decision was in fact equivalent to an almost total condemnation of international loans, from individual to individual, and even from State to State, since sovereignty includes the right to refuse the payment of debts. From then on, capital could no longer enter, for fear of not being able to get out. A situation was sanctioned which was due, partly to the absence of international justice, but also to the relationship of political dependence inevitably created by the loans of the rich to the poor.

It is pretty futile to make a value judgment on these events; rather are we simply recording the death of one form of foreign aid, which in any case had a somewhat agitated time of it when alive.

Loans will still be arranged in other forms, for example by the International Bank or other organizations. For the moment, these are benefiting from the popularity all new forms of credit seem to enjoy, as well as from the prestige that international organizations have in young borrowing countries. And nobody would think of repudiating such loans. As for repayment . . . there is the risk that it may be achieved simply through new loan agreements, with tradition being respected at least that much.

Gifts

The international gift is a fairly new development. The failure to pay inter-allied debts, reparations, etc., after 1914–18 had shown the futility of long-term instalment plans, so that the lender came to think that if he was not going to be repaid he could at least have the satisfaction of a splendid gesture. During the second war, "lend-lease" was a lending in name only. It was a clever platonic satisfaction given to American public opinion, which had been so deeply offended by the non-payment of the first war's debts. Apart from this there were direct gifts from nation to nation during and after the war.

Another reason has been invoked: it has been said that if certain countries grant economic gifts, it is to sustain their vacillating economy, and to avoid risks, by increasing the buying power of the poorer countries. This argument, which has had—and still has—so much success, is a disconcerting simplification and, moreover, relates to pre-war situations which have largely been left behind.

If a country has big financial resources and an economy in slump (one thinks, in fact, of the United States), it is by no means certain that its economy will be revived by such methods. For if the sums loaned are obtained by fiscal means or by long-term borrowings, they reduce the buying power of the nation's own people; it is then a simple transfer. In any case, whatever the origin of these sums, the Treasury disposing of them might just as well subsidize its own poor as those of the foreign country, if the channel has to be artificially maintained. And there are, in the United States even more than in other Western countries, vast areas of under-development and widespread social misery.

It is true that outside gifts are more easily made in kind. If for one reason or another stocks of wheat have been accumulated and are difficult to dispose of, it is in the interest of the owner country to give them to foreign countries, because they could not otherwise consume these goods. But in this case there is no real question of supporting a faltering economy.

It is certainly true to say that almost all the gifts that have been granted in the last twenty years have had some political motive, whether it be the Marshall plan, American aid to Chiang Kai-shek's China, Soviet aid to Egypt or China, or French subsidies to Morocco. Which is tantamount to saying that until now there has been no true, pure gift.

Fearful conditions

Pure gifts, and even low-interest loans, come up against the dreadful obstacle of the conditions on which these are granted. It is usual to assert, in all these cases, that the transaction has no political conditions. Public opinion is ever ready to accept foreign money as long as the political conditions are not revealed, or even better, are strenuously denied.

The giver or lender, however, is very often trying to keep within his orbit a country which is trying to escape from it. The mere fact of granting the gifts is a political act, even if the receiver enters into no legal agreement.

If it were a purely economic gift or loan, the difficulties would begin again:

It is not enough to control the use of funds, to know that they are being employed for a dam, irrigation, etc., and not dissipated in pure loss, because the very gift or loan by relieving public funds allows them a certain relaxation. The carrying out of a useful investment may, by way of corollary, reduce other investments which were very necessary, so that in the end, beyond the documents, everything happens a little as if the loan had been wasted. The relative financial relaxation benefits the courtly bureaucracy that gravitates around the political power, serves to pay useless officials etc. So that even gifts and loans in kind, (machinery, etc.) do not wholly escape from this danger.

Can we look ahead, in the hope that once this political court has been fed—and, after all, it represents only a tiny fraction of the country—the rest of the loan or gift will be put to useful work, that is, to fertilizing the country's economy?

It is a vain hope, and the venture would be a dangerous one. Experience shows how much the needs increase in such circumstances; also, power thus equipped would have recourse to more and more widespread liberalities. The example of the Arab population expelled from Palestine and more or less supported by international organizations is not encouraging.

Here again we come across the need for *responsibility*. If the responsibility falls to a foreign power, even be it an international one, we are back with a form of colonialism, and its attendant inhibition of the protegé. The responsibility must be national; a government must itself feel threatened if it does not succeed in feeding the citizens who have nominated it or tolerate it.

Technical assistance

This new form of assistance has no doubt arisen out of these difficulties. The borrower or assisted nation can distribute, dissipate, eat the dollars, but it cannot consume an agronomist, an electrician, a demographer, a forester, etc., except to productive ends.

Besides, this form of assistance was also dictated by other considerations. The importance of capital in development is less real than that of men.

Men, I repeat, are the important factor. The technical assistance of international organizations lends them. These men are placed under the orders of the national political government, which fact excludes all control of a colonial type, and they render considerable services. But their number is very small so far and they sometimes find it hard to pierce through the layers of bureaucracy in the country where they work.

The aid given by Soviet Russia to China is more technical than economic. This help plays an important part in the development of a country where everything is being started again from scratch, and where many heads were lost in the Revolution.

Another method consists in granting scholarships to universities or technical schools. Some countries are resorting to this procedure, though not without imperialist, cultural or commercial intentions.

General aid

The general problem of collective aid from the developed countries to the under-developed countries has often been proposed (President Truman's Point IV, etc.). The results have gone no further than good intentions and verbal declarations.

Efforts to link such aid to disarmament have hardly been more successful. By each giving up two aircraft of a specifi type, according to Mr. Follereau's demand, the two great nations, the U.S.S.R. and the United States, could have suppressed leprosy in the entire world. All that was needed was a joint consent, which would have left the balance of forces intact. But neither party was willing to give in to this demand, for fear of creating a dreadful precedent, perhaps. An unfortunate decision, for such a precedent might precisely have given the signal for a gradual transfer of military efforts to peaceful works, and a kind of involuntary political thaw.

Alternated threats

The little ones have always suffered for the follies of the big ones, the fable-writer tells us, without perhaps convincing us this time. If they are clever, they can on the contrary profit from them. Follies and passions are forces to be studied, and channelled in the right direction.

Faced with the rivalry of the two big powers and their respective satellites, the under-developed countries can choose between three attitudes:

To enter into the orbit of one big power and try to derive economic advantages from this. Such is the case of Turkey, for example, or of East Germany. It is not always a real option, of course, it can be an imposed solution.

To adopt an attitude of absolute neutrality and refuse all economic aid that is linked with political conditions. This more or less means refusing all aid. Such is the case of India or Argentine.

To practise alternation, threatening each camp in turn with desertion to the other, like a woman between two lovers. Although such an attitude may be dubious from a moral standpoint, it can certainly work, in certain circumstances and for a certain time.

A more useful attitude, however, much more useful, would be for the Bandung world not to demand help explicitly, but to condemn the policy of over-armament which dries up the source of help (see end of book).

Chapter 16

Choices and priorities

THE ONLY choices and priorities I am dealing with here are, naturally, those within the "economic" solution. The big choice between the "economic solution" and the "demographic solution" is left for the end of the book.

Let us suppose that in a certain country we have been able to assemble all production forces—whether interior or exterior—as a reserve of financial means, of human beings Like a skilful tactician, we wish to throw them into the battle at the best possible place, in order to obtain the best result. Policy is the art of choosing, even, let us say, the art of sacrificing.

And what a lot of sacrifices! In an under-developed country, there is, or seems to be, a lack of everything. Whoever is entrusted with the planning, that is to say with the distribution of means, is bound to be assailed with numerous perfectly legitimate claims. Here are the representatives of various departments or social classes, sitting round a table:

We must first feed the inhabitants and develop agriculture, one of them says.

Without industry, says another, we cannot achieve economic independence, or a certain standard of living and full employment.

We must look after the most crying needs, we must train doctors and nurses, says a third, have a little pity.

That's a short-term policy, says another. We must build big hotels to receive rich tourists, so as to improve our balance of accounts, which will enable us to import foreign machines and everything we are short of.

And one voice after another goes up in favour of education, science, laboratories, roads, postal services, drinking water, housing, historical monuments, forests, national prestige, motor energy, etc.

How can one choose and what are the criteria?

Before one can even begin to choose, one has to find a method, a doctrine, so that already we are faced with a choice on the method of choice itself.

Planning of the market

A nineteenth-century economist would hardly have been embarrassed by such a question. Although he would have recognized the necessity for some public effort as regards education or roads, which are public concerns *par excellence,* he would have assumed that the answer lay in that great sovereign, that divinity we call the MARKET. The mechanism of prices and profits, he would have said and demonstrated, will select the most investable activities, which are inevitably in accord with the general interest.

But even taking into account both the good deeds of individual enterprise and the serious weaknesses of a state apparatus, few economists today would support such a "liberal" thesis.

On what principle can we draw an absolute demarcation line? Intervention is a matter of degrees, in a socialist regime as much as in a capitalist regime. The debates on the subject multiply in Poland and Yugoslavia, in China, even in the u.s.s.r. The best solution cannot be obtained with a slide-rule, for it depends not only on natural conditions, the concentration of enterprises, etc., but also on what human beings desire and can endure. A communist organization in the Lebanon would be as disastrous as a laisser-faire policy in Mongolia.

One thing is certain: the under-developed countries must go a good deal further along the line of intervention than the European countries did in the nineteenth century, and often further than present-day developed countries. For one thing, they are new countries and time has marched on. The sense of individual initiative is considerably less developed than it is among Western people. And besides, most of the big decisions of economics are beyond the initiative of individuals.

Agriculture or industry

This question is even older, it takes us back three centuries. We have learnt very little in that interval, since we are still perorating on general principles where particular cases prevail.

Under Stalin, the Soviets created the dogma of heavy industry, generator of independence. It is quite a good prop, a provisionary guide for the first few years, a way of not thinking, a convenience, which, however, should not be abused.

If the world were in a state of absolute free trade, the question of the conflict between industry and agriculture would hardly arise, or would arise in a different way: in which zone can we produce the most goods (in international value, of course)? each country would ask itself. We shall then exchange the goods produced against those we need.

In a regime of total autarchy, with every nation at home only, the choice would be very different, but just as clear. What do we need most? would be the question. Let us produce it. Before making refrigerators, we ought to have something to put inside them.

In fact, however, the countries of the world are all in some intermediate situation, so that the two objectives have to be combined, which does not simplify the choice at all.

In a general way, in the world, the industrial working hour is worth more, and brings in more than the agricultural working hour; this difference, which is equally true inside a country as on the world market, and equally true in a socialist country as in a capitalist country, can easily be explained.

Industry is in the vanguard; it is a point-element, a tapering point; there are fewer people skilled enough for it. The very movement of men from agriculture to industry (the famous professional migration of Fisher, Colin Clark and Fourastié) demands in fact that the workers' income should be higher at the point of arrival than it was at the point of departure, otherwise they would not move in the first place. But this observation and this explanation, far from providing us with the solution, merely emphasize the difficulty.

There are differences of degree, in any case, in industry

itself: the textile industry everywhere preceded the large scale metal works, both chronologically and technically. And wages reflect this difference faithfully.

But what is the use of saying that it would be more advantageous to produce electronic machines than corn, if the people are able (more or less) to produce corn but will not be able for a long time, to fathom the mysteries of electromagnetism?

The difficulties of industrialization can be seen in the futility of the many efforts made by certain developed countries with regard to a specific region. Britanny is still waiting for the industrialists to come and use her rich reserve of manual labour. Bad siting, you may say, and lack of protection. All right; let us take another example. Since the war, the Italian authorities have been trying to industrialize the *mezzogiorno*, that Southern region which has all the symptoms of under-development. Important concessions have been made to any industrialists setting up south of Rome. Their imposing list gave an impression that the whole of Milan and Turin were about to "descend" into those protected regions where manual labour is so cheap and so undemanding. Nor was the problem of raw materials very difficult, since iron works get their coal and their iron by sea, and would therefore be just as well placed in Sicily or Calabria as in Lombardy.

The results, however, have been disappointing, the shows of initiative rare and inspired by considerations other than pure calculations of enterprise (Olivetti). The fact is that *industry is a social environment*. "Woe to the solitary man," says Holy Scripture. The Turin industrialist lives in a coherent biosocial group, in which he finds suppliers, customers, sub-contractors, friends; we will not speak of cultural possibilities in the wide sense of the word, the vital necessity of which can be energetically insisted upon by his wife.

A block installation of numerous industries, more or less interdependent, or of combines, is of course possible, but it requires very powerful backing and forces those concerned to step out of the liberal framework.

It would, of course, be unpardonable for a country with

raw materials, energy and such an outlet at its disposal, not to establish this fertilizing short-circuit. Will a country possessing splendid cottonfields and needing woven cottons for ever send its raw material to Europe and buy the materials at high cost? This is to reduce labour opportunities for its own population without even being able to fall back (taking the process to its logical end) on sending its people to work in those countries which weave for the rest of the world. The mercantiles were wrong in only one thing: they thought too much about precious metals, and too little about people.

I have no doubt said enough to show that an *a priori* choice between agriculture and industry is rather futile, and that the most profitable activities are those calling for particular aptitudes. It is only too evident that an effort must be made in *all* countries not to remain in the agricultural or mining rut. It is also clear enough that an initial protection is needed by new industries; but the danger of the protection-rut is no less alarming. A good government must always react against the easy course; if it cannot afford to do so, it must resign itself to letting individual initiative move forward in a visibly progressivist direction, even at the risk of seeing the rise of industrialization at a high cost, and without large profits. But over all these considerations there hovers the larger problem of training men. Before approaching this, I shall first take a look at the social problems raised by industrialization.

Break-up of civilizations

The quarrel between agriculture and industry should not be considered from an economic angle only. Agricultural life is traditionally bound up with an aggregate of customs and rites that enclose the individual and preserve him from many excesses. The man who goes off to the town, attracted by a higher wage, or publicity, or some other need, suddenly finds that he is free of many social fetters, without at the same time being very clever at profiting from this freedom. This is a classic phenomenon, most vividly described by the term "detribalization."

Urbanization in nineteenth-century Europe was far from

producing very good results: alcoholism, prostitution, various social scourges etc. And yet the change was very much less sudden than that which may occur today in many regions of the globe. It is therefore a question of knowing whether it is wise to unleash individuals into an individualist environment and whether perhaps a transitional social environment ought to be created for them. The communists are evidently thinking about this problem and resolving it through their apparatus. Without wholly identifying communism with religion I would say that it does replace religion in numerous instances. Among the countries with private property, it is in the Belgian Congo that the dangers of detribalization are being fought most intelligently.[1]

People are more valuable than capital

A century and a half of capitalism, dominated by the profit-motive (as opposed to the profit-statement, which is only the instrument) has given rise to the idea that the key to progress is the formation of capital, even of plant and implementation. It is easy enough to reach such a conclusion: when a person wishes to create an enterprise (even if that person is the State), what is his essential concern? To have the capital, the necessary financial means. Once these are assembled, he will always be able to find the personnel on the "labour market," by paying the usual rates for it, or even by paying more, if labour is scarce.

For a nation, the problem is very different.

First of all, the financial capital proper can be created in many parts, through a more or less complex system of credit. But the financial capital is nothing, of itself. An issue of paper, both in a fully employed society and in an ignorant and professionally ill-qualified society, is inflationistic and noxious. But the personnel, or essential production factor, is not un-

---

[1] On this question, and, more generally, on the social problems arising out of development, see *Le Tiers-Monde–Sous-développement et développement*. Cahier No. 27 de l'Institut National d'Etudes Démographiques, a work brought out under the direction of G. Balandier.

limited, and could not be created in this way. The apparent over-population in under-developed countries may seem like a superabundance of people, but I am concerned, naturally in this context, only with qualified personnel. If men are unemployed, it is because they do not know how to labour usefully, how to tame nature, how to work its products marketably.

I shall therefore leave the financial capital aside; and rather consider the respective merits of the real capital, that is, the implementation, in its more general sense, and the qualified personnel.

Here again an illusory perspective tends to give preference to capital. What does a country, a government, need? Money, obviously. A misleading delusion, for a nation. All the experience and all that has happened since the great world slump have shown that men's aptitude is more important than the material.

Every time a country is destroyed by war, whatever its regime may be (Spain, Germany, U.S.S.R., etc.), we are always surprised by the rapidity of the reconstruction. In spite of the loss, not of financial capital but of material capital such as productive machines, nevertheless production rises at record speeds. Until when? Not indefinitely, but until the pre-war level is reached. Once this has been regained, production rises only slowly, re-assuming its secular rhythm. The reason is that this production corresponds to the technical capacity of the people, it represents what they can do.

If you kick an ant-heap, there is a huge destruction. All the ants get tremendously busy around the great disaster. When you return some time later, you find the ant-heap in its previous state, neither better nor worse. That state corresponds to the technical capacity of the ants.

If trained and qualified men settle in a virgin island which is sufficiently rich in natural resources, after ten years that island will be covered with factories, theatres, hospitals, villas, etc. If necessary these men will have borrowed machines and redeemed them in a few years. Have we not examples? Australia, the U.S.S.R.?

If, on the contrary, you give the most perfected electronic machines to an illiterate people and return after a few years you will see the machines all rusted and the people as wretched and ignorant as before. Capital is not useless, but, contrary to general opinion, it is secondary.

It may seem paradoxical that an over-populated country should be short of men. If we Westerners are shocked by such a proposition, this is due to our deplorable habit of counting people as one would count drops of water. The statistics of world unemployment that were widely diffused during the great slump and since ("unemployment has increased," "10 per cent of the workers are unemployed," etc.) somehow strengthened this dreadful illusion. The result was that a surplus of people was assumed to be a durable surplus, the original source of it being a dislocation in the social apparatus, which had simply become a visible manifestation of some structural fault. And the United States thought themselves over-populated! This perspective suggested some purely malthusian remedies: the reduction of working hours, the bringing forward of the retiring age, the driving back of women to the home, etc., which now encumber our legislation.

If the aim is purely social, arising from a positive desire to work for a shorter time, there can be no objection. It is very natural that part of technical progress should be devoted to the extension of leisure. But these methods are more often suggested for economic reasons: to ensure work for everyone, as if work were limited, as if the number of jobs could be determined like the square miles of a territory.

In a modern society, people are much more complementary than they are competitive, they are not simply juxtaposed, they do not just add up, they form an aggregate of several dimensions.

A qualified worker is complemented by several labourers. Together they make a relatively harmonious whole which is resolutely productive. Take away the manual labourers and the qualified or skilled worker can no longer work to his full capacity, his efficiency will be considerably reduced, but he will continue to work. Take away the qualified worker, and you have five unemployed labourers.

The facts observed over the last twenty-five years invalidate all the arguments and forecasts of those who calculate on global population figures and, either out of sensitivity or out of superficiality, take only the visible into account. Unemployment is always visible, but the shortage of personnel is sometimes completely out of sight, so that its precise extent is never seen by the naked eye, however penetrating.

Two eloquent and little known episodes may be cited on this subject:

Devastated Germany

In 1938, Hitler filled the world with his cries about the lack of living space in Germany. More than one Frenchman or Englishman (without having much sympathy for the Nazi regime) came to regret that the treaty of Versailles had taken Germany's colonies from her. "With the Cameroons and Togoland," they said, "Germany would have an outlet and would not seek to conquer other territory."

In 1945, without any regard for such aspirations, the Slavs on the contrary pushed back ten million Germans into a much smaller territory. These ten million people, of which five million were of active age, arrived almost naked, with hardly a few clothes in a suitcase; no capital; their factories, houses and even furniture were left behind. Western opinion forecast vast unemployment in Germany: more people, fewer possessions and less capital, these are the future unemployed. On top of all that, they added, the armament factories have been suppressed. Besides the five million refugees there will be four million unemployed from pre-Hitlerian times, that is, a total of nine million people without work. These words were mere sophistries.

In 1958, this is the situation of Western Germany.

The five million refugees have been integrated; there is no unemployment and the Ruhr has even thought of resorting to Italian immigration. The national income per inhabitant has been recovered and overtaken.

Why this success, contrary to the forecasts of all the doctrines, malthusian, abundantist, capitalist or marxist, contrary even to "common sense" as conceived by the most widespread opinion?

Because these men without capital came with their knowledge, their qualifications. They worked and they recreated the capital that was lacking, because they included a sufficient number of engineers, mechanics, chemists, doctors, sociologists, etc. If five million manual workers had entered Western Germany instead there would be five million unemployed today.

France 1938–9: the unknown recovery

In November 1938, after Munich, the Daladier-Reynaud government sensed the importance of an economic revival of production. In a peace-economy, it was the only way to contain, without too much difficulty, the industrial costs of war. These amounted to about 7 per cent of national production, and it was possible, for the well-being of the French, to double them without touching consumption on condition that national production was also increased by 7 per cent. And if national production increased by 14 per cent it was possible —arithmetically—to triple arms production without impoverishing the French.

Such was the aim; but to apply it was more difficult. Orders went out for the lengthening of working hours beyond forty a week, wherever the need was felt. A storm of protests. Is it possible to be so ignorant of present conditions? said everyone from right to left. As long as there is unemployment, longer working hours will only increase the number of unemployed! Public opinion was unanimous and almost the whole of the government forecast stagnation or a lowering of production. A few months later, in spite of very unfavourable political conditions, industrial production had risen by 20 per cent; the recovery was general and more important still: unemployment had gone down. The proportion of partial unemployed (those working under forty hours a week) had dropped from 20 to 9 per cent.

What happened? By allowing those enterprises which were short of personnel (usually qualified personnel) to work more, these measures created an outlet, that is to say, work for others. Working longer, metal workers bought more textiles, etc. The famous multiplier played its role, but only because the local bottle-necks of manual labour were initially widened.

The French have long been ignorant of this recovery, or else forgotten it.

Application to under-developed countries

Official dogma, careless of experience, valiantly ignored this startling failure of theory, just as it later ignored the example of Germany. But the under-developed countries are not obliged to follow the errors of capitalist countries. If these are incapable of understanding their own system, which has perhaps become too subtle, they should not be astonished if others show a marked preference for a planned economy, an apparently simpler system, easier to grasp in principle. In any case, the priority is quite obvious: qualified men must be formed, in sufficient proportion, and the machine as a whole will get going.

The function sometimes creates the organ, but it takes its time. Help the movement on, create the organ and the function will be fulfilled.

Two objections

There are two kinds of objections to these observations on the necessity of training men:

(*a*) All countries complain of lack of capital; the International Bank for reconstruction is assailed with demands for dollars, far more than U.N.E.S.C.O. or Technical Assistance are assailed for skill.

(*b*) Why speak of priority? Is it not necessary to train men and to build up the implementation at one and the same time, in balanced proportions?

I shall look at these two points:

Capital, money, finance

The "shortage of money" is as general in a capitalist regime as is the lack of means of production in a socialist regime. The finances of all countries are precarious, and expenditure must always be energetically compressed. And besides, those who try to escape from the "shortage of money" by creating it, that is to say, by appealing, more or less deviously, to the bank of issue, very quickly find themselves in a "foreign exchange crisis." This is why international capital and the International Bank are assailed by demands from countries needing dollars.

But these financial appearances mask the real difficulties. What is really lacking are consumer goods, and since an individual or even the State can only get them in exchange for money, penury manifests itself in monetary material.

The statesman will say that in order to build dams, he needs capital. But if we look beyond the appearances: as soon as a government establishes a firm control of foreign exchange, in order to increase the inside demand without letting that demand overflow outside, it has to face "bottlenecks" that slow down production, but do not prevent oversupply elsewhere.

There is, in every country, a limit to the absorption of capital; if some generous Maecenas were to grant credit to any given country, it would be used, certainly, but in a sterile way, towards consumer ends.

Capital can certainly help Egypt to build Assuan. It can enable the country to buy the necessary machines and, if need be, the food or consumer goods for the workers it will have to pay. But the country could also buy fewer American cars and more bulldozers. It could restrict luxury consumption a little. Finally it could buy the machines on credit and pay for them with the gains from the operation.

But if it has not got the necessary qualified personnel, the machines will be badly used, the operation will no longer be profitable. The Bank knows this in advance and refuses credit. It is the men that are lacking in fact, the capital that is lacking in appearance.

The movement is a disequilibrium

It would of course be unreasonable to look after the training of personnel alone and to neglect everything else. To return to the dam in question, men are needed, and material.

But, as I have said, material is more easily borrowed than men. There are two other reasons for a priority in favour of training men.

(a) The movement is a perpetual disequilibrium. Even in a planned economy, the harmony is never complete; the planning office spends its time whipping up the sectors that are behindhand. It is a perpetual disequilibrium that creates the movement.

Now, very little time is needed to create a material that is lacking, but a great deal to train personnel. And if a mistake has been made in the production of the material, it can be rectified, even, if necessary, by destroying the useless machine and passing it through profit and loss. A man, once trained, cannot be destroyed; he is ready, for forty years, to practice the activity he knows, whether it is useful or not.

(b) Governments always have a tendency to demand and to seek money; its fluidity allows every weakness, every easy way out. This natural deformation should be firmly reacted against, in advance, by pushing the training of men a little beyond what seems to be the most balanced position.

Moreover, in the under-developed countries, the general tendency is in favour of legal or theoretical studies, to the detriment of practical and concrete instruction. This has been observed almost everywhere. Such methods give the illusion of cultural development, and create, instead of economic development, an almost permanent political agitation arising from the existence of intellectuals without employment.

Choice of economic investments[1]

Having established this priority in favour of training qualified personnel, let us now look at the choice of the most

[1] Here is the distribution of economic investments proper in

"profitable" investments. The organization, private or public, which is considering an investment, calculates the amount of capital that has to be raised, and computes the annual benefit expected to result from it. So far, no objection.

But if the organization that is distributing the credits (direction of budget, national bank, government, etc., it hardly matters), wishes to classify the investments in order of profitability, and to retain only the most "profitable," it runs the risk of making serious mistakes. What counts is the rate of national interest, not the rate of capitalist interest. A mechanization of agriculture which brings in more money by dismissing workers who will not be able to find work elsewhere, may produce a high rate of capitalist interest. An owner will rightly resort to it; but a nation must beware of encouraging such an investment. I shall call it *recessive,* because it pushes out manual labour. The national income cannot be increased by it, it may even be diminished. Conversely, an irrigation which yields new land for cultivation may be very unadvantageous in capitalist accountancy, but very profitable for the nation; being *processive,* in a country where there is unemployment, it benefits from a very high "multiplier."

But can one proceed to classify investments according to these criteria? Yes, if one had a perfect economic system at one's disposal, with fixed rates of exchange between currencies. In actual fact, the answer is negative; judgment can only be approximate.

---

developed countries, according to Professor Lewis (*Theory of Economic Growth,* p. 210)

	%
Housing	25
Public works and services	35
Industry and agriculture	30
Other economic activities	10
Total	100

In the under-developed countries, the share of public works and services is much lower (13 per cent in the Lebanon, 8 to 9 per cent in Egypt, 5 per cent in Irak).

I must add that, in such a case, electoral and political pressure (if it comes from below) is often exercised in the general interest. Without ever being completely identical, the social and the economic forces here join together more or less for part of the way. Which is another reason for marching resolutely in that direction.

Chapter 17

Results

MANY WORKS have been written on the chances of the "economic solution." Opinions differ very widely, as do the kinds of advice given. But couldn't experience come into the picture? Ten years have elapsed since the problem was first posed, since President Truman's famous Point IV. Would it not be possible to judge and compare the progress made in this decade, especially with regard to the increases in both population and the production of subsistence-means?

Difficulties of observation

There are, in fact, serious difficulties in the experimental method:

(*a*) The ten-year period is in practice brought down to 7 or 8, sometimes less, by the lateness of statistics and basic documents. The assembling of evidence in international organizations inevitably means long delay.

(*b*) Although the increase in population is measured, in most countries, with sufficient and even foreseeable precision, this is not at all the case for the measurement of subsistence production; here documentation is insufficient and of doubtful reliability.

(*c*) Since this production is largely agricultural, meteorological conditions produce graphs that go up and down so jaggedly that it is difficult to perceive general tendencies.

(*d*) The increase in agricultural production, which is the most generally observed, is not absolutely reliable as evidence. On the one hand, it may be more apparent than real, resulting, classically, from the mere improvement in the statistical apparatus, the findings of which become more complete every year. On the other hand, the years following the war were marked by a simple progress of recuperation, after

175

destructions and disorganization that had upset the whole planet. It would be imprudent, in such cases, to rely on a continuation of such increases, or at the same rhythm.

But a converse argument can be put forward: newly created States often find it difficult to get organized. A purely political phase precedes the effort of economic expansion. In such a case, the observed increases ought on the contrary to accelerate in the future.

It can be seen how delicate observation must be. It is not enough to sit at the window and watch the landscape. A complete exploration is needed; and even so it can only be summarily made as yet, so that the perspectives presented must still be rather general.

Overall perspective by regions

The Food and Agriculture Organization (F.A.O.) in Rome publishes yearly figures of the world's agricultural production. Here is a table giving food production by regions. The figures are worked out on a base of 100 for pre-war:

	Pre-war	Average 1948–9 to 1952–3	1953–4	1954–5	1955–6
Western Europe	100	107	123	124	125
North America	100	141	152	150	158
Latin America	100	125	135	141	142
Oceania	100	112	121	121	127
Far East (without China)	100	104	115	116	119
Near East	100	120	144	141	139
Africa	100	125	141	143	140
All above regions	100	118	132	132	135
Whole World	100	110	122	123	126

It is hardly necessary to add that these figures only represent broad categories of measurement. The greatest increase affects Anglo-Saxon North America, that is, precisely the richest region, whereas the weakest increase is that of the Far-East, which is the poorest region. *The wide gap is already visible between famished regions and regions of superabundance.*

But the production per inhabitant is even more interesting. The table overleaf shows it for the same regions, still on a basis of 100 for pre-war.

Below we see three regions that are less well nourished than before the war: Latin America, Oceania (in spite of the favourable influence of Australia and New Zealand), and the Far East. The most progressing regions, Europe and North America, were already the best fed before.

	Pre-war	Average 1948–9 to 1952–3	1953–4	1954–5	1955–6	1956–7	1957–8
Western Europe	100	97	109	109	109	109	112
North America	100	108	120	117	116	121	116
Latin America	100	93	93	95	95	99	99
Oceania	100	93	93	91	93	94	82
Far East (without China)	100	87	91	91	94	95	93
Near East	100	99	113	109	105	112	111
Africa	100	103	110	110	104	106	111
All above regions	100	99	105	104	102	103	101

We may compare the most recent trend, that is to say, since the period 1948–9 to 1952–3, the middle of which is 1950–1. In five years, from 1950–1 to 1955–6, an improvement of 6 per cent—almost negligible—has been observed in the assembly of regions and also in the Far East.

Perspective by countries

Now we can take a more localized view, bearing in mind that the figures are more fragile without the moderating effect of averages. Here are the indices of food production in a few under-developed countries, still worked out on a basis of 100 for pre-war:

	1952–3	1953–4	1954–5	1955–6
Brazil	127	132	138	147
Chili	127	136	136	141
Colombia	170	168	172	179

	1952–3	1953–4	1954–5	1955–6
Mexico	153	159	176	166
Peru	143	150	159	165
Burmah	89	87	87	87
Ceylon	138	143	154	162
India	109	120	120	120
Indonesia	99	107	114	109
Japan	120	107	117	137
Malaysia	104	103	108	108
Pakistan	112	116	118	114
Philippines	142	146	148	150
Thailand	142	163	133	158

In a general way, the countries whose production has most increased are those which are not suffering from over-population (South America, Thailand, Ceylon). This fact is not at all surprising, since there is more free space; but we should beware of turning it into a general and automatic law.

We must, in any case, pay more attention to the production per inhabitant. Here it is, still worked out on a basis of 100 for pre-war:

	1952–3	1953–4	1954–5	1955–6
Brazil	90	92	93	97
Chili	97	102	99	100
Colombia	122	117	119	120
Mexico	105	105	113	104
Peru	108	107	114	115
Thailand	106	120	96	112
Philippines	106	120	96	112
Ceylon	99	100	105	108
Japan	98	94	93	89
India	90	98	97	95
Indonesia	85	91	95	90
Pakistan	91	92	93	89
Malaysia	79	76	78	76
Burmah	74	71	71	70

Even with these hazardous figures, we can see that the situation is far from being brilliant in a large part of Southern Asia: from Pakistan to Indonesia. But through these dry indices we can guess at millions of tragedies in hunger and suffering.

I shall now outline the situation of several individual countries.

Turkey

The statistics we have about Turkey are summary, but enable us to follow the general development. It might be unwise to rely on the absolute precision of these figures, but the general schema is interesting to follow.

The national income (at constant prices, naturally) has increased faster than the population; but since agriculture represents about half that income, the line is not surprisingly rather jagged, so that observation is difficult. Taking the average for 1948–50 and the average for 1953–5, we find an increase of 25 per cent, which is very interesting (more

	Population in thousands	National Income in millions of pounds (at constant prices of 1948)	Income per capita in pounds
1938	17,016	7,524	442
1948	20,049	8,851	441
1949	20,487	7,781	379
1950	20,947	9,147	437
1951	21,545	10,644	494
1952	22,160	11,566	522
1953	22,791	12,822	563
1954	23,441	11,402	494
1955	24,121	12,530	519

than 5 per cent per annum), but it is made bigger by the exceptional drought of 1949; if we discount the latter, the increase is of 12 per cent in five years, itself remarkable enough.

Going back to 1938, we again find an increase of 12 per cent, but in sixteen years, this time. The progress since 1949 may therefore be simply the result of the slow-down during the war and may not continue.

We can see how delicate the interpretation must be. For a closer judgment we would have to know the amount of investments (in proportion to the national income) and the amount of American aid; even if the latter is counter-balanced, pound for pound, by military expenditure inside the country, it nevertheless has a favourable effect, because it improves the balance of accounts and allows for the buying of equipment.

In any case, we have here an example of a country which is not over-populated and which, with the help of considerable foreign aid, has managed slightly to raise the national income per person. The growth in population (about 3 per cent) is rapid and birth-control is hardly in question.

Mexico

The situation in Mexico is better; in spite of a very rapid demographic growth (about 3 per cent per annum), the standard of living rises year by year, slowly, it is true. This is because the little exploited natural wealth is still important and because the increased density favours economic progress. The realization of investments represents 12 to 15 per cent of the national income every year; the income itself rises by about 4 per cent per annum, which leaves a slight bonus for the improvement of the standard of living. The "rate of national interest" from the investments must be between 25 per cent and 30 per cent per annum. These are rough figures which have to be confirmed; at least ten years of fairly regular advance are needed before one can evaluate the general trend.

Brazil

According to the calculations of the F.A.O., agricultural production per inhabitant has hardly changed since the war, as we have seen, and there is even a slight decrease. The data concerning the general national income strike a more optimistic note.[1] Here is the national income in steady prices, on a basis of 100 in 1939:

1939	100
1946–8	138
1949–51	162
1952–3	189
1954	201

[1] *Analyses and projections of economic development. II. The Economic development of Brazil.* Studies by a work group uniting the National Bank for economic development in Brazil and the Economic Commission for Latin America, New York, 1956.

The available quantities per inhabitant seem to have increased by 49 per cent in fifteen years, a remarkable leap which contradicts the pessimistic note of the tables given above. The divergence is chiefly due to the important advances in industry.

Nevertheless, the net investments represent only 10 per cent of the national income. Since this income has increased by about 6 per cent during the last few years, we would have to assume a rate of national interest of 60 per cent, which is really very high indeed. In fact the investments must be higher than is indicated, due no doubt to faults of accountancy.

The calculations have been made ahead to 1962. They forecast net investments maintained at about 10 per cent of the national income and an increase of 34 per cent for the latter in eight years, that is, of just under 4 per cent per annum. The expected rate of national interest is therefore a little under 40 per cent.

This rate is still high enough, though not impossible in a country far from saturation, possessing important natural resources.

There is for the moment no question of birth-control on a national scale in Brazil, any more than in Turkey or Mexico. But the growth in population does cause many difficulties, particularly in education, because it adds its own effects to those of intense scholarization.

India in difficulties

Although its population is increasing less rapidly than that of Turkey or Mexico, India is finding it immensely difficult to emerge from its thousand-year-old poverty.

The lowest ebb certainly seems to have been reached immediately after the war. In 1951, 1,620 calories and 42 grammes of proteins were still reckoned as the average daily ration. The first five-year plan 1951–6 included the irrigation of nearly 17½ million acres; moreover, there was a slight general improvement. Food consumption seems to have gone up to 1,900 calories and 50 grammes of proteins. But the second five-year plan 1956–61 is facing difficulties.

The rise in food prices (from 313 to 408 during the 1955–6 experiment) somewhat contradicts the optimism of agricultural statistics. It may of course be due to monetary circumstances. On the whole, little has been achieved. The country remains at the mercy of unfavourable atmospheric conditions.

General outlook

The situation has not become any worse since the alarum cries of ten years ago; in general, there is even a slight improvement per head. In countries that are little populated, especially in South America, the increase is marked; but the difficulties of population increase supervene, particularly as regards education.

In countries that are already very populated, such as India or Egypt, the improvements are so slow and so delicate that one can hardly speak of a victory over nature, nor even of getting off to a good start. In spite of important efforts, poverty and hunger continue, and moreover threaten the future. The most incontestable evidence is in fact, that the "demographic solution" is more and more frequently resorted to, as we shall see in chapters 21 and 22, in countries which previously vetoed any idea of birth-control. This is the solution to which we will now turn our attention.

PART 3
THE DEMOGRAPHIC SOLUTION;
PREVENTION OF BIRTHS

Chapter 18

General considerations on the prevention of births

THIS IS THE point we have reached:

I am assuming that, in a given country, or region, the population is increasing rapidly enough to raise economic difficulties. The problem of means of subsistence has not been solved, because the inhabitants cannot (or will not) accept the necessary initial sacrifices to meet this increase, and because they are not being sufficiently helped from outside. Therefore production is not stepped up quickly enough, it may even be increasing more slowly than the population, which causes a drop in the standard of living; in brief, I am assuming the failure or the insufficient success of the economic solution.

At such a moment (and perhaps before), voices are raised in that society (or outside it), wishing for, suggesting or advising a slow-down in the growth of population, which means, as we have seen, a reduction in the number of births.

This proposition may also be formulated in other circumstances:

Economic progress (and I mean increase in production) is higher than the demographic growth; the standard of living goes up. But this solution is burdensome, its future is not assured, so that the two following questions arise:

(1) For how long will the demographic growth continue at its present rhythm? At what moment will the rhythm of that geometrical progression be broken, which we know must slow down one day?

(2) In what circumstances will people *spontaneously* resort to the prevention of births, that is, to anti-natal practices?

Even without demographic preoccupations, advanced

groups, feminists particularly, may also arise and demand the propagation of contraceptive methods, for simple reasons of liberty. But such behaviour is only likely in an already fairly developed country.

The questions asked

Finally, whatever the state of economic development, the question of forecasting the number of births may be put forward, if only for the sake of being able to make some kind of judgment about the future. The most liberal person, the most convinced opponent of state intervention, should surely have enough curiosity to wish to know what is going to happen in this or that country, even if it is only to be in a better position to defend his liberal convictions. But some very different questions may also be asked, in the following order:

Can a *spontaneous* lowering of the birth rate be expected? With how much *delay*?

Should one *wish* or hope for it?

Should the government *authorize* methods of preventing births?

Should the prevention of births be *encouraged*? By what means?

No disagreement in principle

I must here emphasize an important point:

Because feeling is often stronger than reason where demography is concerned, many people would like to classify writers as "malthusian" or "anti-malthusian," rather as if they were dividing the good from the bad. Both trends exist of course, and a person's thoughts may come to be dominated by the one or the other. All the same it is not possible to maintain the same attitude, or advocate the same political solution in all countries. The variety of situations demands not only changes of general doctrine, but changes of attitude.

In an ageing population, where couples have only one child and the society is advancing to its own doom, the policy must be to encourage births. This is spiritually satisfying too, since the interest of the moment is being closely bound up with the life forces.

The case of a society suffering from exuberance is more delicate. However unpleasant struggling against life may be, the maintenance and perpetuation of natural fertility is nevertheless undesirable. In its ulterior motives, the malthusian spirit is not always beyond reproach. Mr. X may be sorry for others, but he may also be afraid of having to share with them.

I am here leaving aside all religious or moral ideas, in the strict sense of the words, not out of scorn but on the contrary because of their elevated nature, which is inaccessible to science. And in the end we are obliged to accept the hypothesis of a country which, rightly or wrongly, finds the economic solution unsatisfactory and therefore deems it necessary to resort to the demographic solution.

The arguments that follow are made in the spirit of discovery: to take the mechanism of conception to pieces in order to know it well. Once it is well understood, it is easier to make it function in the desired direction, whether for the increase or the decrease of births.

The reader's opinion on what is or is not desirable may of course remain unchanged. The important thing is to avoid misunderstandings and contradictions, being careful for instance not to imitate the author who after evoking the wretchedness of peasants in India or Brazil then wishes to reject the system of family allowances in France or Belgium.

A clear-cut, single attitude is of course more convenient, more sympathetic, even, more high-minded. But it is also too easy, and not very practical.

No physiological reduction

Dr. J. de Castro, who has written so eloquently on the geography of hunger and fought so courageously for the poor and under-nourished countries, has estimated that a lowering of the birth rate may in fact result directly and spontaneously from economic improvement, through a purely physiological mechanism.

Hunger, he said, over-excites sexual appetites, and the lack of animal proteins increases fertility. Let people be better fed, with adequate rations of meat, and physiological fertility will decrease.

Experience does not confirm this opinion; there is no evidence at present to suggest that well fed populations are physiologically less prolific than others. The French Canadians, for example, who did not resort to birth-prevention for the whole of the nineteenth century, had an extremely high birth rate, in fact the highest ever observed. They also had a fairly high consumption of meat, and therefore of proteins. Then there is the curious society of Hutterites in the United States to-day. They are well-fed, but do not wish to resort to birth-prevention. Their fertility is as high as that of poor countries. The same applies to French, Italian families, etc., who, for religious or other reasons, do not wish to limit the number of children they have.

It is true that well-fed societies (Western societies, for example) have fewer children, in general, than poor and under-nourished societies. But the reasons for this correlation are social. It is in the most developed societies that contraceptive practices are resorted to.

Therefore, apart from surgical sterilization (see p. 227 for the case of Japan) and the eventual discovery of the pill (see chapter 24), there can be no question of relying on physiological sterility. It is the prevention of births we have to discuss, that is, a voluntary limitation in the number of children.

A little terminology

Terminology plays an important role in such delicate questions. When accurate and well-defined terms are used, it is always possible either to reach an understanding, or to diverge usefully to the point where, if experiment is not convincing, the mind can extend the facts as it wills.

But when ambiguous terms are used, agreement becomes impossible, and instead we have only a vast and sterile confusion, inevitably dominated by passions and prejudices.

Few expressions have caused more misunderstanding than birth control. For one thing it can include the various methods enumerated above, especially the last two. The literal translation of birth control as *controle de naissances* is not only a contradiction in terms in French (to control births, in correct French, is to register them, to observe them, in other words, it is the job of the Civic authorities), but even in English the expression is full of ambiguity. Used properly, it ought to mean all anti-natal practices, including provoked abortion, but in fact it is more often used to mean contraceptive practices.

The expression birth control in fact implies sometimes the contraceptive practices themselves, sometimes the attitude or tolerance of the public authorities towards these practices.

It is because of this deplorable expression that the question has remained so static, and has become flooded by more passion than light. It must therefore be banned absolutely and I shall not be using it in the arguments that follow.

The expression "limitation of births" could, if pressed, include the general social aspect, but it is not quite right from the point of view of the family, which may try to space out its births (two years, three years, etc.) without in fact having any idea of limitation. Of course the final result may be a reduction in the number of children they could have had, but that was not necessarily the intention. Similarly a person or a group may declare in favour of contraception without necessarily wishing the number of births to be reduced.

The correct expression seems to be "the prevention of births." It really is a preventive measure. The term has been criticized because of its connotation of disasters and scourges (prevention of accidents, illnesses, etc.). But surely the desire to prevent or delay a birth means that the birth is considered as unfavourable, at any rate if it occurred at that date.

The expression "prevention of births" may itself be insufficient and must be complemented by some sort of indication with regard to the other aspects of the question mentioned above.

The expression "family planning" has also been used, in

imitation of the Anglo-Saxon world. This goes further than simple prevention, but apart from being clumsy, it is also inexact. The objection to it is the same as that which will be made later against the expression "voluntary maternity."

Prevention of Births: Enumeration of Methods

In any society, the number of births depends on the amount of celibacy and the age at marriage, as was shown in Fig. 4. If marriage is the fundamental institution, the births are more or less proportionate to the number of marriages. The age at marriage also plays an important part in countries where there is still natural fertility.

Thus it was that in the eighteenth century, the contraction of marriages later than immediately after puberty could bring down the possible number of children per family from 10.2 to 6.5 (Fig. 4, see p. 66).

Celibacy and the age at marriage may vary spontaneously or under the influence of legislation.

And then there is the fertility of couples:

Every couple in cohabitation is subject to the laws of fertility. The methods known at present to evade those laws are:

Total continence, the method advocated by Malthus. But from our point of view, it is more precisely a question of abstention from natural coitus, and not necessarily from all sexual intercourse.

Periodical continence, based on the woman's periods of fertility.

Contraceptive methods, which prevent conception.

We may distinguish the natural methods, whereby no product is used (simple ablution, *coitus interruptus*) and the active methods, among which the most important is the occlusive diaphragm invented by F. A. Wilde in 1838.

Abortive methods, which mean the stopping of pregnancy.

Provisionary or permanent *sterilization* of one party.

These methods taken all together could further be described as voluntary sterility or, more exactly, "voluntary infertility," if the term "sterility" includes the meaning of permanent sterility.

Physiological fertility

This question is little known, because in some aspects it demands a delicate statistical analysis which no clinical or laboratory research can provide.

A couple living together from puberty to the woman's menopause should have an average of 12 children (12 births, more precisely), if they do not resort to any anti-natal practice. The works of L. Henry and P. Vincent have thrown further light on this. In their different ways, they have both shown that the fecundity of a woman (or capacity to participate in reproduction) does not decline with age, as is so often believed.

For a fecund woman, the probability of conception during the menstrual cycle is about 10 per cent around 17, rises to 13 per cent from 21 to 23, then diminishes only very slowly to 10 per cent at 43. No observations have been made beyond that age.

But the proportion of fecund women decreases constantly, whereas the age of women increases. The combination of these two phenomena has led people to believe that the fecundity of woman decreases with age, but in fact it drops suddenly, on a given day, from 10 or 12 per cent to zero.

A false start: "voluntary maternity"

This expression is often used by people who favour the prevention of births (especially the repealing of measures that forbid it or slow it down, as well as official instruction on contraceptive methods); but it is a most inaccurate expression, which has led to numerous misunderstandings, even, sometimes, to the failure of the very aims pursued by the partisans of contraception.

In most cases, the will is not exercised as regards maternity, but as regards sterility, since the norm is over-exuberant fertility. Of course there are provisionally sterile families that have to make special efforts (medical care, etc.) in order to have children. But in a large majority of cases, children are born to a couple without any will being exercised, as they are born to animals. A couple may decide to prevent birth for a determined period. But they cannot decide to have a child during that period, only to give nature all its chances (a little over 10 per cent per cycle, as we have seen, for women who are still fecund).

A woman cannot decide to have two children after she is 26. All she can do is to have no child before she is 26, by making a perfect use of contraception.

All the preventive methods enumerated above demand a fairly strong effort of the will. In the following chapter I shall return to this point, which dominates the whole question.

In order to see how contraceptive methods may spread in any given country, with or without legal permission, it is useful to know how they spread in the past. Not that the problems remain identical of course, but some of the more profoundly human aspects may be profitably compared.

A strange absence of documents

The way in which human beings give life or refuse to give life is important. The psychologist, the economist, the sociologist, the "politicalist," the historian, the ethnographer, the geographer, etc., are all or may all be interested in this question.

One might therefore expect a huge bibliography on the subject. On the contrary, it is astonishingly meagre. Apart from a few works of feminist or malthusian propaganda, a few medical treatises (more often on abortion than on contraception), a few articles or chapters of works on demography or sociology, there is almost nothing.

On the historical side, there is only one work, which is in English: Himes' *History of Contraception*, which appeared in 1936, is out of print and very difficult to find, even in the United States. But this highly documented work, which talks so much of antiquity and backward tribes, has almost nothing on the development of contraception in France, which is astonishing, since France was the country where the limitation of children within the family first began, in modern times, a whole century ahead of others.

The discretion of writers, indeed, their complete silence, can be explained by the fact that the subject is an extremely intimate one. And yet many doctors, psychiatrists, etc., must have collected evidence on the subject; it disappeared with them, so much so that the National Institute of Demographic Studies found it extremely difficult to find any documentation for its schemes on the origin of contraception in France.

Even erotic literature, Philippe Ariès tells us,[1] and he is the most penetrating writer on the subject, is curiously silent about such practices.

It seems that this literature, once released from social bonds, immediately falls into new constraints (for they are constraints, as I shall never be tired of repeating). Having broken through the sacred gates of social convention, the erotic passes into forbidden domains, but is careful not to describe its fears and servitudes. Medical students' songs are not shy of words, yet they never allude to these practices.

In the end, it is Church documentation which has formed the chief source, however insufficient.

Because of these lacunae, many points remain obscure. For further enlightenment, we would have to plunge into private correspondence, Church archives—if they contain any information on difficulties encountered by confessors in the eighteenth century, etc., in short, we would have to work long and intensively to obtain very meagre information which would only become instructive if considerably less meagre. Such a disproportion may well *a priori* discourage all good will, if research gives such disappointing results so soon.

Pre-medical times

Two periods of history must be distinguished, the medical period, which begins in the eighteenth century, and the pre-medical period, with a high death rate.

Abortive practices can be discovered in most periods and most countries. They were often the result of potions, sometimes of direct intervention. Contraceptive practices, however, are very much rarer in pre-medical times, at any rate effective ones. They are found in certain refined societies (Greece, Rome) that are rapidly turning to decadence. Depopulation

[1] *Histoire des populations françaises et de leurs attitudes devant la vie, depuis le xviiie siècle.* Editions Self, 1948.

and the loss of vitality lead to the eventual disappearance of these societies, so that in fact, only the prolific societies survive, by natural selection.

In the middle ages, and at the beginning of modern times, provoked abortion occurred in a sporadic way, but frequently enough in the sixteenth century for Henri II to issue an edict obliging pregnant women to declare their pregnancy.

On the other hand contraceptive practices were rare. The Church condemns them now and again, which shows that they had not completely disappeared, but the very tone of these reproaches, and their lack of frequency, shows that the danger was not very great. They occurred chiefly among prostitutes and in debauched quarters. The birth rate remained very high, and was reduced only by celibacy or the death of partners.

Medical times

New trends appear in France in the eighteenth and even in the seventeenth century; in particular, the famous letters of Mme. de Sevigné are quoted. These practices spread from 1750, so much so that before the Revolution numerous writers were mentioning them (Cerfvol, Moheau, Restif de la Bretonne), without however approving of them, even when atheist or anti-clerical. Such machinations "cheat Nature," which is a criminal act in a society where religion in the real sense has been replaced by "natural religion."

Two questions, one social and the other technical, arise out of this development, which is peculiar to France and perhaps to a few neighbouring regions (Geneva).[2]

Why did married couples change their behaviour?

What did these practices consist of and how did they spread?

One thing is certain: The desire to limit the number of children began among the rich, that is, the nobility and the bourgeoisie. Logically one would expect the opposite: poor

[2] Louis Henry, *Anciennes familles genevoises. Etude démographique, xvi–xx siècles*. Cahier No. 26 of "Travaux et Documents," P.U.F., 1956.

families without the means to rear their children being obliged to stop having them. But logic is often violated in matters of contraception.

Rich families not only enjoyed a certain liberality of spirit with regard to morals and religion, and conditions of comfort lacking among the people, but their needs were also very widespread. A child rivalled other satisfactions; the desire for luxury and enjoyment was opposed to the desire for posterity. Moving in fairly dissolute circles, and in social freedom, women tried to complete that freedom.

The most plausible explanation is as follows: contraceptive practices, or at least some of them, came from circles of prostitution and debauchery where they had existed through the centuries; from there they passed into loose adulterous liaisons, by simple superficial contact, according to Chamfort, then into the conjugal home itself. The most used methods were ablution and withdrawal (*coitus interruptus*) possibly also the sheath.

In the nineteenth century, France's lead over other countries is emphasized. The first writer who seems to have approved and advocated these practices is Etienne de Sénancour,[3] not of course for demographic reasons, but for the sake of masculine politeness and gallantry. The birth rate went down more or less constantly in France, while it remained level in England until 1875, in spite of the propaganda of Place, Drysdale, etc., and in Germany until 1900. In England it was the famous trial of Annie Besant that brought contraception into general use. Denounced as an obscenity, it caused a scandal, which was precisely what was needed, the problem being ripe. The publicity of the trial had a decisive influence. The whole of civilized Western Europe and the Anglo-Saxon countries more or less follow that movement.

As in France, contraception began in rich and cultured families, spread only very slowly into the lower middle classes, then into the peasant and working-classes.

Then the movement spread to other less developed coun-

---

[3] *De l'amour considéré dans les lois réelles de l'union des sexes,* 1806, pp. 148–53.

tries: Central Europe, Anglo-Saxon countries, temperate South America, French Canada, etc.; the lower birth rate became the clearest test of what we called development today.

During the whole of the "demographic revolution," the birth rate in any one country was in inverse ratio to the economic and social level. A slightly different trend prevails in very developed countries: the lowest rates are found in the fairly cultured middle classes (clerks, officials). They have the needs of the rich and the means of the poor, and a greater fear of social downfall than others, so that families from these classes frequently stop at the first child. The situation can therefore be summed up as follows: at first, sterility was an appanage of the big bourgeois, rich, educated and irreligious; today it is particularly marked among lower grade civil servants, providing, of course, that they are not fervent catholics.

Methods used

Like all techniques, those aiming at the prevention or limitation of births have progressed; the primitive *coitus interruptus* may well remain much the same as in Onan's day, but ablution has benefited from the development of spermicide products, and occlusive gadgets have been much perfected. Finally the Ogino and Kraus discovery—as yet incomplete—of the ovular cycle has led to the technique of period continence.

A fairly rigid discipline of restraint is needed for all these practices—we shall return to this problem in the next chapter. That is why abortion spread even in the countries where contraceptive practices are authorized and even encouraged. Abortion is a painful solution, often arising from the failure of precautions and contraceptive practices.

Favourable factors

Why did the limitation of births begin in the superior social classes which had a high standard of living and some education? This difference of behaviour arose out of intellectual dispositions, and a spirit of foresight and prudence, but also for materialistic reasons. In peasant families, the child had long been considered as a kind of property that could bring income, for he worked from the earliest age. This habit of making children work naturally spread to the new industries, without really causing any scandal, except retrospectively. Compulsory education changed the family's economic balance-sheet without at once changing the attitude and behaviour that resulted from it.

But in non-manual environments, one factor rapidly grew in importance, and this was "social capillarity," to use a term of Arsène Dumont. The reduction in the number of children arose out of the parents' worry about their children's prospects of climbing up and their own fears of sliding down. Education became even more important than saving, in all clerical, white-collared families.

In these conditions, the reduction in the number of children has not been accompanied by a lessening of affection towards the child, as it was in the eighteenth century; one might even say that the family has been reduced to one or two from an excess of affection, concentrated on one or two.

Leisure, culture, comfort, foresight, education of children and social ambition, together with a weakening or changing religious or traditionalist spirit, these are the main factors that played their part in countries affected by the "demographic revolution."

Unemployment

This social phenomenon must be considered separately, and a clear distinction must be made between the acute unemployment of industrial countries and the chronic underemployment of agricultural countries.

Unemployment has a sterilizing effect as a whole. Logically it should be only the unemployed man, who deprived of resources, fears the arrival of children; but there is no evidence of this at all. During the acute crises, like that of 1929–35, the birth rate lowered throughout the whole population, not only among those threatened by unemployment (industrial workers), but among officials assured of employment.

Crisis unemployment in fact has a profound emotional effect on the population, especially if it lasts more than a

year. There is a general impression that people are supernumerary, that society cannot contain any more. Not only
are there fewer marriages, which is understandable in such a
pessimistic, anguished atmosphere, but even those couples
who feel stable and secure about the future start putting off
having children. It is difficult to describe just how this collective psychosis gets transferred into individual behaviour, but
the most suggestive phrase is that so often heard during the
slump: "Why bring future unemployed into the world?"

Agricultural under-employment does not have the same
effect. It may of course retard marriage in families above a
certain level, with the young people waiting to get established
and often waiting a long time, from lack of land. But in very
poor families, without any foresight, this kind of unemployment does not cause any prevention of births.

I shall be dealing later with a more particular factor:
medical and sanitary progress.

Resistance factors

These forces, driving towards new ways of life, were bound
to meet with resistance factors and types of inertia that have
retarded the movement, so much so that it has not reached
its completion in a single country.

These factors are tradition and habit on the one hand, and
the sexual instinct on the other. The religious spirit is not the
only cause. "Cheating nature" seems at first a sort of sacrilege
that is bound to bring bad luck. The birth of a child has for
so long been thought of as the very type of the happy event,
the gift from heaven, the "benefice," that it is difficult to
change, in a few years, a state of mind so deeply rooted in
the past, when fighting against life seemed a senseless act,
diabolical and linked with Evil.

Medical and sanitary factors

In general, the lowering of the birth rate and the lowering of
the death rate went together. We say "in general," and not
always, because the countries of Western Europe, apart from
France, did experience a lowering of the death rate before
the lowering of the birth rate. The law that relates the two

phenomena is incontestable, as we shall see, but the fact that a disconnection can take place is of capital importance. It constitutes, in fact, the cause and substance of this whole work.

The first effect of medical progress itself was to increase fertility, by reducing the cases of physiological sterility and venereal disease, and prolonging the life of couples. But at the same time it encouraged new attitudes towards the number of births accepted in the family. I say "number of births" and not "number of children," because the family which in the past gave birth to six children, in fact raised only five up to one year of age, and three up to marriageable age. The final result is about the same as that obtained today by the family giving birth to three children; therefore, the family which now still gives birth to six children, that is, which apparently has not changed its behaviour at all, in fact faces a far heavier task: more children to bring up and to a higher age. It was therefore "normal," if not inevitable, that the number should be reduced.

Another point: in earlier times, say before the Revolution, the responsibility of having children was, contrary to appearances, much smaller than today. Not only did children work young, so that they ceased to be a burden, but even the rearing of them was less trouble: breast-feeding and rudimentary care. The diffusion of even very rough principles of hygiene meant more time given to children, who thus became more "important," took more time, place and trouble, and therefore became less numerous.

On a more general level, the fight against death may have played an important part in the sense that it was already a first revolt against the divine will or destiny. Here we may cite the theory of Ariès.

It was not till the eighteenth century that society undertook a systematic struggle against death, and therefore against nature. The debates on inoculation against smallpox, among others, are characteristic. But by seeking for techniques to fight nature, man also made the techniques of fighting against life seem less absurd, and less sacrilegious.

In a general way, hygiene is easily opposed to nature. The

bidet appeared in France at the beginning of the eighteenth century. In its triumph, it became a symbol, the very testimony of comfort for hotels and tourist associations in France.

As for the sheath, which was first invented as a preventive against venereal diseases, it was condemned by the Church, because it opposed divine penitence and encouraged sin. Naturally it also became part of the struggle against undesired life.

The prophets proved wrong

The preceding summary, though simplified, shows numerous opposing forces and cross-currents in a sometimes disorientating complex. And in fact, many of them were simple failures of forecast. These failures had a strong influence on the prognostications, not only of public opinion, but also on that of the experts.

According to a very widespread view, the reduction of births would lead to the impoverishment of families. This thesis is closely related to that of pauperization, which confuses the relative and the absolute, and always finds much support in the most various social categories. The thesis hardly matters, only its usage, which can be recognized precisely by the forecasting. But does a general improvement in the standard of living cause a rise in the birth rate, as public opinion so often believes? If there is any evidence of such a correlation, it must be only of exceptions to the rule.

In 1936, wage-earners benefited for about a year from a notable rise in their purchasing power, which was then lost again by a rise in prices; but the birth rate showed no rise; it did rise, however, when family allowances, that is, differential wages, came into being.

And here is an expert's forecast, which is equally false:

During the first war, the birth rate collapsed among the belligerents and lowered in neutral countries. Would the same not occur during the second war 1939–45, since the same essential conditions obtained: separation of married couples and general insecurity?

On such apparently solid arguments, the demographers forecast a reduction of births among the belligerents and even among neutrals. But although the birth rate did go down in some countries (notably France), there was on the contrary a general rise in others. Moreover, the fertility of couples not separated by the war increased almost everywhere, and this phenomenon counterbalanced the reduction arising out of separations.

The chief explanation, produced retrospectively, is as follows: in 1913, in most countries, the birth rate had remained at levels which no longer corresponded to actual conditions of life or states of mind. In 1938, the situation was almost the reverse: the economic crisis of the preceding years had reduced the birth rate to below the level of balance. Wars always precipitate events, like a jerk at the rusted needle of a barometer.

1939 also marked the end of unemployment, a much more sterilizing factor than war.

Conclusion

Contraception is one of the most delicate subjects in existence; the very fact that it is not widely known in the scientific sense, has led to very prejudiced opinions, often expressed with a lightness that contrasts with the seriousness of the subject. But with careful observation of the past and present we may evolve a few rules or useful principles. I shall now show how the problem presents itself in under-developed countries, first examining the attitude of the couple, the family, and then the collective attitude of governments and public opinion.

Chapter 19

The attitude of the individual and of the couple to the prevention of births

IN THE HISTORICAL SURVEY of the preceding chapter, I described the conditions in which families resolved to reduce the number of their children, in certain countries and certain social classes. Rather than expound an *a priori* theory of contraception, I would like to report a few significant episodes, that occurred recently in the under-developed countries, and throw considerable light on the whole question.

The Egyptian guide

I hope the reader will forgive me for starting with a personal anecdote, but it is the best way of taking him to the very centre of the debate:

I was in Egypt in 1949, and was lucky enough to find an excellent guide. He was very correctly dressed, spoke good French, and knew a great deal about the monuments of Luxor and their history. He contrasted strongly with the innumerable ignorant and ragged cicerones who offered their services, and would send them packing without compunction.

One day (although he had no idea that I was a demographer), he suddenly told our group: "You see, I have two children and I am quite resolved not to have any more." On being pressed further, he added: "I was born in a peasant house no better than the one I showed you yesterday (a real hovel). I will also show you my present house, which is made of stone. It is not luxurious, but I can live in it, have light in it, and my books. How did I get to that point? A little luck perhaps and a great deal of work. I learnt ancient history, English, French, and I am now learning Italian. I intend to give my children a similar education, so that they will not fall back to my earlier level and my previous house. For this, I have calculated, I cannot have more than two."

And as we were listening to him with the greatest attention, he forestalled an imminent question by adding: "I am a good Moslem and visit the mosque every day to pray."

This man, both simple and civilized, was uttering one by one the very words on which a whole doctrine of contraception may be built, words that more or less give the key to economic development and the answer to over-population.

The sermon in the hovel

Here is another real-life anecdote:

A well-intentioned American was talking, in front of me, to an Indian teacher, and insisting on the lack of foresight among the masses, who are multiplying without a thought for the future. The Indian replied in this strain: "These are people who have no satisfactions, no pleasures in life: deficiency of food, ragged clothes, and let us not speak of housing. No pleasure at all, except sexual enjoyment. No power, except paternity. And you want to come and deprive them of this only pleasure, this only power, for the sake of a much respected logic?"

This episode shows us a trend exactly opposite to the above: instead of spontaneous success from within, we see the failure of outside efforts, however well-intentioned.

The abacus

Here is another episode from India. In 1952, Nehru's government appealed to Dr. Stone, the great specialist in contraception. The idea was to make an experiment on a "sample" of 1,000 women, all volunteers, by applying the method of periodic continence.

The doctors and nurses taught the women how to follow the calendar so as to regulate their sexual intercourse in the home. First obstacle: these women had no calendars, and most of them could not read. With great presence of mind, the doctors then gave them all an abacus, of the kind used by children or billiard-players. "Every day, you will slide one ball from right to left, and when all the balls are on the left, you may resume sexual relations with your husband." Unfortunately, some of the women then regarded the abacus as a pure piece of wizardry. If sterility was to be acquired when all the balls were on the left, all they had to do was joyfully to push the whole lot to the left . . . many of the women were pregnant at the next consultation.

Polls on opinions and attitudes

The polls undertaken in various countries, Porto Rico, Japan, Ceylon, India, etc., teach us one important thing. Many women (or men), when asked how many children they would like to have, do not give a high figure; but when they are asked whether they intend to act in such a way as not to by-pass that figure, they either give a negative reply or simply do not understand the question.

Here is the result of a poll carried out by S. I. Chandrasekhar and Mulkta Sen in India: People of various classes were asked how many children a forty-year old woman ought to have had (that is to say, a woman nearing the end of her procreation period). These are the answers in averages:

Rural	3.4 children
Urban lower classes:	
Moslem	4.8
Hindu	3.4
Hindu upper class	3.2

The number of children considered desirable is notably lower than that produced by natural fertility, particularly among the Hindu population.

In a general way, people willingly admit the possibility of limiting the birth of children, but express no positive will in that direction. La Fontaine's woodcutter may well count his children, together with his creditors and his toil, as part of the burden that makes him long for death. But it would not occur to him for one moment to limit that burden himself by resisting nature.

There is thus a marked difference between the desired number of children and the *actual* number of children; this difference is the opposite of that observed in developed countries. In France, the ideal number of children, according to a poll carried out over a representative sample of 2,553 people,[1] is very near 3 (average 2.85). But the actual number of children, per complete family, does not reach 2.5, and this figure includes an appreciable number of children who were not expressly planned. This is then the order:

Ideal number in society,
Actual number,
Number desired oneself.

But this state of mind is not absolutely general. Leaving aside people's attitude to the ideal family size for society, we may distinguish three phases in the attitude and behaviour of a couple with regard to paternity:

(a) A positive desire to have many children.

(b) A positive desire for a limited number of children, but with insufficient will to satisfy that desire for limitation.

(c) A positive and strong enough desire to limit the number of children.

The two positions a and b represent profoundly opposite attitudes. Between the two, there is a large zone in which the will does not assert itself very clearly.

I will take these three stages in turn.

First phase: a positive desire for a numerous posterity

This desire expresses first and foremost the instinct for reproduction of the species. Death has long been so powerful, so triumphant, that any act of life is considered as a happy thing in itself.

Religions support this instinct; birth is a divine gift, a victory against the forces of evil. The cult of the family and of ancestors has the same effect. To have a child, and especially a male child, is to live on and prolong oneself. Everything happens as if the successive generations together make up one huge living organism that renews and perpetuates itself.

[1] Alain Girard and Louis Henry: *Les attitudes et la conjoncture démographiques: natalité, structure familiale et limites de la vie actives. Population*, January–March 1956.

The economic point of view does not always contradict this attitude. In primitive agriculture, the child is a factor for surplus production, a useful piece of property that can even be hired out or sold. The authority of the *pater familias* makes him feel that his wealth increases with his power, even when this identification is far from being assured.

And yet at the same time, as a contradiction which is only apparent, the child does not hold an important place; it is loved, yes, but barely looked after. Those who rely on nature for the giving of life also rely on it for its continuation. Besides, a child has hardly been weaned when they are already thinking of the next.

Second phase: fear of a large family, without positive will to limit it

Here we meet the factor that is so often observed in polls of opinions and attitudes.

A poor and ignorant couple does not have the necessary will to resist the sexual instinct. Living from day to day, and close to nature, they are deficient in the necessary spirit of foresight; having nothing to lose, they do not seek to preserve.

In order successfully to limit the number of children, a strong and sustained exercise of the will is needed, fed perhaps by a lively fear of unbearable burdens which can even become an obsession. Now, all contraceptive methods include some imperfection which demands continuous vigilance. Nature is always there, ready to take its revenge.

An American doctor, when consulted by a father of four who was finding it extremely difficult to bring them up, advised him to think hard, in the moment of orgasm, about his financial resources and the number of children he was capable of feeding. A little while later the father came to announce his wife's fifth pregnancy. "Didn't you follow my advice?—Yes, I did, but at that moment I had the feeling I could feed a vast number of children."

Even when there is some kind of will, it meets with considerable material difficulties in a poor population—lack of comfort, or the cost of gadgets or products. In an over-crowded house without sanitary installations, and in full promiscuity, the will melts, only too easily giving place to resignation, fatalism, and the absence of reaction which is a well-known feature of pauperism.

In some under-developed populations, a limitation of births can arise from certain taboos, especially with regard to intercourse during the feeding period. These taboos, the origin of which is disputed, can replace individual will or at any rate create a provisionary fear, more lively even than that of a developed family, at the prospect of an additional birth.

Third phase: firm will to limit the family

At this stage the economic concern is dominant, or, more exactly, the concern about social rank; the fear of going down is then sufficiently strong to provoke powerful reaction, even a violent one. It is the classic manifestation against any sliding; one has to be tough.

This reaction generally occurs more quickly in the woman than in the man, in a homogeneous couple where both members have reached the same degree of evolution, as was the case in French high society in the 18th century. In the under-developed countries, this differentiation is usually counterbalanced by the woman's inferior cultural evolution, but it can be found in group manifestations. Feminist associations nearly always head a movement favouring the prevention of births.

Here then is a ready-made indirect method for governments to encourage such prevention, without even pronouncing the word: they can develop the education of girls. But before we go further into the necessary policies, we must see how that positive will to limit the number of children can be put into practice.

Contraception and abortion

Most people, in most countries, regard abortion as less commendable or more condemnable than contraception. This is particularly true of countries with a basically Christian morality. Moreover, the woman runs far fewer risks, both for her health and her reputation, by resorting to contraceptive practices. It is therefore astonishing to see so many abortions, even in countries where contraceptive practices are not illegal. To understand this attitude, so apparently illogical (as always), we must once again turn our attention to the question of will.

The contraceptive practices that are known at present all presuppose a constant and renewed effort, a sustained and unfaltering will.[2] One single weakness may be fatal, but it may not be; thus a false security is created, which causes a gradual relaxation, leading to the feared pregnancy.

Abortion, however, means only one decision, painful, of course, and dangerous, but urgent and decisive. If the fear of a child is strong enough, it wins right out, especially if the social ambiance is not too hostile. This is the case in Japan; surrounded by nurses and assistants, impressed by the whole hospital apparatus, the pregnant woman easily resigns herself to an operation that demands only passivity. And the very easiness of this method leads people to neglect the austerities of contraception.

Without pushing the comparison too far, we may recall the painful servitudes of dieting and the high number of surgical interventions used to correct the failures of preventive practices.

Should we then conclude that people, or, more exactly, women, prefer abortion to contraception? As far as intentions are concerned, the reply is negative; in practice, and judging by results alone, it looks like yes, but the word "prefer" is inadequate.

---

[2] Coitus interruptus reduces sexual pleasure. The Ogino method demands constant attention and even, for real efficacy, the daily taking of temperatures. Ablutions sometimes mean shortening the act. Occlusive diaphragms must be fitted initially by a stranger, and they can be rendered useless by a mere inflammation, so much so that doctors recommend the simultaneous use of two and even three methods, which mean more restraints.

Child-care, allowances, instruction

As we have seen, the child does not have an important place in families of natural fertility. What a contrast with the parents of the only child, who live in anxiety of the slightest indisposition and tremble at the slightest risk!

One of the ways of encouraging the limitation of families is to teach child-care. When a woman has learnt of all the ills that threaten her child, she feels morally constrained to lavish all possible care on it; this further leads her to fear the arrival of a younger child, which would mean giving less time to, and in a way sacrificing, the other one.

Knowledge of child-care has another effect: it produces a certain consciousness of the value of the child. The word "consciousness" is not perhaps very well chosen, for the process is very often unconscious. But this new consideration for human life, this esteem given to a being who previously had very little, does contribute to the necessary change of mentality.

Family allowances, on the other hand, do not, in underdeveloped countries, exercise the populationist influence so easily attributed to them by European public opinion, which is ill-informed on these questions. In France, the family policy which was decided on in 1939 and later reinforced gradually up to 1946, did not produce more large families. Its influence was felt almost only with regard to the second and third child, and slightly with regard to the fourth, but no further.

The family allowance, in a population with a high fertility, is justified by social considerations, but meets with strong financial obstacles. It does not increase the birth-rate, since the latter is already maximal, and only slightly reduces infant mortality.

It could, however, help to slow down a progressive lowering of the birth-rate. But even here, the influence is not necessarily inspired by "common sense," that sentiment which causes so many mistakes, as regards voluntary birth. It all depends on the intensity of the movement. The effect of the family allowance is to give a value to the child, and especially an importance, unsuspected by the parents. If it is modest (and how could it not be?) it inspires a calculation which previously would never have entered their heads. "This child brings us so much a day, but how much is it costing us?" The answer is easy: the child is "a deficit." Such a conclusion was heard many times, from the lips of French parents when family allowances began, around 1925. These in fact accelerated the awakening of consciousness and no doubt provoked a sort of revelation in certain families. A much more intense degree of family aid had to be resorted to in 1939 for a very different psychological process to begin: the weakening of the malthusian determination.

Therefore, it would not only be inhuman to refuse all family aid in undeveloped countries, on the grounds that it would tend to increase the number of children, but the argument itself is far from being convincing. Care must of course be taken to see that the given aid is not too natalistic in its effect; but by "getting the family out of the hole," some forms of aid may contribute to a spontaneous reduction of births, which is always more pleasant than a reduction under the direct influence of authority.

Action in favour of instruction is one of the most useful: a rise in the cultural level is at least as necessary to the training of foresight as a rise in the economic level. The instruction of girls is, as we have seen, particularly effective. Moreover, compulsory education is opposed to the use of a child as an economic unit and therefore helps to modify the age-old conception of the child as wealth, or as income-bringing property, if I may be pardoned the expression.

The ground prepared

When the standard of living and, especially, the standard of culture, are sufficiently high for fatalism to give way to foresight in all families, when women gain independence or are ready to do so, when the care given to children is rational and sufficient, the ground is favourable to the limitation of births. The advice given in special clinics, the sale of contraceptive products, and a good propaganda showing the dangers of an over-rapid growth in population, all these can have a palpable influence.

And since a reduction in births itself leads to an improvement in the standard of living, the process is self-generative.

The standard of living of an increasing population may be represented by a curve, or more exactly by a series of possible curves in time. Such a curve may show a critical point. If, in spite of its progression, the standard of living remains below this point, the malthusian process cannot get started, the population growth wins and the standard of living plunges back into the depth of poverty. If, on the contrary, that threshold is passed, the malthusian process leads to an accelerated improvement in the standard of living.

In a very poor population, the prevention of births may still be attempted, but must be aimed especially at the leisured or middle classes, who can then serve as an example to others. If the standard of living manages to rise, time will have been saved.

Quite often, the economic level and the cultural level increase together as parallels; but if a choice is necessary, it is the cultural level which ought, preferably, to be encouraged.

Some opinions

The views I have just expounded are only partly personal. Those who have seriously studied the question (they are rare, it is true) are agreed on the essential points. They all regard a reduction in births as desirable, in countries where fertility has remained at the physiological level, but none of them conceal the difficulties any propaganda for contraception is bound to meet among poor and illiterate people.

Some of them insist less than I have done on the necessity of first raising the economic standard, and lean more heavily on the cultural level, or rather, on the customs and traditions as a whole. Here, for example, is Professor F. W. Notestein:[3]

[3] Frank W. Notestein: *Summary of Demographic Background of Problems of Under-developed Areas;* Millbank Memorial Fund. Communications presented to the annual conference, 1947, p. 10.

Human fertility . . . responds scarcely at all in the initial and often superimposed stages of such changes—changes that too often influence only the externals of life and leave the opportunities, hopes, fears, beliefs, customs and social organizations of the masses of the people relatively untouched. These latter are the factors that control fertility and since they are unmodified, fertility remains high. . . .

The opinion of Mr. Frank H. Hankins is much the same:[4]

Experience shows that a population cannot be forced or induced to use contraceptive measures so long as traditional attitudes prevail. It also shows that they will come into almost universal use in spite of much opposition if the surrounding cultural influences are favourable. The experience indicates also that the trend towards the small family system precedes rather than follows widespread propaganda by birth control organizations, though this latter may speed the process. Family limitation is thus a folkway, emerging slowly in answer to widely felt need in a culture traditionally opposed to it, but receiving in due time the blessing of moral and even religious approval.

The Rockefeller Foundation commission which studied the problem of population and public health in the Far East in 1950, wrote in its report:[5]

The fact that folk methods of contraception of proved effectiveness were matters of common knowledge for centuries before they were generally used is a sufficient proof that the critical element in the delayed decline of birth rates were those of motives rather than of means.

[4] Frank H. Hankins: *Under-developed Areas, with Special Reference to Population Problems,* International Social Science Bulletin, Autumn, 1950, vol. II, No. 3, p. 315.

[5] Marshall C. Balfour, Rogers F. Evans, Frank W. Notestein and Irene Taeuber: *Public Health and Demography in the Far East,* 1950, p. 10.

These writers are encouraging a few illusions on "the undeniable efficacity" of the processes known throughout the centuries, as also on the possibility of generalizing their use. Visibly inspired by a strong desire to see the birth-rate of these populations go down, they imagine the sudden generalization of procedures that are of doubtful efficacy and have only been practised by an infinitesimal number of people. In Western Europe too, certain methods were practised from immemorial times; nevertheless they were not generalized for a very long time, and even that took a preliminary economic and cultural revolution.

The divergence between writers on the subject is therefore only a matter of degree; but this divergence may nevertheless lead to very different forecasts; those authors who dwell more on traditions than on the economic cultural level, have great faith, for example, in industrialization and urbanization.

Here, on the other hand, is the conclusion of N. K. Sarkar on Ceylon:[6]

> It is obvious, therefore, that a birth control policy only achieves limited success unless the long over-due economic-social-cultural revolution is carried out in all its aspects and society is modernized at a rapid rate. Even if a birth control policy were otherwise acceptable, the cost involved would be a serious obstacle to its introduction, especially when the need for capital in industrial development is so great and its supply so scarce.

Here again we meet the economic obstacle, which was somewhat under-estimated by the other authors quoted above.

Experience seldom permits precise conclusions. But excessive faith in contraceptive propaganda seems more dangerous than the opposite excess, because it may lead to the neglect of economic investments, a relaxation of the efforts always needed for any such undertaking.

Sarkar goes on, still about Ceylon:

[6] *The Demography of Ceylon*, 1957, p. 246.

It is argued further, that industrialization would lead to a decline in fertility, as it has done in Europe and Japan, and the problem of surplus population would solve itself.

This, however, is a drastic simplification of the problem. Industrialization is not easy to attain in the conditions in which the under-developed countries are today. The difficulties are great, the efforts needed to overcome them must be strenuous and prolonged, and the moral support required from the entire population must be unstinted.

To appreciate and judge the difficulties is the best way of surmounting them.

Chapter 20

The reactions of power and collectivity to contraception

FROM IMMEMORIAL TIMES, governments have been populationistic. The attitude starts at the patriarchal and tribal stage. The birth of a child is a sign of wealth and power for the head of the family or the head of the tribe. Since death was a scourge to be feared, birth was a blessing; this is the traditional position.

The chief in power is much more anxious about an insufficiency in the number of his subjects than about excess. Property is more or less identified with power and this confusion continues well into feudal times.

Thus the absolute ruler, who exercises power without being subject to its duties, seeks an increase in numbers; he is a populationist. We shall see how this works in various examples.

Absolute domination

In the family framework, the concept of power and domination is opposed to the economic concept. In the days when children remained under the direct and strict authority of the father right up to their marriage, the concept of power was easily the strongest. The emancipation of children contributed to the lowering of the birth rate, by emphasizing economic questions. If these were to dominate as sole factors, outdoing both the need for affection and the desire for authority, the optimum would be zero; it would mean the childless family. In our times, the effectiveness of family allowances in certain families can be explained by the relative conciliation they achieve between the economic concept on the one hand and the concept of power together with the need for affection on the other. These allowances cover, even in France, only a part of a child's needs. But by increasing the total of family goods, allowances paid in kind increase buying power; when another child comes, the welfare decreases but power increases. It is true that here power is not exercised on the children themselves. But the more the emancipation of children progresses, the more necessary it will be materially to help the parents, who are further and further away from domination. On a wider scale, the patriarch looks favourably upon any birth within his tribe, because it increases his power which is, in any case, identified with his wealth.

But here is a very different example:

In the classic administrative set-up, any official at the head of a department wishes to increase the number of people under him. The attitude is logical, since all increase gives him a wider base and—in general—more widespread power. Of course, the administrative chief is far from absolute power, but his domination is not rigidly matched with specific duties. If an extra person is placed under his orders, he is not obliged to cut down his own salary in order to pay the new man. In private enterprise, however, or in an organization that is sufficiently autonomous and interested in its output, the boss on the contrary tries to reduce the number of people devoted to any one task.

Let us now look at a more important example, or at least an example nearer to the subject, that of the landowner, of a feudal type, or even the absolute sovereign or the strong nationalist government.

The feudal lord

A dominant class that exercises power in an absolute manner is populationistic. The number of writers are legion who have echoed Bodin and said that the strength of a sovereign is measured by the number of his subjects.

It is in the interest of those in power to have a large number of people working for them. But should this number surpass all reasonable need? Should the ruler not fear that an excessive multiplication might generate a defective state of sanitation that would hardly favour high production? In theory, it is so. And in practice, any animal-breeder knows that he must not go beyond the number that will assure him the highest income. Why then were not the lords and sovereigns moved by similar considerations?

Their position can be explained thus: the owner of a farm limits the number of his domesticated animals, but allows all game and useful wild animals to increase. The gardener prunes his fruit-wall, but lets the trees out in the open develop as they please. The border-line between marginal and submarginal lands (or activities) is not very clearly marked, so that this reserve population is ill-defined.

On the other hand, the number of slaves must be limited. The populationist concept of domination found a remarkable advocate in the eighteenth century: in his three works,[1] Turmeau de la Morandière, a gentleman demographer, develops it explicitly, and with a cynical ingenuity that makes his works more instructive than those of more clear-sighted but more bashful authors. He writes with candour: "Subjects and cattle must be multiplied." No author has defended the doctrine of domination with more brutality; but many had the same ideas and put them forward less clearly and less frankly.

For the absolute ruler therefore, free workers are never too numerous in practice. For rulers with more foresight, the only care to be taken on behalf of the ruling power is to avoid too great losses, to preserve that truly vital element below which the output would decrease too greatly. "The common people are useful, therefore we must see to their preservation," said Boulainvilliers.

Thus, absolute authority desires numbers; numbers not only enrich and strengthen power, they also flatter vanity.

Relative domination: appearance of Malthus

The ruler's attitude changes when his domination becomes less absolute, when the subject, instead of being a source of wealth, starts becoming a burden.

[1] *Appel des étrangers dans nos colonies*, 1763, *Principes politiques sur le rappel des protestants en France*, 1764, *Police pour les mendiants*, 1764.

This is what happened in England at the end of the eighteenth century. The Poor Law imposed charges on the rich. With this change in the advantage of the ruling class, the domination was no longer absolute, and the limitation in the number of births became, if not imperative, at least advisable.

This conversion of the ruler to malthusianism is echoed, almost identically, both in the family and on the global scale. As long as the father of the family enjoyed absolute authority and made his children work, and as long as strong inequality was tolerated inside the family (children left without care to scrap for miserable bits of food outside), it was in the interest of the father to have a large family.

But as soon as the child has to be better looked after, goes to school and gets emancipated fairly fast, the attitude changes.

The malthusian reflexes of family paternalism can also be seen in colonial paternalism: from the moment the subjects become burdens, their increasing numbers cause concern; some reduction becomes desirable, if not in the actual number, at least in the rhythm of its increase.

These paternalistic malthusian preoccupations are seen on yet a wider scale: the fear of world over-population. From the moment that the commercial, if not the political domination of the Western people was no longer absolute, and that various forms of assistance, however incomparable to the Poor Law, came to light, the fear of excessive numbers began to preoccupy many people.

It is in the richest country particularly, that is to say in the United States, that the fear of having to feed needy populations, and the even more acute fear of having one day to make room for them, through immigration, in their vast unexploited territories, logically set this malthusian reflex in action.

The young under-developed nations

The primitive attitude is inevitably found in present-day young nations. Proud of their new existence, they willingly put prestige before the desire to improve the standard of living of individuals; this distinction, or even, this opposition between the two objectives does not, in any case, stand out very clearly to the men in power, since the working masses have not achieved a sufficient degree of emancipation. The society being still vertical in structure and rigid in its stratification, it instinctively seeks its well-being in a base that is as large as possible. Religions follow the same trend.

Even the most far-seeing hesitate before the malthusian attitude, which seems an insult to nature, if not to divinity, as well as a reproach to those individuals deemed excessive, and an attack on the greatness of the nation.

These countries are in fact at the Jean Bodin stage; the only difference is that their death-rate is that of Pasteur's time, or even of Fleming's and not that of alchemy.

Any pressure, any advice, even on malthusian caution, coming from outside, may, in such conditions, provoke a reaction exactly opposite to that desired, should the approach be clumsy or too direct.

> La superbe simplicité
> Demande d'immenses égards. . .
> (Superb simplicity
> Requires vast deferences. . .)

I have often noticed this reaction, even among Indian intellectuals only too anxious to understand their country's economic difficulties. Faced with over-direct advice from well-intentioned Americans to reduce their birth rate, they react vigorously. "India," they reply, "will soon be in a position adequately to feed a much large number of inhabitants." An emotional reaction, of course, boastful even, and inspired by national pride, but a reaction which is almost fatal, especially when the advice comes from a country that is developed, moralizing and protective.

The "colonized" countries

It follows that a colonized country will be all the less able to accept the lessons of the dominating country on this point. Take the case of Algeria: the French power there is in fact less threatened by the revolt than by the demographic growth. The revolt is in any case the result of demographic pressure; a peasant without work is only too ready to seize the gun that will feed him; the lawyer without clients is an essential agent of revolutions. In others times, extermination would have been the specific solution of the dominating power, as it was in the United States, Canada, Australia, etc. Since this cannot be used in our day, the logical solution for the dominating power threatened by subversion seems to be the reduction of a surplus birth-rate.

Now the difficulties enumerated in the previous chapter, on the possibility of spreading such practices among a wretched population, are here increased by a collective reaction which would certainly have occurred if the thing had been attempted. "Not content with oppressing us," the Algerians would have said, or the Tunisians, or the Moroccans, "the French attack our vitality, our race." And big words like "genocide" or "biological warfare" would certainly have been uttered, especially on the international platforms. All the moral and religious authorities would have risen against this "attempted murder of a whole people."

In Canada, after the Treaty of Paris, the English naturally did not think of introducing malthusian practices, before Malthus' famous work had appeared and a whole century before the English themselves began to reduce the number of their children. But the high fertility of the French Canadians was one of the manifestations of the national and religious reactions against the risk of assimilation by the dominant and heretical power.

In India, the English would have met the same resistance, if they had made any attempt to force the ideas now held by Nehru. Of course the Indian head of state and numerous intellectuals who follow him found the inspiration for their anti-natalist policy in their Anglo-Saxon heritage. But they were able to "take possession" of their own problem. Now that they themselves had the responsibility for the poverty of their country, they could no longer resort to a simple vindictive attitude. They were now in the position of "relative domination," and therefore recognized the necessity of malthusian practices. Ghandi had the success of great men, namely, he died at the right time.

The example of Japan, which will be described in the next chapter, seems however to give the lie to these observations: it was in mid-American occupation and on the suggestion of American demographers that the policy of "eugenic protection" was decided in 1948. But the Americans had the good sense to appear as little as possible and to let national organizations do the work, once those responsible at the top had been convinced. In any case, the circumstances were rather special:

First of all, abortion—the chief method in the system—is deeply rooted in the Japanese consciousness: having been alternately tolerated or forbidden throughout the centuries, it did not, in 1948, have the same effect of destructive surprise that it would have had in other countries.

Secondly, Japan was hit violently. For half a century it had sought to meet its demographic expansion with the conquest of territories and markets, then suddenly it was reduced to its own frontiers and even a bit less than that, and had to find work for masses of returning soldiers or colonizers. The shock was such as to provoke a profound reaction in the national consciousness.

Finally, the docile and imitative character of the Japanese people easily lent itself to an experiment of this nature.

This example should therefore be interpreted with some caution.

The middle east on fire

The Middle East countries are all on the alert. Whether their position is defensive or offensive, justified or unjustified, one worry remains: the struggle against Israel. Without this major preoccupation, which is further fanned by the rivalry of the great powers, the economic concern would have prevailed and might have suggested a reduction of the dangerously exuberant birth rate. An effective campaign for the prevention of births could hardly have succeeded as long as Suez was owned by a foreign company. In any case, it was demographic pressure itself that pushed Nasser to power, and the fact that he could not feed his subjects adequately which led him to seek a prestige success and to snatch at the few resources that lay to hand. If the population had been sparse and decimated by illness, a Farouk would still be on the throne.

Movements favouring the prevention of births in Pakistan still come up against the nationalist spirit, which does not burden itself with calculations or weighty arguments; hence it has been stated in all seriousness that the question cannot be examined before the population of Pakistan has, in numbers, equalled that of India.

There are many unknown springs and motivations in any collectivity, which set up this or that current of opinion. Neither the population nor even the rulers of the United Arab Republic need have the slightest consciousness of their demographic growth to take up an imperialistic attitude. This attitude would in any case become, if not more violent, at any rate more active, if Israel showed any signs of weakness or disintegration. It is the coexistence of pressure and depression that causes storms.

The communist position

Marx denounced the existence of a reserve army of workers always ready to depreciate wages, but he attributed it to capitalism and not to over-population. Such an attitude was violently opposed to Malthus and his successors.

But Marx was cautious about the problems of population, about which he knew little, and which he had certainly not studied as deeply as his opponent Malthus. The essential thing was to fight and destroy the false Malthusian remedy, or, more exactly, the argument that in effect protected the regime of private property.

With the progress of the struggle against mortality, the premisses were modified in such a way that the initiated expected an inevitable revision of this attitude from one day to another. The only unknown factor was the date when the change would occur.

As soon as it had freed itself from Soviet authority, Yugoslavia took a more advanced position: China (next chapter) adopted a frankly malthusian attitude as soon as the planners began to see the citizens as a burden, though different motives were invoked. The very notion of demographic investment produces a malthusian argument.

The two currents

Any collectivity, and in particular, a nation, may pursue two objectives: the individual standard of living, and power or prestige. These two objectives dictate the policies of different population. It is easily demonstrated that the optimal economic population, that is, which ensures the highest standard of living, is less numerous than the optimal power population, that is, which ensures the greatest power (which is not necessarily military power; the Sputnik is also a collective object).

Therefore, a population that seeks to improve its standard of living (Western democracies) is less natalistic than a population which seeks (or whose government seeks) to increase its power. And conversely, a population often instinctively aims at the objective which most corresponds to its monetary state, so that it may turn imperialistic with relative over-population, when already at optimum power.

Periods of political tension and troubles push the economic level to the background and therefore favour the natalistic attitude; in calm periods, on the contrary, economic questions are again brought forward into actuality. This is the moment when malthusians and moderators have the best chance of being heard.

Individuals and governments

There remain the relations between the attitudes and behaviour of the individual (or couple), on the one hand, and the official doctrine of governments or ruling classes on the other.

Appreciable divergences may occur: in France, the prevention of births was practised with considerable effects, as we have seen, from 1750 and throughout the eighteenth century, without anyone actually advocating the limitation of children as Malthus did. During the whole of the nineteenth century and part of the twentieth, the birth rate continued to go down although officialdom upheld the traditional encouragement of births.

In England, on the other hand, where Malthus was followed by influential neo-malthusians, it was not until the trial of Annie Besant, in 1875, that individuals changed their behaviour at all.

Today, the governments of India, Japan and, no doubt, China, are in advance of individuals. The conflicts and divergences that occur in all countries are obscured by a constant confusion between the demographic point of view and the family point of view, because the dogmatists are unwilling to accept the idea that these two objectives may in those circumstances lead to very different solutions.

Chapter 21

Two anti-natal policies: Japan and China

WHEN THE WAR WAS OVER, no under-developed country was thinking of reducing its births; such a proposition, fought by Marxists, by Ghandi, by the Catholics, would have seemed sacrilegious. We should remember, too, that in European countries the prevention of births spread against the will of governments.

Twelve years later the situation is very different: in two large Asiatic countries, one capitalist, the other communist, the most anti-natalistic policies ever to have seen the light of day are being applied, while many efforts, often private, are being made in the same direction in various other countries.

This chapter will describe the Japanese policy and its results as well as the policy and attitude of the Chinese government.

JAPAN

Japan is the first non-European country to have broken with the traditional policy of the emperors, based on power and the numerousness of subjects. Circumstances imposed the reversal.

When the expansion and the modernization of the Meiji era began, Japan already had a very dense population: 235.69 inhabitants per square mile, that is, considerably more than present-day France, which is richly endowed by nature and part of whose population is complaining of demographic saturation.

With this high density of 1872, Japan started off on the kind of expansion that several European countries had already been undertaking for over half a century. In Europe itself, and, naturally, in the United States, faith in continuous progress was still more or less intact. But many maturing ideas were about to change family behaviour fairly rapidly. Japan on the contrary, behaved, in this sudden enterprise, like a new country; its type of government and institutions were inclined towards demographic expansion, more or less like those of France in the time of Louis XIV, or those of certain very newly created countries today.

Thus, neither in the family, nor in the national collectivity, were conditions favourable to the conversion which was about to occur in the various European countries. In 1901–10, the birth rate was still 32 per 1,000, while the United States were already at 30, England and Australia at 28, Sweden and Belgium at 26; parity was still retained with Germany and Italy (33), Spain (31), and the Netherlands (31), but the trends were very different. One generation later, around 1930, Japan was still at 32, but Germany had dropped to 17. the Netherlands to 23, Italy to 25. As for the countries in the vanguard of the movement, France, England, Belgium, Switzerland, Sweden, etc., they had already progressed to about 15 per 1,000, a figure which no longer ensured the renewal of generations and which meant the ageing of the population rather than its growth.

If we are looking for an abridgment of history, we can see Japan joining a brilliant procession, without noticing that on this essential point, it is undergoing a gigantic conversion.

The collapse of the imperialist solution

In the second war, the movement could certainly have continued for some time; the 518 inhabitants counted per square mile were not living solely on that square mile, but also on commerce and colonization, the two going together. Japan was trying to follow the example of England in the preceding century: to live like a metropolis, like a town, like a factory, thanks to what other regions were bringing in, if not to their detriment. The second war was in a way the logical consequence of that attitude: had it been successful, it would have enabled Japan to pursue this policy; but the defeat knocked the whole system to pieces, and suddenly revealed an awesome gap between men and resources.

Having thus long sought the solution in imperialism and the exterior outlet (for men and especially for goods), Japan found itself face to face with the collapse of this policy after the second war. Like France, but in the opposite direction, it had made the mistake of dissociating itself demographically from other countries in mid-development. In both cases the final result was catastrophic.

After the second war, both countries undertook to correct their error. In Japan, the risk of a sudden and intense over-population became so acute that many eyes were opened.

American technical advisers acted at that moment, and with the necessary discretion.

Besides, over-population and the practices used to fight it had deep roots in the country; abortion was more or less endemic. In certain periods the emperors strictly applied the edicts forbidding abortion and infanticide; then, when over-population was particularly severe, they turned a blind eye and relaxed the vigilance.

The eugenic law of 1948

The "law of eugenic protection," promulgated on the 28th June 1948, dressed up an essentially quantitative objective in qualitative clothing. The objective: to reduce the number of births.

First of all, particular cases were foreseen in which the doctor would have the right to practise the sterilization of an individual. Furthermore, contraceptive methods were encouraged and taught. Finally, abortion was authorized in certain very widely interpreted medical and social conditions.

The results

This is the number of births and the birth rates recorded during the last few years:

| | *Births* | |
	in thousands	per 1,000 inhabitants
1940-1	2,180	30.2
1948	2,681	33.7
1949	2,697	32.8
1950	2,337	28.2
1951	2,138	25.4
1952	2,005	23.5
1953	1,862	21.5
1954	1,765	20.1
1955	1,727	19.4
1956	1,660	18.4
1957	1,600	17.5

The year 1948, the point of departure of the law is, in fact, a bad date for comparison, because the birth figures were still swollen by the return of soldiers and prisoners. It is best to compare with the pre-war 1940–1, remembering however, that the results were obtained in less than ten years.

In 1958, ten years after the promulgation of the law, the birth rate was about 45 per cent lower than the pre-war rate. Fertility (the number of children per marriage) has probably decreased further. Never has such a rapid lowering been observed in any country.

What caused this steep drop? Abortions or contraception? On facing page are the compared results of the decrease in births and the official numbers of abortions.

The decrease of births is inferior to the number of abortions. And yet the births of 1949 were still swollen by nearly 500,000 by the return of soldiers and prisoners! How can we explain this anomaly?

(*a*) Official abortions have, for one thing, replaced clandestine abortions.

(*b*) Two or several abortions may take place in order to avoid one birth.

Nevertheless, this comparison does not leave much room for contraceptive practices. The Japanese authorities admit

228

	Decrease in births compared to the year 1949	Official number of abortions
1949	—	246,104
1950	360,000	489,111
1951	559,000	636,524
1952	692,000	798,193
1953	835,000	1,068,066
1954	932,000	1,143,059
1955	970,000	1,170,143
1956	1,037,000	1,159,288
1957	1,097,000	(1,150,000)

that the lowering of the birth-rate is due chiefly to abortion.
This is what Mr. Ayanori Okasaki, director of the Institute
of Population Studies, has said on the subject:[1]

> The limitation of births spread in both town and country.
> But as the method of usage was not diffused widely enough,
> the efficacy of the drugs was reduced and the number
> of undesired births[2] increased. This leads one to believe
> that these births were suppressed, in a large majority of
> cases, by abortion . . . so that the number of abortions
> was unexpectedly increased. In the final analysis, the
> strongest brake on the Japanese birth rate was, contrary to
> expectation, abortion and not contraception.

And he added moreover that the shortage of traditional
housing was a serious obstacle to the generalization of contraceptive practices. These observations are of great interest:

Abortion remains important, even in countries where contraception is officially encouraged. Many illusions are enter-
tained in France about the possibility of suppressing abortion
by the free sale of contraceptives. Of course there is a great
deal of difference between France and Japan, but certain facts
remain.

The preceding remarks are of course only valid for the

[1] *Histoire du Japon: L'économie et la population*. Editions de
l'I.N.E.D., Paris 1958.
[2] Presumably "undesired conceptions" is meant.

classic contraceptive procedures, all imperfect and all demanding restraints that lead sooner or later to negligence. The sterilizing pill (see chapter 24) could change this one day. The Japanese authorities have in fact called in Dr. Pincus and asked him to proceed with experiments. The results have not yet been published.

Another method used is sterilization with a view to protect the health of mothers. The slight decrease in the number of abortions since 1955, the maximum figure, is not, according to Mr. Okasaki, due to a wider diffusion of contraceptive measures, but to eugenic sterilizations. Here is the increase in numbers since 1949:

1949	5,356	1953	31,162
1950	10,792	1954	36,601
1951	15,409	1955	41,273
1952	21,241	1956	42,662

Unlike abortion (two abortions may avoid only one birth, if they occur at an interval of a few months), sterilization can avoid two or three births and therefore be numerically equivalent to several abortions.

It may however happen that an abortion badly carried out leads to permanent sterility. The advances made in antibiotics have greatly reduced this risk, but it cannot be negligible in a country that has gone over so fast to mass abortions.

However that may be, Japan seems to have attained its main objective: the stopping of the populationistic tide by considerable reduction of the birth rate. But there remain several black spots in the demographic future of the country. I shall look at these now.

Quo non descendam?

For a young population, a birth rate of 17 or 18 per 1,000 means in effect a low fertility, hardly sufficient to ensure the renewal of generations. Comparing the 1,600,000 births of 1957 with an adult generation: those who are about 25 years old to-day number about 1,700,000 to 1,800,000 persons, and are already more numerous than the young; and the young will be further decreased by mortality. The young population will therefore diminish, not only relatively, but absolutely.

There is no reason to suppose, at the moment, that the lowering birth rate has reached its lowest point. The advice given since 1948 did not have immediate effect, and some of these effects may be only just beginning in the more remote districts.

Mankind is pitifully lacking in experience on such a new subject; it is unlikely to have learnt, all in one go, how to manage this instrument faultlessly.

Growth all the same

Steep though this lowering may be, it has not been sufficient to stop demographic growth. We can see the mechanism of division by age group operating under our very eyes: the Japanese population is so young that it has a very slight death rate: 8 per 1,000. A static population (in the demographic sense), with such a low mortality would reach an average life of 125 years.

The Japanese average life, however, is only 66 years. In a static population this would correspond to a death rate twice as high as this, that is, 16 per 1,000.

The difference between the theoretical death rate and the actual one results from the youth of the population; so that for the moment, the total population is still increasing by 900,000 persons each year, that is, by about 1 per cent. If this rhythm were kept up this would mean a doubling of the population in 70 years. But if the birth rate continues to go down or even if it stayed at the present level, the rhythm of growth will slow down, on account of old age, and, therefore on account of an increased death rate.

Forecasts to 2015

The institute where problems of population are studied in Tokyo has produced forecasts to the year 2015, based on the following hypotheses:[3]

[3] *Histoire du Japon*, op. cit., pp. 161 et seq.

(a) Mortality at every age will continue to decrease until it reaches, in 1965, the present rates of New Zealand, when it will then remain constant.

(b) The rates of fertility at every age will reach, in 1965, those that Sweden had in 1937, and will then remain constant.

Which hypotheses give the following results:

| | Population (in thousands) | Per 1,000 inhabitants | | |
		Births	Deaths	Increase
1960	93,800	17.1	8.4	+8.7
1970	100,700	15.3	8.8	+6.5
1980	106,500	14.3	10.3	+4.0
1990	108,500	12.0	11.9	+0.1
2000	107,000	11.3	14.0	−2.7
2010	102,700	11.1	16.6	−5.5
2015	99,600	10.9	17.9	−7.0

As we can see, the death rate increases and even doubles in 45 years, in spite of an increasing longevity; this seeming paradox results from the ageing of the population.

The population would pass through a maximum around 1990 and would then start on its steady decrease.

These provisional forecasts may of course be contradicted in one direction or the other.

But for a long time yet, this over-populated and relatively well "organized" island will have to face a fairly rapid increase that is the result of a sort of acquired speed.

This is not the main risk. We can easily imagine the production of subsistence-means doubling in 70 years so that the Japanese will be assured of their food. But the sudden slowing down will provoke a considerable ageing.

Ageing

We must repeat that the ageing of a population is the result of a lowering birth rate and not, as common sense would believe, of a lowering death rate and an increasing length of life. Since the Japanese lowering of the birth rate is the fastest ever witnessed in any country, ageing will also bear all records for speed. The word "speed" is of course relative, and should not be misunderstood—such phenomena occur implacably, at their own rhythm.

The proportion of sexagenarians, still 7.9 per cent in 1954, will slowly reach that of Western populations (16 per cent and on the increase).

Here is the probable development of the population by age-groups, on the preceding hypotheses:

	0 to 15 years	15 to 60 years	60 years and over	Total
1955	33.4	58.6	8.0	100
1960	29.9	61.4	8.7	100
1970	22.1	67.2	10.7	100
1980	20.9	66.8	12.3	100
1990	19.1	65.6	15.3	100
2000	16.9	63.7	19.4	100
2010	16.7	59.0	24.3	100
2015	16.7	57.8	25.5	100

The proportion of under-fifteens will halve, while the proportion of old people will triple. This is the classic pivot movement (greatly amplified) around the medium ages, who by 2015 return to much the same level, in relative value, as the one they started from. Fewer children than old people, an awesome prospect. If the demographic movements are slow, their power may lie in their very slowness. The ageing of the Japanese population will lead to profound changes in institutions and pose entirely new problems, which run the risk of being attributed to secondary but visible phenomena, as they are in France.

Sooner or later it will be necessary to provoke a sharp rise in the birth rate, that generator of new burdens, ill-accepted and ill-understood by the population.

On the best hypotheses, the shock undergone in the twentieth century can only be assuaged in two or three centuries, as far as the division by age groups is concerned.

General view and conclusion

The example of Japan is instructive from many points of view. It has shown that even in a relatively developed, and reputedly docile population, the diffusion of contraceptive practices meets with enormous obstacles (in the present state of these practices) and that abortion is easier to introduce and manipulate than prevention.

This experiment, moreover, which is taking place under our very eyes, has shown up the accordion-like effects of a sudden change in the birth rate. When Japan has reached a new and more stable situation, it will have a population which will be both more numerous and more aged than the old one. But the risk of a permanent decline, on account of old age, cannot be ignored.

CHINA

Like Japan, China is a country with a long tradition of over-population. Over-population was already worrying an emperor of China 24 centuries ago. More recently, Sun Yat-sen, in 1894, paid some attention to it. Not so the rulers when communism took over. Initially, "there was no problem." The Chinese attitude was modelled on the Soviet one.

The first measures of a demographic nature concerned only marriage and the ban on concubines.

For an outside observer, however, it was pretty certain that the growing awareness of the problem would soon change this theoretical attitude. The only difficulty for this observer, as we have said, was to foresee the date and the scope of the change.

The stages of conversion

In August 1953 the cabinet seems to have sent instructions to the Minister of Health advising him "to assist the public in the prevention of births." This declaration, vague anyway, remained secret for a long time, and has not been confirmed.

The following fact is more reliable: on 18th September 1954, at the first re-opening of parliament (the People's Congress), the deputy Shao Li-Tsu, who represented small parties, suggested limiting the number of births, for health reasons. This proposition was not passed, but it was reproduced in the People's Daily of Peking. Shao Li-Tsu has indefatigably continued his propaganda ever since.

It cannot have been unsuccessful, because in December 1954, Liu Chao-li assembled some doctors in Peking to study the problem, at a conference which ended up in a study committee; in March 1955, the Central Committee of the Communist Party sent a few directives to its branches, concerning the prevention of births. In the meantime, the question had been aired in the publication *Youth of China*, 16th February 1955, by Chou Ngo-feng, who explains the various contraceptive techniques.

Nevertheless, until this moment, the argument in favour of contraception was still imbued with the ideology of the bourgeoisie, in spite of its defenders' precautions. Many orthodox communists, some of them highly placed, had not yet been converted. The differences of opinion were severe, even in the heart of the government.

The great conversion took place just about at this time, say 1955–6:

The Democratic Federation of Chinese Women announced, in its paper *Woman of New China*, that it was about to start a movement to encourage the limitation of births. At the same time, some attempt was made to reconcile this new attitude with classical doctrine. Such for instance was the aim of an article in *Studies* (Hsüeh-hsi), signed Yang Ssu-Ying, on the malthusian theory of population.

In October 1955, the Vice-premier Mr. Chin-yi, made an even clearer declaration to a delegation of French women: "It is not possible to go on producing children without any kind of limitation. Over-population is bad for the home, the children, and the country" (text quoted in *Libération*, 9th November 1955).

The legislation on abortion and sterilization was broadened in early 1956, in a liberal direction, in favour of mothers with four children, women over thirty, sick and poor women, and students.

The Health Minister's campaign for limitation of births was amplified and made more specific in mid 1956. The most important thing, everyone said, was to look after the health of the mothers.

At the eighth congress of the Communist Party, in September 1956, Madam Tsu Chang, First Secretary of the Commission on Female Labour, declared: "We must react to the desire of many of ourselves and a large part of the masses, who wish to limit the number of children."

At this same congress, in his proposal for the second five-year plan, Mr. Chou-en-lai declared: "For the protection of women and children, for the upbringing and education of the rising generation, and for the health and prosperity of the nation, we are in favour of some adequate regulation of reproduction. We are entrusting the Ministry of Health with the task of putting into action a positive programme for the prevention of births, by means of publicity and practical measures."

Mr. Chou-en-lai made similar declarations to Mr. Thapar, an Indian high official, stressing that overpopulation is not a problem peculiar to capitalist societies. This is an important innovation in communist doctrine.

Finally, in March 1957, the promulgation of the law authorizing, with certain reservations, the sterilization of both sexes and abortion, coincides with the widening of the campaign in favour of contraceptive practices.

Moreover the legal age of marriage has been set back. A boy may not marry under 20, or a woman under 18. These figures are fairly high for a country where the custom of young second marriages was very widespread.

The doctrine

So, in spite of some persistent opposition, the revolution in attitudes is an accomplished fact. How do the Chinese justify it?

As in Western countries, there is a certain troubled confusion at the presence of so many different angles to the question: the health point of view, especially the health of the woman; the home equilibrium, especially the economic equilibrium; the population increase and the economic problems arising from it.

Nevertheless the confusion seems to have been less great than in the West, because the various perspectives all lead, at least for the time being, to the same conclusion: births must be decreased.

It was the health point of view, naturally, which was put first, followed by family considerations and the difficulties of raising numerous children. These arguments did not directly clash with the classical anti-malthusian doctrine.

But later the problem of overpopulation was clearly set forth. The authorities established the distinction—often omitted in the West—between the number of inhabitants and the rhythm of increase, emphasizing very properly that the Chinese are not too numerous but are increasing too rapidly. In 1958, after an exceptional harvest and much individual success, Chinese home and foreign policy was an outburst of pride and enthusiasm. This exuberance had its repercussions, not on the policy of contraception, but on the interpretation given to it. It was no longer a question of danger from overpopulation, but of protecting the health of the mother and the family equilibrium.

This extremely skilful development of attitude enables the Chinese rulers more or less to respect the marxist doctrine, while actually pursuing a malthusian policy.

Demographic investments will be much reduced, but their reduction will seem to be a simple consequence of the health policy.

Until now, the Soviet reactions to these changes have remained very discreet.

The end and the means

In August 1957, Mr. Ta Chen, Chinese demographer, brought some very interesting specifications on desired objectives to the international statistical congress in Stockholm.

The birth rate must be reduced by 50 per cent in the next ten years. This objective was decided on after considering various factors: traditions in marriage and family matters, medical and hospital equipment, cultural, economic and social conditions of the people, the conservatism of peasants, and means of communication in remote districts.

A reduction by 50 per cent in a space of 10 years has never been achieved by any country, Mr. Ta Chen observed. In Japan, however, the birth rate fell from 34.3 per 1,000 in 1947 to 18.4 per 1,000 in 1956, and to about 17.5 in 1957. But the point of departure for 1947 was abnormally high, because births had been particularly favoured by the return of soldiers to their homes.

From the three methods envisaged—the setting-back of the marriage age, abortion, contraception—the third must in theory have the first place. Apart from publicity and propaganda there is also a wide distribution of contraceptives. These were planned, in 1957, for 25 million couples (the total number of couples below 45 years of age must be about 100 million), and include 80 per cent sheaths, 10 per cent spermicide jellies, 5 per cent pessaries, 3 per cent diaphragms and 2 per cent other gadgets or products.

During the first three months of 1957, the sales of the State medical and pharmaceutical company of Peking reached 4,310,000 sheaths, 46,500 pessaries, 80,000 tubes of jelly, 569,504 boxes of pessaries. Medical teams visited factories, offices, the country (on market day) in order to teach the use of contraception.

Classical abortion is not recommended, but is authorized in certain cases, as is sterilization.

The lowest marriageable age, which has been the subject of lively debates, has been set back to 18 for girls and 20 for boys. It may even be later, the rulers think, thanks to the lengthening of studies and the granting of professional employments to young men and especially to young girls in the towns. Students are only allowed to marry when they have obtained their last diploma.

Since the burst of confidence of 1958, Mr. Ta Chen has been disgraced, but the objectives which he indicated seem to have been upheld, though now they are called "forecasts."

Probable development

What will this policy produce? On the one hand, there are the traditional obstacles to the introduction of contraceptive practices in a little developed and largely peasant population. On the other hand, there are unusually favourable conditions: a meticulous people mad about hygiene, the power of the political apparatus, and a certain rise in the economic and cultural level.

The Chinese birth rate will decrease. But at what rhythm?

The situation is completely unknown, the subject exceedingly delicate, on which highly authoritative prognostications have failed in the past.

Dr. Chou tells us that the birth rate went down considerably at Tientsin in 1955 and 1956; but this isolated result is vague and hardly proves anything.

The forecasts established by the Chinese authorities in 1958 calculated 700 millions in 1962. This figure means a steep drop in the birth rate, even more rapid perhaps than that indicated by Mr. Ta Chen.

Assuming that the birth rate really drops by 50 per cent in ten years, there would be the same dangers, in almost identical terms, as those already envisaged for Japan, namely:

(a) The difficulty of checking the fall, once begun, at the level considered desirable.

(b) The notable growth of the population, despite this drop.

The decrease of 50 per cent would still leave the birth rate at a level just above 20 per 1,000, whereas the death rate would no doubt go down fairly rapidly to 8 or 10 per 1,000. The residual increase of more than 1 per cent per annum (instead of the present 2.5 per cent) would still be considerably higher than that of Western populations, which are provided with capital. This growth would require larger and larger demographic investments.

(c) A rapid and significant ageing of the population, which would pose fearful problems of a social and political nature.

In chapter 24, we shall see what consequences this may have in the world, and especially how it could affect the Communist position.

Chapter 22

Other anti-natal efforts:
India and various countries

No COUNTRY has pushed an anti-natal policy further than Japan and China. But a slow progress is made, the general trends of which we shall describe, paying particular attention to India.

INDIA

There is no doubt that India is the poorest country in the world, the country where poverty is most widespread, both in the towns and the villages. Moreover, since China went over into the Communist camp, India is the most important country in the non-Communist world, with the most acute economic problem.

A few factual premisses

The population rose above 400 million in 1958. The density of 310.8 inhabitants to the square mile is about 50 per cent higher than that of France.

Growth is less rapid than in other countries, because of the very wretchedness, which causes death and perhaps also physiological sterility. But, as we have seen, poverty does not stop procreation, while people living in abject misery are enabled to live much longer today, thanks to the progress in medicine and hygiene. Moreover, a slight economic advance would cause a further reduction in the death rate, thus setting up an auto-resistance. I shall now set out the problem in more detail.

The death rate

The death rate in India is not exactly known, because many deaths are not officially registered. I must therefore make an approximate estimate. For the period 1941–51, the recorded rate was only 19.4 per 1,000; but this should be raised by more than half, which gives just under 30 per 1,000, a considerable figure, one of the highest in the world.

This death rate must go down in the next few years, even if the economic level does not improve palpably.

Here is what Mr. Gilbert Etienne has to say on the subject:[1]

> In 1952, malaria caused at least a million deaths a year, and 100 million Indians, that is nearly a third of the entire population, were affected by it. Numerous anti-malarian teams are now operating, in vast regions where entire villages are cleansed with D.D.T. According to the report on the second five-year plan (1956–61, p. 544), the struggle in the first year was conducted over an area covering about 60 million malarian inhabitants. 20 million were cured.
>
> Since D.D.T. destroys many other parasites besides the anophelous mosquitoes, it will encourage other advances in general hygiene.
>
> Besides malaria, there is tuberculosis:
>
> At the end of the first five-year plan, in 1956, 70 million people had been examined, and 25.5 million vaccinated with B.C.G. During the second plan, the entire population under 25 was to be examined and vaccinated if necessary.

The number of deaths from the plague fell from 8,230 in 1951 to 1,031 in 1954, and to 44 in 1957. This evil that spreads so much terror now belongs to the past.

Interesting though these results undoubtedly are, these various measures in a way only make a first stage. And the health policy goes further. Here is Mr. Gilbert Etienne again:

> Besides the direct struggle against diseases, there are also the indirect sanitary measures in villages and urban zones. In the "Community Projects" programmes (a system of communal rural development), great priority is

[1] *La population de l'Inde: Perspectives démographiques et alimentaires. Population,* October–December 1957.

given to the sanitization of villages: accesses to wells are being cleaned, drains are being covered, houses are more frequently whitewashed or covered with dried mud. In the towns, the struggle against slums continues, fairly slowly, for it requires much larger financial means than mass B.C.G. vaccinations or D.D.T. campaigns, but there is a distinct movement in the right direction, which has every chance of developing.

An analysis of these various factors leads us to believe that the death rate must drop much more rapidly than is foreseen by the statistical departments according to the 1951 census. Only a recurrence of the disasters that hit India between 1891 and 1921 could contradict this expectation.

In any case the death rate in this type of country cannot be judged over a short period. As we said at the beginning of this work, if the population of the world increased only very slowly between Roman times and the eighteenth century, it is because natural increase was slowed down by a high accidental death rate: wars, epidemics, famines. Public order is re-established in that country and naturally we are working on a hypothesis that peace will be maintained. Epidemics have been drastically reduced, at any rate the more murderous ones.

There remain the famines. India is not at the mercy of bad harvests and dry seasons; and these eventualities seem much less fearful than they used to be. With improved transport it is possible to relieve a threatened area fairly quickly. The world will not allow millions of men to die in too visible a manner. In a case of acute distress, neither Communists nor Capitalists would fail to help India (or any other country), if only for political reasons.

Finally we may recall that famines are only rarely caused by one bad year, but more often by an unfavourable cycle (see p. 38). A shortage that is not itself very serious compromises the sowing, leads to earlier harvesting than is wise, etc., setting up a whole process that used to be fatal but can now be avoided.

This greater solidarity (whatever its motives) and the existence of food reserves in the world allow one to hope that acute famines will soon have run their course.

Consequently the death rate, estimated at nearly 30 per 1,000 in 1951, must go down considerably. Even without any palpable improvement in the standard of living, it may fall to 20 per 1,000 in the very near future. In their prognostications, Messrs. Coale and Hoover assume that the expectation of life at birth will rise from 32 years today to 52 in 35 years, which would give a death rate of about 15 per 1,000, that is to say, that of France on the eve of the Second World War.

Birth rate and fertility

For lack of precise statistics, the birth rate must also be estimated. From 1941 to 1952, only 27 births per 1,000 inhabitants per average year were registered; but this figure must be raised by more than half, to allow for the unregistered births, which gives a birth rate of over 40 per 1,000. This is the norm of under-developed populations. The birth rate cannot have varied much since 1952.

Since it was impossible to establish detailed global statistics in this vast mass of 400 million inhabitants, partial polls and investigations were undertaken. In any case the Indians are excellent mathematicians and statisticians.

Here are the results of an investigation carried out over 1,018 women of Lucknow and Kampur, in 1956–7:[2]

These are the number of children of women over 45, according to the religion:

Hindus:		
Superior caste	7	children
Inferior caste	8.5	"
Moslems	8.4	"
Christians	5.8	"
Together	7.8	"

[2] J. N. Sinha: *Differential fertility and family limitation in an urban community of Uttar Pradesh. Population studies*, November 1957.

The number of children in the inferior classes is very high. The slight difference is more emphasized in a division according to ease of living:

Class I. Rich	6.5 children
Class II. Middle	7.2 "
Class III. Poor	8.2 "
Class IV. Very poor	8.3 "

The investigation also established the percentage of women who, at some point in their lives, resorted to contraceptive practices:

Hindus:	%			%
Superior caste	20.2	I. Rich		32.7
Inferior caste	—	II. Middle		23.3
Moslems	4.6	III. Poor		9.1
Christians	23.1	IV. Very poor		—
Together	10.6	Together		10.6

Here the differences are even more marked, contraception being relatively widespread in the superior castes or the rich classes, but unknown at the other end of the social scale.

Collective official efforts

The government is more and more determined to encourage contraception. Besides, the efforts in this direction are by no means new. In 1933, the *Conference of the Women of India* passed a resolution that the prevention of births should be included in the municipal health services. In 1938, the Congress had created a "planning commission" which proclaimed the need for spacing out births and for spreading contraceptive products.[3]

But these trends met and still meet with a strong opposition from traditionalist groups and from the followers of Ghandi. Ghandi went even further than the Catholic Church and would allow only continence for slowing down the birth rate; moreover, these modern ideas suffered from having been more or less inspired by the British occupation. Independence has gradually removed these obstacles and the ideas have made their way.

[3] See J. Sutter; *l'Eugénique,* p. 118 (Cahier No. 11, Institut National d'Etudes démographiques, Paris 1950).

Some, like the princess A. Kaur, will only admit the Ogino method. Dr. Stone carried out an experiment to that effect (see p. 203). But there is an active minority in favour of family planning by all the known methods. Demographic experts, whether they are statisticians or doctors, are agreed on this point.

The Bombay Government, which opposed positive contraception for a long time, has now opened urban and rural clinics.

The second five-year plan[4] even allows a sum of 50 million rupees (about 90,000 dollars), to open clinics for contraceptive advice. In 1958, the Minister of Public Health decided to distribute contraceptive products free in thousands of villages. In the state of Kerala, bonuses are given to people who get themselves sterilized.

Research has moreover been done on the sterilizing pill, in particular by Dr. Sanyal. In 1958 a high official stated that India needed a dozen factories to produce contraceptive pills. This somewhat vague declaration can at least be interpreted as an intention.

We should not, however, expect a rapid decrease like that of China or Japan. Contraception will spread easily only among families enjoying a certain ease and a certain cultural level. The Parsees, who are a high caste, have long ago reduced their birth rate to the level of Western populations.

Medical improvements may even, in an initial phase, cause an increase in the birth rate through the reduction of miscarriages, dead births and physiological sterility.

Forecasts

The forecasts attempted by the official census office were based on too slow a decrease in the death rate, which was bound to be surpassed. It is better to rely on the forecasts of Messrs. Coale and Hoover. If fertility were to remain constant, the population would double in 30 years, reaching 800 million just before 1990. With a birth rate diminishing from 43 to 24 per 1,000, that is to say, fairly rapidly, the popula-

[4] *Second Five Year Plan*, p. 554, Delhi, 1956.

tion would still increase by 64 per cent in the same interval of 30 years, reaching over 650 million, or double the population of Western Europe, by about the same time.

A considerable growth is to be expected in any case.

General outlook

The idea of contraception was almost non-existent twenty years ago; ten years ago it encountered strong and apparently insurmountable opposition. And yet the idea made its way, from the sheer pressure of facts and also thanks to independence, which gives a nation a sense of its responsibilities. Under British rule, it would have been easy, with a population so ignorant of demographic facts, to misrepresent any government initiative as a sort of genocide or biological war.

Even so the economic advantage that would result from a limitation of births does not solve the problem, since such a movement can only succeed in populations that have a higher economic and cultural level.

A slight economic progress has been recorded in the last few years, as we have seen. It is encouraging, but quite inadequate. This whole business, like many others, is a matter of time. It is not enough to pronounce in favour of this or that solution; one must also see to it that the solution is achieved in time. The danger is not of a famine reducing the population back to its ceiling, as it used to be, but of multiplying in abject misery which is just discreet enough not to hold the attention of or provoke help from the developed countries.

OTHER COUNTRIES

Japan, China and India represent more than 1,100 million inhabitants, about 40 per cent of the world population and more than half the "Tiers Monde" of under-developed areas. Those are the countries (together with Porto-Rico) which have made the most determined efforts to reduce their birth rate.

Nevertheless in other countries, the idea of preventing births, once entirely out of the question, is slowly making its way, under cover of feminism or the difficulties raised by the population increase.

In Egypt, for instance, Dr. Kemel Abdel Razzek, director of educational and health services, declared himself in favour of planned parenthood.

In Ceylon there exists a "Family Planning Association" and seven contraception clinics are functioning in Colombo.

In Pakistan, there is a similar movement: associations for family planning, advisory and teaching clinics, and official subsidies. In the clinics of Lahore, the number of consulting patients rose from 1,500 in 1953 to 5,695 in 1956.

The Koran makes no explicit pronouncements against contraceptive procedure, and some interpretations of the text can even sound encouraging.

Finally there are the people's republics, which are forced to react in spite of communist doctrine, because of the increasing number of clandestine abortions and the national economic difficulties resulting from them. Official preoccupation has been most marked in Poland and Yugoslavia.

The ideas therefore develop gradually under the pressure of necessity. Governments no longer show the same repugnance and are more willing to give some sort of help, as yet modest in most countries, towards the diffusion of contraceptive practices. This trend can only increase:

(a) the inadequacy of economic progress leads people to seek other means,

(b) the reduction in the death rate continues,

(c) the diffusion of knowledge slowly makes its way,

(d) the example of China will have a contagious effect.

The development of ideas does not necessarily mean a complete adoption of the "demographic solution," nor, especially, its success. Only in China and Japan has the decision taken been a large-scale one. Moreover, in the present state of contraceptive practices and of poverty among the populations in question, all the obstacles mentioned in chapters 18 and 19 will subsist. Success will be easier in the middle or leisured classes, but they represent only a small part of the population. But the movement should be followed with the greatest attention.[5]

[5] For further reading see *Population*, 1958, special number on the U.S.S.R.

Chapter 23

Communist doctrines and attitudes

I PREFER TO SPEAK of a communist doctrine, rather than a marxist doctrine, because the latter was never as explicit on the subject as the former.

Against all malthusianism

In 1947, at the United Nations Population Commission, the Soviet delegate Mr. Rabichko spoke unequivocally. "We consider any proposition formulated by this commission in favour of limiting marriages or births in wedlock as barbarous. Overpopulation is only a fruit of capitalism; an adequate social regime (socialism being understood), can meet any increase of population. It is the economy which should be adapted to the population, and not vice versa."

This view was often repeated, in almost identical terms (Malishev, Riabouchkin, etc.) at other sessions of the same commission, at the Economic and Social Council and at the World Congress on Population in Rome in 1954.

"There cannot be any surplus population under a socialist regime, in spite of rapid demographic growth," says the Great Soviet Encyclopaedia.[1]

This was certainly not the first time that the socialists attacked the malthusian concepts. For a long time, these concepts were directly inspired by the fear that property-owners felt of having to share their goods with the poor who had become too numerous. Marx and the Marxists, like others (Proudhon, etc.) assumed that overpopulation was caused by private property.

Against the "belly strike"

Nevertheless, towards the end of the nineteenth century, the

[1] Article on *Overpopulation*, vol. XXXII, 1955.

more advanced doctrinaires, socialists or anarchists, were declaring themselves in favour of birth-limitation, a sort of "belly strike" to avoid producing "cannon fodder" and "labour fodder." The great schism was already being formed on this point. Rosa Luxembourg and Klara Zetkin argued against the birth strike on the grounds that numbers were a decisive factor for the working-classes in their fight for liberty. Devaldès[2] gives two explanations for their attitude: a deep trust in providence as regards the generosity of nature, and the need to keep up the misery in order to foment the revolution. This is the classic opposition between revolution and reform: to blow up the whole thing rather than amend it. These two arguments are often transposed to an international scale.

Interior divisions

In all countries, the social democrats favour the prevention of births. Some of them even admit abortion and all are fairly broad with regard to sexual morality. Their aim is still the equality of the sexes, an ideal which often leads them to neglect the child.

Official communists took up a very different attitude. In 1950, under the auspices of U.N.E.S.C.O., P. Vincent and Alva Myrdal published their work *Are We too numerous*? in which the problem was set out scientifically on a world scale. The Soviet press treated the authors as "backward bourgeois," apparently ignorant of the fact that one of these was a communist.

In 1956, the disagreement was even clearer, for numerous communists in France, doctors particularly, declared themselves in favour of diffusing contraceptive methods, while Thorez and officialdom kept to strict orthodoxy. For the first time, *Libération* and *l'Humanité* were out of unison (see below).

I have already noted the case of China and mentioned that Poland and Yugoslavia have recently shown concern about the danger of overpopulation.

[2] *Croître et multiplier, c'est la guerre*, Paris, 1933.

With the lowering death rate, the possibility of a steady growth at the necessary rhythm becomes more and more problematic. We have reached the point when a population can increase by 3 per cent per annum and even more. An economic development may of course support such a rhythm for a little while, but not indefinitely.

How then can we explain the intransigent Soviet attitude? There are three possible explanations.

Environment, ignorance, political attitude

Any doctrine must be inspired by the environment of the doctrinaire. Everyone tends to generalize what he sees immediately around him. The Soviet Union has immense raw materials at its disposal, especially in Siberia; its territory is under-populated. Transport in particular, would be more profitable if there were a greater density, and if the means of communication were more frequently used.

Moreover, the Soviet population was reduced between 1941 and 1945, and to a very serious degree. If we assume the official results of the 1939 census and the 1956 estimate are correct, we have to conclude that the war losses rose to about 35 million, divided as follows:

Military deaths	8 to 9 million
Civilians killed by war	4 to 5 "
Civilian excess mortality	8 to 9 "
Lowered birth-rate	11 "
Emigration	3 "
Total	34 to 37 million[3]

It is hardly surprising that such a bleeding of the population should have led to strongly natalistic legislation (special decorations for "heroic mothers," etc.) and a populationist doctrine.

This environmental influence is all the more decisive in that studies in population have hardly been pushed forward

[3] Alfred Sauvy: *La population de l'Union Soviétique*, July-August-September 1956.

in the Soviet Union. Elementary facts such as ageing and the influence of composition by age-groups seem to be almost unknown by specialists, who are in any case not numerous. And all in all, the doctrinaires seem a little ingenuous in their attitude.[4]

Apart from ignorance of numerous facts there is also a very summary knowledge of capitalist doctrines: At the Commission on Population—which had at least some value as a field of confrontation—the Soviet delegates were constantly reproaching the delegates of capitalistic countries for holding static doctrines on optimum population which in fact had been abandoned for some years. To-day, as we have seen, the leading concept is that of an optimal rhythm of increase. Moreover, the search for a static optimum may well lead to

---

[4] Here are two absolutely authentic anecdotes which show the primitive elements in the Soviet position:

In 1949, in Geneva, a sub-commission on the demographic dictionary was functioning side by side with the Commission on Population. The words to be included in the dictionary were being debated. The inclusion of purely demographic terms, such as birth rate, death rate, etc., raised no objections. But then the doctrinal terms were discussed, such as "malthusianism," "prevention of births," etc. The Soviet representative protested: "We simply cannot allow such abominable words into an official United Nations dictionary." The French representative observed that the word "sin" was very likely to occur in a religious dictionary. This argument having failed, the British representative observed that the word "fascism" could hardly be left out of a dictionary of political science. After a moment of reflexion, the Soviet representative approved, thus: "Agreed, but only on condition that the definition should be written by an anti-fascist." The manichean position is incontestable.

In 1950, the question of the statistical definition of the living child came up. The question has been pending ever since the origins of the civil state, and is not without importance, for the statistics of birth, and especially of infant mortality are not always comparable from one country to another, at least not without the appropriate correctives. Dr. Pascua, representing the World Health Organization, read out the definition suggested by this organization. It was precisely worded, and contained the terms "matrix" and "expulsion." The Soviet representative was indignant over this "veterinary style," and strongly objected to the use of such bestial expressions with regard to the human species.

the conclusion that an increase in population is necessary, as is the case in France.[5] This ignorance can itself be easily explained:

It is not surprising that research has not been much encouraged on a problem which did not exist in the initial doctrine. And whereas the researches on physical sciences or the sciences called exact sciences can be pushed, in such a regime, without risk and even with profit, it is extremely adventurous for a researcher to lead the way in the social sciences, since he runs the risk of being alone and unfollowed, should he disprove some well-established political doctrine. Even if there were no particular official line to be feared, there is still a certain inhibition that bars all progress: it is better to rely on pure science and hope that it will produce the economic benefits.

For many advanced doctrinaires, it would be enough to change the word "Providence" in the populationist doctrines based on divine goodness ("Behold the fowls of the air . . . your heavenly Father feedeth them"), and replace it with the expression "scientific progress," to get a conformist text.

Finally there is the attitude the communists have often been reproached with, not only by conservatives, but by social democrats and anarchists like Devaldès:

"Misery must be kept up, the pressure must be maintained in the boiler until it bursts." This attitude is transposed to an international scale today. The problem of the social classes has faded before that of Nations, whether colonized or not. The most unenlightened American worker knows that his wage is twenty or thirty times higher than that of the Burmese or the Egyptian. Any English labourite knows that Malaya is a mine of dollars which the United Kingdom needs.

This revolt of the under-developed countries, which crystallized at the congresses of Bandung and Cairo, is carefully nurtured by the Soviet Union. The classical attitude is thus maintained on the international scale: blow up capitalism first

[5] With regard to France we should mention that in 1950 the Soviet delegate put forward the name of Paul Reboux as one of the chiefs of the French demographic school.

and then see. The Soviet Union has never expressed regret for the excessive birth rate of an under-developed country, it is poverty that is denounced and blamed on capitalism only.

It might be objected that the Soviet worker's wage, though by no means equal to that of the American, is considerably higher than that of the workers in under-developed countries. Does not the U.S.S.R. run the risk of having to impoverish itself one day in order to help the poverty-stricken masses?

I think this objection has some validity, but it has none whatsoever in the Marxist perspective; pushing the transposition of the national to the international a little further, we can see the U.S.S.R. playing the role held by the communist intellectual in a capitalist country. Personally, he enjoys better conditions than a worker, but he thinks that capitalism must be overcome. The redistribution of wealth will in any case lead to a levelling upwards, not a levelling down. The U.S.S.R. (like the salaried intellectual with the workers) has concentrated on avoiding "production relationships" with the under-developed countries. Outside trade is slight, the loans granted are so liberal they are more of a gift than real loans with interest rates. Besides, the difficulties between debtor and creditor begin only when the balance of accounts is reversed, and the creditor no longer accepts or is no longer in a position to grant new credits. The U.S.S.R. is in the splendid period of international transactions.

The Chinese obstacle

It is more then, a question of attitude than of true doctrine; but this position has been compromised by the policy of the Chinese People's Republic. For here are orthodox communists asserting the possibility and even the existence of a durable overpopulation in a socialist regime, and assuming that the realization of plans for the improvement of well-being is illusory if the population continues to increase at a rhythm of 2.5 per cent per annum. The Chinese position was good. Impossible to continue animal prolificity once death is more effectively fought. But this is precisely what capitalist demographers have been saying over and over again since the war, whether their beliefs were frankly "malthusian" or whether they favoured a certain slight increase in the population.

There will always be some way out; communist countries, they will say, do not struggle against overpopulation, but for the liberation of women.

This skilful position allows a transition. Nevertheless the planning of the regime is the least advanced as regards forecasts. Ageing phenomena are more or less unstudied. The Soviets will sooner or later have to drop their traditional distrust of demography.

Advantage to communism?

But let us look further: I will assume that in ten years, the Chinese Republic, whether or not recognized by the United States, and her satellites, has succeeded in reducing her birth rate by half, according to the present plans, or at any rate by a large proportion, while India and other countries are still burdened by the weight of their own exuberance. Communism could then announce that it alone has contained a fearful evil that had been denounced in vain by a capitalist system incapable of curing it.

And by an irony of history—one has ceased to count them—the communist regime would draw an advantage out of an error and would boast of having conquered a social evil, the very existence of which it had denied.

Soviet growth

It remains to be seen whether the Soviet Union will accept the thesis of an optimal rhythm of growth for itself, and whether it will look favourably on a slow-down of its present growth. This being of 1.5 per cent per annum, the demographic investments must represent about 6 per cent of the population. But given the low density and the wealth of the natural environment, this figure of 6 per cent may be considered as a maximum. I will assume a figure of 5 per cent; it is not an insupportable burden, especially if the expense of armament is reduced and if methods are found to build mass housing.

But the birth rate might go down spontaneously from the effect of development itself, and especially the diffusion of culture. It has already come down to 12 or 13 per 1,000 in Leningrad, that is, to a level half as low as in the U.S.S.R. as a whole. What will the official attitude then be: resignation or reaction?

The question is already current: official abortion has been readmitted and family allowances have not been maintained at the level of 1944. As regards abortion, the measure is apparently only aimed at directing and improving the conditions for practices which had spread spontaneously. But the great birth fever of 1944 has certainly fallen.

The spread of clandestine abortion has led to a reaction in favour of contraception. In December 1957, the U.S.S.R. invited Dr. Stone, the American specialist and propagandist, to demonstrate his methods. Madam Kovriguina, Minister of Public Health, denounced the gynaecological troubles caused by abortions and showed the need for active research into contraceptive methods, which had to be effective, satisfying and inoffensive.

Even so, propaganda continues in a natalistic direction.

On the 7th February 1955, Mr. Khrushchev spoke to young people who were about to leave to colonize new territories:

"A man who founds a family is a good citizen. Our country will become all the stronger with a more numerous population. The bourgeois ideologists have adopted anthropophagous theories, among which is the theory of overpopulation. They ask great questions on how to reduce the birth rate and reduce the growth of the population. With us, comrades, the problem is quite different. If another 200 million were added to the 200 million which we already number, it would be very little!"

He then justified the tax on bachelors and childless families:

". . . If each family has only one or two children, the population will not increase, it will decline. But the development of society is our concern. That is why a family must have three children and all will be well!

Some people ask: why should a man who has two children or even none pay the tax? This is why. In our country, there are people who do not marry or who have no children when they do marry; we will not ask why. But such people live in society and benefit from all the good that society puts at their disposal. Then the man grows old. Who then will look after him when he will have lost the capacity to work?"

These words are already five years old, but there has been no perceptible change on this question.

The argument about old-age pensions deserves attention. It is not only new in the Soviet doctrine on population, but it is not very well understood in capitalist countries. Relying on the legal and financial aspect, most people believe that the pension is earned because it is written down in all the accounts and legal documents. The socialist perspective emphasizes the fundamental fact much more clearly: whatever the nature of their rights, inactive people live on a deduction from the production of the active people.

The very vigour with which the tax on bachelors and the populationist doctrine are defended by the rulers would be enough to suggest that the limitation of families is spreading gradually. The phenomenon is probably most marked in the towns.

Communist attitude in capitalist countries

Although this book is devoted to under-developed countries, the Marxist doctrine on contraception, or rather the communist attitude to it, in Western European countries is by no means irrelevant.

The schism between what one may call the right-wing intellectual and the main party has been even clearer, in effect, than over the repression of Hungary.

The quarrel began in France, over a book called *Des enfants malgré nous*, by J. Derogy, member of the Communist Party. His arguments in favour of freedom in contraceptive matters found complete support from socialist circles, and also from intellectuals in the Communist Party. But Mr. Thorez and Jeannette Vermeersch replied in the name of pure dogma "against the reactionary neo-malthusianism" (see especially *l'Humanité*, 2nd May 1956). Among the arguments were the following:

(*a*) The condemnation of Vogt's malthusian book, *La Faim du monde*, and of Vogt's disciples.

(*b*) The need for a sufficient birth rate. "A country that has stopped having children, a country consisting of a growing population of old men, would be a country without a future, a condemned country. We have other ambitions for France."

Mr. Thorez addressed himself to Mr. J. Derogy direct, in the following words:

". . . Instead of getting your inspiration from the ideologists of the greater and lesser bourgeoisie, you might perhaps have done better to ponder on the article that Lenin devoted to neo-malthusianism, in which, with his usual clairvoyance, he defined the position of communists, as Marx and Engels had done in their day when they too were struggling against the theories of Malthus.

The petty bourgeois, Lenin writes, despairs of his future, and seeks salvation in the limitation of births. The worker, however, knows that his class will triumph; therefore he is the most bitter opponent of neo-malthusianism. He struggles that his children may be happier, and with his battles he prepares their victory.

While stigmatizing the repressive laws of the bourgeoisie which hit the unfortunate and demand their abolition, the communists condemn the reactionary concepts of those who advocate the limitation of births and thus seek to turn the workers away from their battle for bread and for socialism. 'Birth control' cannot assure young couples of their lodgings; it cannot give a mother of a family the means to bring up her children decently.

. . . We are fighting that all women may know the joys of maternity in the best possible conditions, we are opposed to the regime that condemns them to hunger, piles them up in slums, drives them to abortion. . . .

All the same, the Communist Party was unwilling to take up the same position as the Catholic Right and therefore proposed a law which authorized official abortion in certain conditions, though it condemned the diffusion of contraceptive practices. The difference is in fact an important one: for while it is difficult to limit and to localize contraceptive practices, abortion can remain the instrument of a well defined policy; moreover, official abortion means that clandestine abortion can be fought more rigorously.

Another work appeared at about the same time, *L'Epouvantail malthusien*, under the signature of Jean Fréville, conforming to the purest orthodoxy. The conclusion is, in fact, as follows: "In a classless society that will provide work for everyone, and will adapt production to its needs, there will be neither relative overpopulation, nor absolute overpopulation" (p. 302).

But in the introduction to the work, no doubt written later, the difficulties with regard to China, the density factor and the high birth rate, are taken into account. Demographic policy, it is emphasized, must follow local conditions. There is an allusion, moreover, to the "harmonious family." Some reflexion seems to have occurred between the work and its introduction.

The Chinese conversion is gradually forcing marxism to change its position, and to tone down judgments too visibly inspired by the desire to fight capitalist malthusianism, and also to insist on certain aspects which until then had only been evoked with the most extreme discretion.

An exchange of views[6]

Here I should mention another statement of position, more recent and less brutal than the official declarations to the United Nations. When the review *Voprossi Filossofi* asked me for an article on "the relationship between demography and social sciences in capitalist countries," I wrote this article specially for Soviet readers, and insisted on the strictly accurate and whole reproduction of my text.

[6] *Population*, 1958, special number on the U.S.S.R.

My conditions were respected, and the article appeared in January 1958, together with a critique by Mr. Arab-Ogly. The critique was very courteous in manner and very severe in matter. The author had unfortunately not always understood the full meaning of the propositions he was analysing. The desire to condemn capitalism *en bloc* is so strong that the nuances within its function are difficult to seize. For naturally if an author shows that there may be some dispositions in a capitalist regime that are more favourable than others, he is suggesting or admitting the possibility of a certain *reformism* which is contrary to revolutionary doctrine.

In spite of these misunderstandings, the attempt must be made again. It would have been surprising if one article had proved sufficient to modify opinions that are mostly dogmatic. The mere fact that a dialogue was begun may lead to more fruitful exchanges. But the Western communists are the missing link in the chain. They are the ones who ought to ensure communication so that disagreements can be localized; unfortunately their fear of being taxed with heresy keeps them in the wholly optimistic paths.

Chapter 24

The developed populations

ALTHOUGH THIS WORK is essentially about rapidly increasing countries that are hit or threatened by over-population, indeed, that might actually be stifled by their own birth rate, some attention must also be paid to the developed populations, especially to those already fairly populated European countries. A few indications have already been given in chapter 6; here we shall deal with the main characteristics.

High density, slight growth

The high density has been counter-balanced by intense development; moreover the demographic growth is slow from now on, while the standard of living rises steadily. So that it has been said: there are two sorts of populations, those where riches increase but not men, the others where men increase but not riches.

Towards 1950, however, there were cries of alarm on the over-population of Western Europe, especially in Germany and Austria, which were invaded with refugees and "displaced persons." England, too, was threatened, after the second war. The population of this country, even more than that of others, had been based on the domination of the world under various forms. It was feared therefore that the loss of colonies, of markets, of property, etc., would put these countries in a difficult position by producing surplus population.

Gradually, however, these threats diminished and unemployment was held in check. Even in Northern Italy the situation improved. France took in 300,000 Algerians and could take in many more, if need be, its territory being so under-populated.

Holland (see chapter 6) is in fact the only developed country to suffer from a certain absolute over-population; a very relative situation in any case, which leaves the inhabitants with a much higher standard of living than that of under-developed countries.

If France knew how to discern its own interest, it could moreover provide numerous working opportunities for the inhabitants of neighbouring countries.

Over-population is therefore almost non-existent among developed populations; but another danger threatens them, or, more exactly, they are already infected by another evil, namely ageing.

Ageing

This is usually the name given to the increase in the proportion of aged persons in the population. The proportion of 6 or 7 sexagenarians per 100 inhabitants is a constant, a norm in countries of high fertility, which we find in present-day under-developed populations as well as in eighteenth-century France or England. This proportion has risen to 15 or 16 per cent and will reach 20 per cent in several countries by 1980.

Stronger still, is the increase in the proportion of the very old, who are nearly all totally inactive and even have to be looked after. For every 100 Frenchmen there were less than 4 octogenarians in about 1789, today there are 18, that is, four and a half times more.

This is a remarkable psychological case: The most ancient and durable phenomenon, which is also the best measured and the easiest to foresee is almost unknown to public opinion, even to enlightened opinion. Why? Because it is regarded as "unpleasant" information, which should not be propagated.[1]

But here is another curious fact: ageing as a phenomenon is little known by the public, as opinion polls show. And more: if you inform someone of this fact, tell him that the proportion of old people has strongly increased, and ask him why, even the most enlightened person will reply that it is the effect of penicillin and medical advance, in other words, the lowering death rate. This seems so much "like common

[1] For lack of space I cannot here develop the precise sense of the word "unpleasant," but the reader may like to follow this up in my essay *L'opinion publique* (P.U.F. Collection *Que sais-je?*).

sense" that expert demographers believed it for a long time and some remain unconvinced to this day. But the works of J. Bourgeois-Pichat, L. Tabah, L. Henry, etc., have shown decisively that the decline in mortality has saved more young people than old ones, and that although it has increased the number of old people it has not increased their *proportion*. Hence the common illusion. And by a paradox which becomes less mysterious on examination, the actual effect of the lengthening of life has rather been a rejuvenation.

Ageing has widespread material and moral repercussions. The material ones chiefly concern the increase of inactive old people and, more concretely, the problem of old-age pensions, which is much misunderstood and studied but superficially, again on account of its "unpleasant" character. But the moral repercussions are even less known. The loss of vitality is felt only in the long run; that is why it has affected France before other countries.

The burden on the active population

The question has already been mentioned in chapter 6; ageing increases the cost of non-activity. I shall begin by measuring the intensity of the phenomenon.

In these countries, taken as a whole—Germany, France, England, Italy, Holland, Belgium—the active population is to increase by 2.5 per cent from 1957 to 1980, whereas the whole population will increase by 5.5 per cent and the inactive population by 7.5 per cent. The increase is three times faster than that of the active population.

The number of active young people is going down, but because of the lengthening of education, the number of inactive young people will still go up. No counterbalance, therefore, is to be found here, on the contrary.

The essential role will be played by the aged inactive people, for their number is to increase by about 30 per cent in less than a generation. Thus the active persons whose number will have increased by 2.5 per cent will have to bear a burden increased by 30 per cent.

In England at that moment, there will be two inactive aged

persons supported by five active persons, if the legislation on pensions remains the same as it is.

Moreover, ageing will take place even within the active population, so that the number of workers over 40 will increase to the detriment of the number of workers under 40.

All these hypotheses could in any case be very much eclipsed by reality if the struggle against senile death were to enter a successful phase (the cure of cancer, for example, to which we shall return later).

The transfer

This increasing burden of inactive persons hardly moves public opinion at all; first they try to deny its existence with every conceivable argument. Some rely on a faulty financial prospect and assert that there is no burden. When old people build up capital or a pension fund, they say, there is wealth and so no problem. This is to confuse rights with facts, morals with practice. Any inactive person is paid for by the active ones, whatever the legal form of the deductions made (income, rent, social security, etc.). The only exception concerns the durable goods collected by the person (furniture, linen, books, etc., and, possibly, the house).

According to one very widespread argument, technical progress enables or will enable us to meet the increasing costs. The argument is only valid for a collectivist regime (and even so, ageing means that less is earned for the producers). In a capitalist regime, the argument is invalid because it neglects the behaviour of the active person and, in particular, the "psychology of the fraction" and that of the transfer.

If, tomorrow, the number of aged inactive people rises from 25 to 35 per 100 active people, the relationship of incomes between active and inactive will have to be maintained (pensions, for example, represent 60 per cent of wages); and a larger deduction will have to be made from the income of the active persons—21 per cent instead of 15 per cent. Such transfers are not made easily. The tendency is to assure workers of a kind of productivity-dividend. In other words, active persons want to relate their income to their production.

The same difficulties recur, in fact, at a higher level.

Thus, the ageing of the population sets problems of redistribution between active and inactive persons, however high the level of wealth produced, however developed the technical progress.

If cancer disappeared

Until now, the lowering birth rate has been, as we saw, the only cause of demographic ageing. But nothing proves it will always be so. A reduction in the number of births will always have the effect of amputating the base in the pyramid of age groups, but it could also happen that the lowering death rate might also push in the same direction, swelling the top of the pyramid without palpably changing the base. Infant mortality can hardly change more than it already has, but senile mortality is an important and almost virgin field.

If cancer were conquered, or even arteriosclerosis, the number and proportion of old people could increase rapidly and considerably, especially the proportion of the very old, over 80, who are entirely paid for by collectivity. Very delicate problems would then arise, soluble of course, as long as the developed populations still have wealth that is ill-used or wasted, but provoking violent controversies as soon as the innovation destroys existing institutions, which happens whenever there is progress.

Moreover, a grave danger would appear, disguised as a false solution! The European populations would be tempted to act as they have acted already: maintaining both their total population and the total of inactive persons, and counterbalancing by a reduction of the young, that is, by a lowering birth rate. This apparent equilibrium obviously covers up a tragic decline. The piece of coal retains its weight and even its brightness as it burns, until the moment when it suddenly collapses into ashes. This risk is often forgotten by a Europe gripped with other worries, but it ought to be much more studied.

The birth rate

Even without such an eventuality, which is as yet problematic, the question of the birth rate might well be reconsidered by this heedless Europe, which is so much concerned about its standard of living, and so little about its chances of survival.

In 1935, some exceedingly pessimistic prognostications were made; terrible calculations showed that if the past trends continued, the population of most countries in Western Europe was doomed to decline and to a severe ageing. This forecast was too pessimistic, as we know today, because it was inspired by economic conditions which, all in all, could not last for ever. With full employment and a few measures in favour of the family, the renewal of generations is once again assured in Western Europe as a whole, and this, together with the lengthening of life, will give a certain increase for a generation at least.

After this hollow followed by a bump, will the secular tendency towards a lowering birth rate start again?

In certain social classes, such as the comfortable middle classes, the lowest point seems to have been reached. The economic factors which weighed so heavily may of course still play their part. On a purely economic level, the ideal optimum would be the childless family. But other factors are there. The need for affection, the desire for paternity, induce nearly all families to want a child. The second child is often also wanted, for various reasons: the desire to have a boy (or a girl), to avoid the inconveniences of having an only child, the desire for balance; but quite often even the second child is born without being actually wanted.

With the third child, these positive forces subsist in a much weaker form, while the economic and other worries increase: housing, education, and various expenses, take a more important place, so much so that in most cases the third birth is not positively desired.

But the belief that maternity is always positively desired or refused (see chapter 19), is a fundamental error only too frequently made by propagandists of contraception. If the conditions of life are not too hard, the family lets children come, by simply relaxing the tough precautions taken to postpone the birth. Consequently, it is not certain that the lowest point has been reached even in these classes. Technical progress in contraception or even in abortion may gradually reduce the number of births that occur without being positively wanted. I shall return to this question in the next chapter.

All the more reason then, to expect a lowering birth rate in the less developed social classes. The rural exodus transforms a relatively prolific peasant family into a family of workers or clerks, with a more malthusian behaviour. The lengthening of education, even when free, further emphasizes and prolongs the cost to the family.

Freedom of conception

In some countries, Protestant ones especially, all contraceptive products are sold freely (in so far as they are not considered harmful) and all medical advice about them is authorized.

A couple or a woman alone may then try to have the number of children they want by taking advantage of existing techniques.

This freedom is in fact part of the liberal and democratic spirit, each person having the right to do what does not harm others.

This very solid position, however, has raised several objections: leaving aside confessional questions (in particular, Catholic objections), there are the following:

(*a*) The demographic objection. It is essential for society or the national group to ensure its survival. One might retort that society only has to assure advantages to the family, or rather, sufficient compensation, and plenty of children will be born. But since society always calculates very meanly. it prefers to have undesired children than to pay the price of fully desired children. This is pure social hypocrisy, which contraception propagandists rightly emphasize, though unfortunately they neglect to ask at the same time and with the same vigour for pro-family measures as well as the free diffusion of contraceptive practices.

(*b*) Full freedom of conception is not yet with us. The propaganda leads people to believe that perfect procedures exist. This can produce an excessive trust in the virtue of present techniques, and a revival of abortion, as in Japan.

(c) Difficulties arising out of misunderstood freedom. Many young couples postpone the birth of a first or second child and then, having become sterile, are eaten up with regret. The psychophysiological equilibrium of the family is not assured till after the third child. Many are the trials and tribulations undergone by inexperienced couples.

These last two objections are not decisive. Marriage has never been made compulsory on the pretext that the bachelor might later regret his bachelor state. There is therefore no reason to control the freedom of couples. But advice should be given, to guard against the only too frequent carelessness of users.

Severe ageing

A new wave of ageing, arising from the possible cure of cancer or other senile diseases, would have its effects in various directions.

From a strictly materialistic point of view, the adult population would tend to refuse the surplus burden, and this would lead to a reduction in the burden of the young; this compensation may occur within the family budget itself, or in the accounts of social security. Already today family allowances are constantly being reduced in France (in buying power and in proportion to wages), although the budget is on the surplus side, because it is used to make up the deficits caused by sickness and old age.

In this way, after being the result of the lowering birth rate, old age might well become the cause of it; and since all reduction of the birth rate *ipso facto* leads to further ageing, the process would be continuous.

Of course, populations hit in this way would react sooner or later. But they might not have the necessary vitality and the reaction might come too late.

These demographic questions always embarrass the developed countries. In a way, they are disagreeable. Demographic phenomena are slow and therefore not well known. And because they are not well known, their consequences appear discreetly, until the time when a big sacrifice is necessary to cope with reality.

The equilibrium of populations can only be assured by a certain degree of social hypocrisy: society being niggardly, it relies on family affection, sometimes on ignorance, to resolve the most important problem, namely the survival of its own collectivity.

Attempts at awareness are very rare; and England was all the more praiseworthy when it created the Royal Commission on Population, which examined the problems with great attention. But the Commission passed away and the problems remain.

Attitude towards non-developed countries

The great capitalist powers have been hit in two ways by the growth of non-developed populations.

(a) The general revolt of colonized or dominated countries was fed or reinforced by the demographic growth, a deep and underground phenomenon which is always under-estimated.

(b) The fear of excessive growths has inspired malthusian ideas. These are invoked in the very title of this work, and have inspired all the biological research to find a sterilizing pill. But as we have seen, it is a very delicate business to try and express these malthusian ideas with regard to other populations, and they are more or less doomed to failure in the case of countries that are not yet self-governing.

Finally, I must repeat, it is absurd that an excessive exuberance in this or that far country should produce fear and malthusian reactions with regard to its own birth rate in a country that already has a low fertility. Such primitive reactions show a strange lack of self-knowledge.

Chapter 25

The sterilizing pill

DURING THE LAST FEW YEARS, laboratory researches have been made to find a substance which in small doses would ensure the partial sterilization of the man, and especially, of the woman. The discovery of such a product could be extremely important and would completely change the whole problem of contraception. To this end, a substance would have to satisfy three conditions:

(*a*) It must be totally harmless apart from its temporary sterilizing effect.

(*b*) It must be convenient to take, for example, as a pill (and not as an injection).

(*c*) It must be moderate in price.

Present state of research[1]

There are four methods of affecting the physiology of reproduction by direct action on the organism:

(1) Action on the male reproductive cells (formation or migration).

(2) Action on the female reproductive cells (formation or migration).

(3) Action on the fertility process itself, including the constitution of new cells.

(4) Action on the initial development of the embryo.

The first procedure means action on the man, the other three on the woman. The first three are of a kind to prevent conception, the last is abortive, which is why it is more likely than the others to raise moral and religious obstacles.

---

[1] Some of the facts that follow are taken from Dr. Jean Sutter's *A la recherche de la pilule stérilisante. Population*, July–September 1957. See also Dr. Logroua-Weill-Halle, *De la liberté de la conception à l'étranger*, Paris, 1958.

The researches have mostly been undertaken in India (Nag, Sanyal, Chosh) and in the United States (Pincus, Sieve, Nelson, Wilkins, Stone, etc.), but also, apparently, in Germany and the Soviet Union.

Until 1955, it was the fourth procedure which seemed most likely to succeed. But in 1956 and 1957 the researches of Pincus and his collaborators began to throw new light on the second and possibly the third.

The progesterone treatment, in injections or by mouth (Pincus) seems to have given conclusive results. The sterilization achieved with the women treated was followed by several pregnancies after the treatment had stopped.

The rumour even spread, in August 1957, that the battle had been won, that the products would soon be on sale in the United States. But less favourable news filtered through later.

Everyone knows how cautious any experimentation must be. Results as conclusive as those of Sieve, from the action of phosphorylated hesperidin on three hundred men, cannot have been reproduced by other researchers. With the human species, not only must confirmation be obtained by counter-experiment, but one must be certain that no physiological trouble will appear at the end.

Pincus has tried other bodies related to progesterone as well as non-steroids (cirantine, meta-xylohydroquinone, already tried by Sanyal, etc.), with positive results.

Other experiments (Thiersch) have used antihormones, antibodies and antimetabolites (azaserine, etc.). But this is for the fourth procedure.

Possible consequences

As often happens, discovery goes in leaps and bounds, capriciously, with alternating hope and disappointment which do not facilitate prognostication. But assuming for a moment that a sterilizing product satisfying the conditions given at the beginning of the chapter will be discovered and launched fairly soon, what will follow?

We must distinguish the developed from the under-devel-

oped countries which are in general over-populated and increasing too rapidly. First the latter:

The under-developed countries

Without positively desiring to have many children, poor and
ignorant couples do not have the material or moral "means"
to resort to the contraceptive practices which are known at
present. The appearance of a sterilizing pill would considerably change the situation by inverting the order of desires; it
would be enough not to want children for that negative wish
to be implemented. An intense propaganda would in any
case be made, either for commercial or for political reasons,
and funds would be devoted to the diffusion of the product.

In spite of forgetfulness and wrong usage, the pill would
certainly reduce the birth rate of these countries. By how
much? It is very difficult to say, for the changes would be
numerous and beyond our experience. In any case, the lowering would be gradual, and this would enable governments
to examine the situation and to take the appropriate action.

This lowering would at first have favourable economic
effects: people would be better fed and production would
benefit from this. New problems would come up, of course,
but the vicious circle of poverty and numbers would be
broken.

The developed countries

In the developed countries, quite a large number of children
are born without having been positively desired. The sterilizing pill would enable couples, not of course to order their
births according to a pre-established plan, but to prevent or
postpone any unwanted birth. How far would this method
reduce the number of births? Here again, the question is
very delicate. But a reduction of 10 to 20 per cent is quite
possible.

In countries with a very low birth rate like Sweden, where
there is total freedom in contraceptive matters, or in Wallonia,
the lowering would of course be less significant than in countries like Poland or even France. But even in these countries

there has been some development of abortion; legal abortion has been authorized for social reasons in Sweden, in precise ratio to the spread of clandestine abortion. And we can be pretty sure that not all women who have conceived without positive desire resort to this solution.

According to the Indianapolis investigation, which was the most widespread ever made and with perfectly efficient methods, on the effects of contraception, the fertility of relatively fecund couples has probably been reduced by 17 per cent.

Now this concerns contracepting couples who are already entirely free to resort to all the classic contraceptive methods. In a country like France, or Belgium, or even Germany, the reduction would be greater, about 20 or 25 per cent.

In fact, the sterilizing pill would strongly reduce the number of abortions and lead to a considerable—and dangerous—lowering of the birth rate.

Such a lowering would once again compromise the maintenance of populations, and this time it would be in a dramatic and spectacular way. Several countries would have a large deficit (Germany, England, Belgium, Sweden, etc.), and Western Europe as a whole would plunge even further into the ageing process.

To restore the balance, great increases in maternity and family aids would have to be granted, and these are costly measures, difficult to impose on an aged population very much attached to its standard of living.

Another consequence of family planning would be the irregularity of births from one year to another. Favourable periods, with full employment, would be marked by numerous births and followed by hollow periods, which would cause durable and inconvenient dents in the pyramid of age groups.

The "moral" point of view

I do not here intend to touch on what is properly called morality, nor on the viewpoints of the various religions.

It is from a strictly pragmatic and utilitarian point of view that I am entering such a controversial debate.

When mankind suddenly has to face the danger of a continuous sliding-down, it looks for footholds, or stopping points that must be as clear as possible.

In the matter of births, there are two clear discontinuities: conception and birth. The first is clearer than the second— at least for biology, and contrary to appearances. From the moment the gametes unite, new chromosomes are formed and, consequently, a new living being.

The second discontinuity differentiates abortion from infanticide. Many countries have become less and less hostile to abortion and even organize it officially, without showing the slightest indulgence towards infanticide. A purely pragmatic reasoning might, however, lead to exactly the opposite conclusion:

When the child is born alive, it is possible to judge whether it is ill-formed and, therefore, to act less blindly than in abortion. But not only are the parents' dispositions already playing their part (the mother has suffered, she loves), but also the fear of sliding (where would the massacre of innocents stop?) which makes any man's life sacred.

It is quite obvious that morality will develop with technique and with biological discovery. If abortion is already less condemned than it used to be, it is not only because the religious spirit has weakened, but also because of medical progress and the almost complete disappearance of childbirth infections, thanks to antibiotics.

An impossible ban

The sterilizing pill will raise a fearful problem for religions, and especially for the catholic religion, as well as for some governments that are resolutely anti-malthusian. But though religion could, in certain cases, exercise enough authority over its faithful, no law would be strong enough to forbid the pill, no frontier too closely guarded to prevent it from filtering through. Very soon the partisans of the pill would have a fine time demonstrating that it is much better to produce the pill officially inside the country than to lose duties or risk the introduction of ill-controlled and possibly harmful products. Even in a completely closed economy public opinion would exercise a strong and efficient pressure; the only obstacle the pill would in fact meet is the doubt that would subsist for a time as to its harmlessness.

Transition

In any case, the pill will not burst forth "like thunder in a serene sky." Not only will numerous trials and even years of waiting be necessary before its harmlessness can be quite certain, but there will also be reticence among the public: rumours will run wild, as with any product, so that its diffusion will be only gradual. Governments will therefore have time to change their legislation and to restore upset balances. But minds develop so slowly in demographic matters that legislation is usually too late.

Other biological discoveries may be made; but since I have no desire to launch out into science fiction, I have been content to describe some of the possible effects of a change which is already envisaged; these effects are so considerable that they might well, one day, completely alter the problem of what we call world population.

PART 4
SUMMARY AND CONCLUSION

Chapter 26

Summary and conclusion

HAVING REACHED the end of this exploration, I ought perhaps to formulate some judgment, which could simply be one of observation with an outline of the developments to be expected. But we must go further than that, and indicate the actions to be taken by the actors in this vast drama, so charged with hopes and dangers.

Abnormal vitality

The salient fact, as we have seen, is the divergence of rhythm between the means of giving life and the means of supporting it. Since medical progress spreads faster than economic progress, part of mankind runs the risk of becoming the victim of its own exuberance. A so-called under-developed country, with the death rate that Western people had half a century ago, the standard of living the West had under the Revolution and the birth rate of the Western middle ages, finds it difficult not only to follow in the path once covered by the developed countries, but also to emerge from its own millenary poverty, which can no longer be regarded as a durable norm.

Against all logic, the poorest countries have much heavier generative burdens than the rich countries. Natural fertility doubles the population in each generation.

Now, a population which doubles with each generation must more than double its production in the same time, or else reduce its rhythm of growth by controlling the careless generosity with which it gives life. These are what we have called the economic solution (part 2) and the demographic solution (part 3).

Risks and rigours of the purely economic solution

The "economic" solution assumes a considerable effort and indubitably relies (for all countries) on outside aid. It is not only a question of over-population in the static sense, as is so often supposed, but of *speed of growth*. Even a rich country would find it extremely tough to have to meet a doubling in each generation, particularly with regard to education and housing.

Countries which still have vast natural resources in reserve, like South America, manage to keep up or even to raise their standard of living. In the Far East, the results are less encouraging and the future looks dark.

In any case, even if these countries manage to keep their head above water, even if poverty can be reduced, there still remains the danger of a growing divergence between countries of unequal development, with all the political consequences of such a divergence.

Never have men been so near and so far from each other at one and the same time; the era in which means of communication are multiplying, distances shrinking, Nations uniting in a communal organization, and the slightest difficulty in any point of the globe resounds in all its parts, is also the era in which men are more unequal than ever before nature, and in their needs, and in life.

Illusions about the "demographic" solution

With all these difficulties, countries are one by one turning to the second solution: the prevention of births, the voluntary limitation of the family. This question provokes, almost everywhere, the sharpest misunderstandings as well as the most profound errors; on economic questions, there are of course numerous divergences on the priorities to be established, but all voices, even the least expert, agree on the necessity for investments and improvements, that is, long-term efforts. The prevention of births, however, produces puerile and passionate reactions.

First, a prognostication: the reduction of births will happen anyway, some day and somehow. The conflict is not about the probability of this certain event, but about its date, the form it will take and the question of whether it should be encouraged.

The most common error consists in thinking that a mere

law or decree will solve the problem. More than one French-man gets out of the difficulties of Algerian development with the mere phrase "birth control," which betrays an almost total ignorance as well as a strong desire to be rid of an awk-ward problem which might well dictate a political solution very different from the one he hopes for.

And in fact, malthusian propagandists have regarded this demographic solution particularly as a means of eluding economic difficulties. Like Malthus, their main concern is to avoid a painful sharing out of riches.

This over-direct and interested propaganda has slowed down the development of awareness about the problem more than it has advanced it. In these poor countries, it is experi-ence and economic concern which first lead intellectuals, then responsible politicians, to envisage some action in favour of family planning. But economic concern is never uppermost in a period of political tension. Here then is one policy that can be recommended to the developed countries, or, more exactly, to the great powers: they should calm the trouble spots instead of stirring them up.

The success of contraceptive propaganda among the ignor-ant and unlettered masses is at present over-estimated. The example of Japan is fairly eloquent.

Both solutions necessary

The economic solution is not enough, and the demographic solution demands a preliminary or at least a simultaneous, economic development. Both solutions must therefore be studied and envisaged.

An intense economic effort means a real social revolution inside the country, with the consumption of secondary neces-sities being replaced, in money, in products, in men, by in-tense investments to develop the land and instruct the people. If, in the leisured classes or the developed countries, the chief object of the birth-prevention policy was to contract out of the duty to human solidarity, it might lead to a dangerous and dramatic situation.

The question of knowing whether the prevention of births should be encouraged must be put more clearly. The religious or civic customs and traditions of any given country cannot be ignored. In any case there are some humane methods of encouraging the prevention of births, such as the diffusion of general instruction, the teaching of child-care, etc., which remove or soften the propaganda's hardness of heart, and even ferocity, which are only too often present even in the best intentioned persons.

Mr. Pierre Gourou, who has written such remarkable books on tropical countries, has made similar observations, and shown that under-developed countries need not necessarily follow the aims and the exact stages of present developed countries, but simply orientate themselves towards cultural progress.

The developed countries

What are the rich and developed countries doing to face this rising poverty? Some, in the Anglo-Saxon trend, try to stop it with propaganda in favour of the limitation of births; others, following the u.s.s.r., intend to use this eruptive force to blow up capitalism, which is doubly engaged in the adventure since the countries in question are (with the exception of China, North Korea and North Vietnam) under a regime of private property and the capitalist countries still have powerful interests in those regions.

So here again, a century later and on a much vaster scale, we come across the conflict between Marx and Malthus.

The calculations of both camps are niggardly and unedifying. Helping under-developed countries but confining one's help to war subsidies and malthusian advice is tragically puerile. Trying to blow up a regime, in the atomic age, is a dangerous game. Even a murderous revolution is defensible, on condition that some people remain in the world to apply its principles. It is not enough to be in one's rights, or to believe one is. When one has been run over and crushed to death by a car, it hardly matters whether one had the right of way or not.

Moreover, it is possible to assert that both camps are neglecting their common interest: to help people out of the rut. A common interest, a common enemy, is one of the conditions necessary to a relative union. But neither camp seems to have any real consciousness of this common interest, this common danger (the rise of poverty). The political men who govern on both sides are quite unable to take action, for they are prisoners of their principles, of their staffs, of public opinion, of their use of time. The action must come from elsewhere, until the day when the light will dawn in their minds, perhaps as a result of some fortuitous incident.

Various projects hope for the transfer of financial resources from ruinous armament to economic aid for under-developed countries. Some have even passed the fearful hurdle of day-to-day politics, without however reaching the stage of really serious debate. It is public opinion which must be convinced.

The governments of the under-developed countries in the Bandung group could also play an interesting part: the useless sword-dance over dying colonialism might with some advantage be turned into a violent cry of protest against full-scale armament, accompanied by a constructive transfer plan. These countries could then exercise a constant pressure on both camps. The courage is certainly there.

Ignorance and awareness

The evolution of ideas is slow, the facts move faster than the development of awareness, because education in both camps has strangely neglected questions of population. The average man blushes if he is caught out not knowing the ministers of Charles IX, or the classification of vertebrates. Having received certain notions in various domains, he assumes that these are part of any reasonable culture. Demography, on the other hand, is a barbaric science, without teachers or pupils. Since no social duty is based on the subject, it is permissible not only to be ignorant, but also to express any opinion about it, however unscientific, however unsupported by even an elementary knowledge of facts.

Such ignorance is easily perpetuated; sciences like demography, which were unfortunate enough not to be presented, in full harness, at the grand review and classification of sciences in the nineteenth century, now beg in vain at University gates. A few alms from time to time, but no rights of citizenship.

In this way mankind may meet its end through its own lack of awareness.

How could it be otherwise, when ministers, parliamentarians, directors of academies, high councils, etc., are all more often than not ignorant of even the elementary premisses in this barbaric science, asserting their right to ignorance and thus ensuring its splendid continuity?

The population resolutely ignores the population, and runs ahead to its doom, eyes shut, head low.

Are they asleep?

Among those who have denounced the gravity of the situation most strenuously, most convincingly and with the highest moral purpose, we must mention Mr. J. de Castro. We will end by quoting him:

> The reality of universal poverty has split the world into two groups of human beings: those who do not eat, and those who do not sleep. The first group inhabits the poor countries, and considers itself crushed in its wretchedness by the economic oppression of the great industrial powers. But in those regions favoured with wealth, lives the group of those who do not sleep, because they are tormented by the fear of a revolt on the part of these miserable people, and the weight of their conscience deprives them of rest.

I agree with my generous colleague about the group of those who do not eat, but I emphatically do not agree with him about the group of those who do not sleep. No, Mr. Castro, the weight of their conscience does not deprive them of rest. They sleep. They sleep in peace . . . if we can call it that.

Index of Proper Names

Index

2431